#6
11/22

CHAPMAN-ANDREWS
AND THE
EMPEROR

CHAPMAN-ANDREWS
AND
THE EMPEROR

by

PETER LESLIE

Pen & Sword
MILITARY

First published in Great Britain in 2005 by
Pen & Sword Military
an imprint of
Pen & Sword Books Ltd
47 Church Street
Barnsley
South Yorkshire
S70 2AS

ISBN 1 84415 257 X

A CIP catalogue record for this book is
available from the British Library

Typeset in 11/13 Sabon by
Phoenix Typesetting, Auldgirth, Dumfriesshire

Printed and bound in England by
CPI UK

Pen & Sword Books Ltd incorporates the Imprints of Pen & Sword
Aviation, Pen & Sword Maritime, Pen & Sword Military, Wharncliffe
Local History, Pen & Sword Select, Pen & Sword Military Classics and
Leo Cooper.

For a complete list of Pen & Sword titles please contact
PEN & SWORD BOOKS LIMITED
47 Church Street, Barnsley, South Yorkshire, S70 2AS, England
E-mail: enquiries@pen-and-sword.co.uk
Website: www.pen-and-sword.co.uk

Contents

Glossary

Amh:		There are widely different transliterations of Amharic terms: those used by Chapman-Andrews have generally been followed here.
Arab:		Arabic; often colloquial Sudanese terms.
Ind:		Indian; Indian terms were often in widespread use in the Middle East and Africa.

Abba	amh	A priest
Abuna	amh	Coptic Archbishop- appointed from Alexandria
Amhara	amh	Ethiopian ruling group, hence Amharic, the language
Azaj	amh	Commander
Banda	amh	Irregular Ethiopian units, usually part of Italian forces
Bandararchin	amh	"Our Flag"- Allied propaganda news-sheet in 1940/1
Bimbashi	arab	Egyptian Army title – company officer -usually British
Dafardar	ind	Indian Army term for NCO
Dejazmatch	amh	Ethiopian Military title- sometimes translated as General
Dergue	amh	Group of officers who ruled Ethiopia from 1975
Dhobi	ind	Laundry or washing
Echege	amh	The senior Ethiopian post in the Church, also Itcheguey

Fitaurari	amh	Ethiopian Military Title, equivalent to Commander
Fukara	amh	A Rally e.g. to greet the Emperor
Ful Sudani	arab	Sudanese dish of beans
Gibbi	amh	Nobleman's residence – used of Imperial Palace in Addis Ababa
Gumz	amh	Nilotic tribe living on Sudanese/ Ethiopian Gojjam border
Hamla	arab	Literally a load. In this context a camel caravan made up of a number of camels and their herds.
Hamlagia	arab	A unit, usually of ten men, of camel transport men
Ingerra	amh	A sort of pancake-like bread made from grain
Itcheguey	amh	see Echege
Kaid	arab	General Officer Commanding, in Sudanese Army
Kenyasmatch	amh	Ethiopian Military title, often Commander of Imperial Bodyguard
Khor	arab	Dry river bed
Lij	amh	Ethiopian noble's title, sometimes translated as Prince or "the Honourable"
Murasla	arab	Guard or servant
Negus	amh	King
Negus Negast	amh	King of Kings, hence Emperor
Ras	amh	An Ethiopian Noble title, sometimes translated as Duke
Raz	arab	A unit of measure
Shankalla	amh?	A tribe from Western Gojjam
Shid	arab	A day's camel caravan march
Shifta	amh	Ethiopian Bandit
Tej	amh	An Alcoholic mead made from fermented honey
Wat	amh	An Ethiopian dish, very spicy.

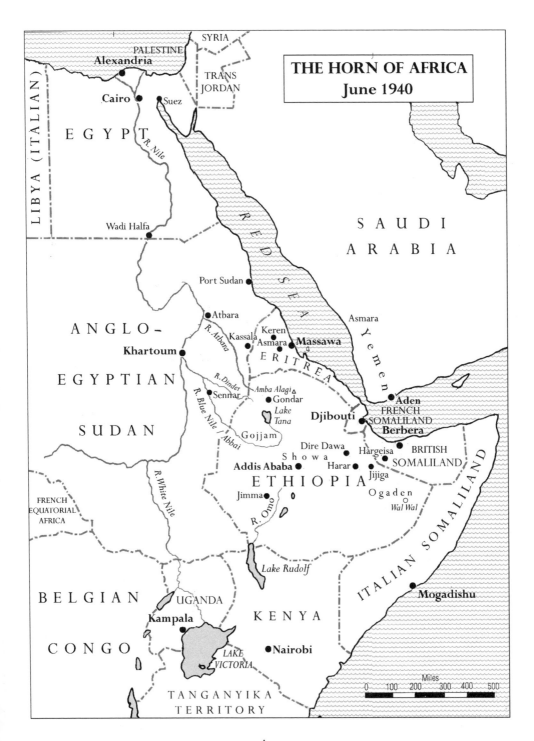

THE HORN OF AFRICA
June 1940

SYRIA
PALESTINE
Alexandria
TRANS JORDAN
Cairo ● ● Suez
LIBYA (ITALIAN)
E G Y P T
R. Nile
SAUDI ARABIA
Wadi Halfa ●
Port Sudan ●
R E D   S E A
ANGLO–
Atbara ●
R. Atbara
Kassala ●
Keren ●
Asmara
Asmara ●
● Massawa
EGYPTIAN
Khartoum ●
E R I T R E A
Yemen
R. Dinder
R. Blue Nile / Abbai
Sennar ●
Amba Alagi △
● Gondar
Lake Tana
Aden ●
Djibouti ●
FRENCH SOMALILAND
SUDAN
Gojjam
Berbera ●
Dire Dawa ●
Hargeisa ●
BRITISH SOMALILAND
R. White Nile
Addis Ababa ●
S h o w a
Harar ●
Jijiga ●
FRENCH EQUATORIAL AFRICA
E T H I O P I A
Jijiga
Jimma ●
O g a d e n
Wal Wal ○
R. Omo
I T A L I A N   S O M A L I L A N D
Lake Rudolf
BELGIAN
UGANDA
Mogadishu ●
Kampala ●
K E N Y A
CONGO
● Nairobi
LAKE VICTORIA
Miles
0   100   200   300   400   500
TANGANYIKA TERRITORY

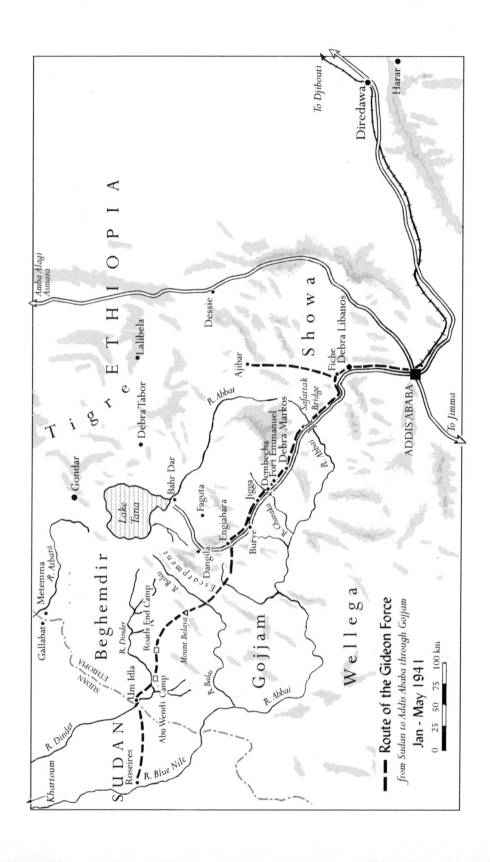

To Djibouti

Diredawa

Harar

Amba Alagi
Asmara

T i g r e   E T H I O P I A

Lalibela

Debra Tabor

Gondar

S h o w a

Dessie

Debra Libanos

Fiche

Ajibar

R. Abbai

Safartak
Bridge

ADDIS ABABA

To Jimma

Bahr Dar

Lake
Tana

Faguta

Dembecha
Fort Emmanuel
Debra Markos

R. Abbai

Jigga

B e g h e m d i r

Metemma

R. Atbara

Gallabat

R. Dinder

Roadis End Camp

R. Balas

Um Idla

Abu Wendi Camp

Mount Belaya

Engiabara

Dangila

Burye

Charaka

R. Abbai

G o j j a m

W e l l e g a

R. Balas

Khartoum

R. Dinder

S U D A N

Roseires

R. Blue Nile

SUDAN
ETHIOPIA

Route of the Gideon Force

from Sudan to Addis Ababa through Gojjam

Jan - May 1941

0   25   50   75   100 km

Introduction

Sir Edwin Chapman-Andrews had always intended to write up some of the more interesting and historic parts of his life and to that end had kept a variety of papers, letters and other records. After his retirement he planned to write some sketches on three men who had played an important part in his life: Wingate, Thesiger and Boustead, but retirement turned out to mean a life full of business interests and charitable work and time slipped by. When in his 70s he started sketching in outline how he might bring together his own memoirs, he realized from enquiries at the Foreign Office how many records had been destroyed or 'weeded', which he told an old colleague was 'really quite scandalous', – and how much work would be involved. By then his health was failing and in 1977 he suffered a stroke from which he never really recovered. On his death in 1980 Lady Chapman-Andrews was approached about Sir Edwin's records and consulted me, as I had married Charlotte, their elder daughter, five years before. It is only now that I am fully retired that I have been able to discharge my promise to her to take on the work of writing them up; she had died in our house in 2002, aged 97.

I have called this book *Chapman-Andrews and the Emperor* since Haile Selassie and Ethiopia filled such a long and central role in his life, including the dramatic march with the Emperor under Gideon Force to recover his country in 1941, covered in his diary. It is no coincidence that the three names of Wingate, Thesiger and Boustead were all associated with those days. I have also tried to use his own words, wherever possible, whilst bringing in the other records which he had carefully retained, particularly concerning his service in Egypt and the Sudan. What is missing is his own intimate knowledge and his own elegant and forceful prose. Sir Edwin was, as diplomat, famously discreet and kept confidential information within his own remarkable memory and only rarely in his papers. I have tried to give the story historical form and to provide such notes as I felt necessary to give coherence and explanation. Whilst I have made use of the many books on the period, I have not undertaken much original research, but have relied particularly on three very valuable sources: Thesiger's *The Life of My Choice*, Anthony Mockler's *Haile Selassie's War* and David Shirreff's *Barefoot and Bandoliers*, which gives a first-rate and thorough account of Gideon Force, particularly from the military point of view.

Haile Selassie's personality commanded the respect and admiration of many British people in a way not easy to explain. Sir Edwin was a very loyal British public servant and wrote that he 'learned early on not to become attached to places or indeed foreigners (except for dear old Haile Selassie)', but it is clear from this story how much the Emperor meant to him. However, there is no doubt that his own loyalty was to the British Government and that he was well aware that the Emperor kept his own cards close to his chest and had only one ambition: to keep Ethiopia independent and under his control, whilst happy to make use of others. Sir Edwin would have been happy that he did not long outlast the Emperor whose fate he greatly mourned.

I am grateful to the Imperial War Museum for their help and for allowing me to include a number of photographs from their archives. I am also grateful for permission to include a photograph of Sir Hugh Boustead from The Special Collection and Western Manuscripts, Bodleian Library – located in the Middle East Centre, St Anthony's College, Oxford: Boustead Coll. 2/14 (AP 25).

I want to express my gratitude to his sons and daughters for all their help and advice, to my brother-in-law, David Chapman-Andrews, for all his help with the illustrations, and, above all, to my wife Charlotte, but for whose encouragement this book would never have been written.

Chapter One

Ethiopia 1929

Just before Christmas in 1929 Chapman-Andrews, aged 26, was posted, rather to his surprise, from the Levant Service in Egypt to the Legation in Addis Ababa and thus started his lifelong association with Ethiopia.

Great Britain had had diplomatic relations with Abyssinia since the 1880s when the Emperor Menelik had given a large area near what was to become his capital, Addis Ababa, to Queen Victoria for a British Legation. The mysterious, independent and Christian Kingdom of Prester John and Rasselas had fascinated the British since the 18th century and several explorers had tried to penetrate it, with varying degrees of success. As British interests in Africa, particularly in Egypt, and the Route to India had increased, we had briefly come to blows, but with little lasting ill will. Not so the Italians who, following their seizure of Eritrea, had received a bloody nose in 1896 when they were defeated by the Ethiopian Army at Adowa. In 1906 and again in 1924 the British Government had indicated to Italy in rather imprecise terms that they regarded Eritrea and Abyssinia as within the Italian sphere of influence, provided that Italy recognized Britain's interests in the Nile waters and Lake Tana.

Whilst Abyssinia appears to have become Christian in the early centuries after Christ and claimed a long line of independent rulers, it had, in fact, had a very chequered history with many small tribes and dynasties fighting each other, more like Anglo-Saxon Britain than the centralized feudal kingdom to which successive 'Emperors' aspired. At one time their rulers had claimed control over much of the Northern Sudan as well as the largely Muslim

1

Red Sea Coast which had brought them increasingly into conflict with Egypt and, during the Mahdist period, with the Sudan. The fact that the Coptic Patriarch of Alexandria was, and had always been, the supreme authority over the Ethiopian Church was an added complication in relations with Egypt.

It was no different during the 50 years before Chapman-Andrews came to Addis Ababa. The last strong ruler, the Emperor Menelik, who had greatly expanded Ethiopia's borders, had died in 1913 and, for want of an obvious heir, his daughter Zauditu had become Empress. For the next 17 years various Rases and nobles, often related by marriage to Menelik, had struggled for power. An added complication was that one of them, a grandson, Lij Yasu, had turned Moslem, to the disgust of the Ethiopian Church and the main nobles, who had ejected and imprisoned him.

In this situation Ras Tafari, the grandson of the King of Shoa and a cousin of Menelik, slowly emerged as the main contender. He had received part of his education at the French Catholic Mission at Harar, where his father, Ras Makonnen, had been Governor. He played a long and astute game, slowly eliminating his rivals by death in battle or by making them allies, often with the help of suitable marriages. Wilfred Thesiger, whose father had been British Minister in the First World War, recalls an early memory of the victorious army returning to Addis Ababa with their prisoners in chains. Not much had changed by 1930 and one of Chapman-Andrews' first experiences on arrival was of seeing the Minister of War returning from the north in Abyssinia's only aeroplane after a triumphant campaign, bearing the severed head of Ras Gugsa, Ras Tafari's latest challenger. Two days later the Empress died, leaving the way clear for Ras Tafari to become Emperor.

With his French education, intelligence and inquisitiveness, Ras Tafari had acquired a wide understanding of international politics and the threats against which his country needed to be protected. These included not only Italy but his colonial neighbours France and Britain, which also had an interest in the Nile waters. In 1923 he ensured that Abyssinia became Africa's only member of the League of Nations. In 1924 he took a delegation, consisting mainly of rivals he did not dare leave behind, to Europe and was greatly impressed by the experience, not least by his realization of how little attention or interest was paid to him and Abyssinia by the

Great Powers, beyond the formal courtesies. He decided to use his coronation as an opportunity to give Ethiopia a higher profile and issued invitations to leading governments, rightly imagining that none would wish to be left out. Among other points which the new Emperor wished to make was that his country was called 'Ethiopia' and not the Arabic 'Abyssinia' by which it had been known hitherto in Europe and the Arab Middle East.

Throughout his long life the Emperor Haile Selassie, as Ras Tafari became at his coronation, was faced by challenges of one sort or another and, until almost the end, managed to overcome them with enormous political skill and his magnetic personality, as he imaginatively tried to bring his large and disparate Empire and extremely independent and ungovernable peoples into the 20th century. Against this background it is not surprising that those who did not know him, and this included the European rulers of his neighbours, remained for long doubtful of the durability of his Empire and whether it had really changed its medieval spots. This is evident in much of Chapman-Andrews' description, written many years later, of his first experiences there.

At the British Legation

'Very shortly after my arrival, I was presented to the Emperor (then Regent) together with the rest of the Legation staff, by Sir Sidney Barton [the British Minister]. It was at some Ethiopian occasion and the Emperor received the Corps Diplomatique sitting on the throne in the Old Gibbi, raised on a dais. I distinctly recall his features, serene, something of a mystical quality about them. His eyes, in particular, I remember; they seemed at that time to be purple, but, of course, they were in fact dark brown. He seemed a majestic figure; there was a divinity about him that doth hedge a king. He seemed to be with, but not of, us who assembled there to pass before him and bow. But I thought that when my turn came to make my bow and my name was called by Sir Sidney Barton, he seemed to glance at me and take me in with his eyes for the moment I was before him.

'In May 1930, I accompanied the Minister on a trek though Harar and Jijiga to Hargeisa, Sheikh, Berbera and returned to Addis via Aden and Djibouti. I acted as A.D.C., private secretary, diplomatic secretary, interpreter, the lot. We took ponies by train

3

from Addis. It was a two-day journey to Diredawa, where we were met by Consul Plowman from Harar. We had a small escort from the Legation guard, Bengal Lancers they were, three troopers, I think, under a *Dafardar*. We spent the night in Diredawa at the local hotel and sent our tentage and baggage on early next morning by camel towards Harar. We ourselves, with Plowman and the escort, set off after breakfast, overtaking our baggage caravan in the foothills. We had, of course, to walk and lead our horses most of the way up to the Pass, for the track was narrow and in places quite steep. The motor road today takes its winding way by easier gradients than the old bridle path. The Minister and Plowman reached Haramaya late in the afternoon and spent the night in what was no more than a rest house there beside the lake. I myself arrived about sunset, having lingered behind to shoot the odd duck which were quite thick round the edge of the lake. I remember getting three or four shoveller, the last of the migrants moving north. These we had for dinner grilled over the charcoal in the rest house.

'We rode on next morning reaching Harar in time for a late lunch. The Minister stayed in the house, which I myself was to occupy later when I was Consul there during the Italian invasion, but I pitched a tent and slept in the garden. I think the Plowmans had a nanny and children so doubtless that was the reason why I could not be accommodated, but I preferred this arrangement. We dined that night with the Governor of Harar Province, old Dijaj Gabre Mariam. We rode on next day to Jijiga, spending a couple of nights on the road. There is a photograph of the tented site which was called "The British Vice-Consulate, Jijiga". Lieutenant Colonel A.T. "Sandy" Curle CBE, DSO, was Vice-Consul. I had not previously met him but we have been close friends ever since.

'We sent our animals and tentage back from Jijiga and travelled the rest of the way to Berbera in trucks which the Governor of Somaliland, Sir Harold Kittermaster, had sent. In British Somaliland we were his guests.

'In September 1930 I had a spell in hospital in Addis Ababa but was up and about again though by no means really fit at the time of the coronation.'

The Emperor, or Ras Tafari as he still was, was determined to use his Coronation as an important internal and external political statement that he was indeed the rightful heir of a long line of past Emperors, ruling over a large and long-established state. This was far from the case and thus the Coronation itself and the ritual was designed to reinforce the myth of the 'apostolic succession' from King Solomon. He took the title 'His Imperial Majesty Haile Selassie 1, Conquering Lion of Judah, Elect of God and King of the Kings (*Negusa Negast)* of Ethiopia' and laid down the principle of primogeniture, which had not existed before in Ethiopia. All the Rases and leading figures were summoned to appear at the Coronation, suitably dressed and titled in the highly complex Ethiopian tradition and to join the important international witnesses of the event. The claimant, Lij Yasu, remained well hidden away in his prison.

The Emperor's visit to Europe in 1924 and the invitations to national events that he had received had confirmed him in the need for international recognition and good relations. The Coronation offered an opportunity to put his own importance and that of the Africa's one ancient independent state on the map. Invitations were issued to foreign Heads of State and Governments as well as to the Press. The British Government decided to send a strong delegation led by the young Duke of Gloucester, King George V's third son, together with the Governors of all Ethiopia's British colonial neighbours, Sudan, British Somaliland and Aden. Italy, not to be outdone, sent the Prince of Udine, the King's cousin, and an even larger delegation; France was represented by Marshal Franchet d'Esperey and Germany, Sweden, Belgium, the Netherlands, Japan, Turkey, Egypt, Greece and the USA all sent delegations. The Emperor was clear that his country should be called 'Ethiopia' rather than the latinised arabic 'Abyssinia' by which it had been generally known in Europe hitherto; this had little immediate effect on his guests or the Press. *The Times* was still using the two names indiscriminately 30 years later, although the rest of the world had adopted 'Ethiopia' by the Second World War.

In Addis Ababa roads were tarmacked, buildings upgraded, electricity introduced, and fences shut off the poorer areas, which meant much of the City. The Emperor acquired from Germany the Imperial coach of Kaiser Wilhelm II; special coronets were ordered from London and a sceptre and orb were sent as a gift from the British Government. The young Duke of Gloucester telegraphed his father, George V, 'The gifts were much appreciated and

Emperor made cordial speech of thanks. Coronation tomorrow. All Well. Harry'. Careful planning and attention to protocol, always a feature of the Imperial court, ensured that the guests went away after ten days of celebration duly impressed. The British marine band and the four RAF aeroplanes from Aden attracted much attention. Chapman-Andrews attended the Coronation 'with other officials from the Legation Staff, accompanying King George's special representative, the Duke of Gloucester, and Sir Sidney to the Cathedral. I was quite near the Emperor, say ten yards away, at the moment of the actual crowning. The Emperor had kept vigil in the Cathedral all night and the Coronation service had begun sometime before the special delegation and the other invited were admitted. I was much struck by the close parallel between the Coronation ceremony and our own in England.' This was not surprising, as the Emperor had ensured that the traditional Ethiopian religious service and ceremonies had been updated to make it a more European event; his father, Ras Makonnen, may well have impressed his young son with accounts of Edward VII's coronation which he had attended in 1902. The international guests were generally impressed by the splendour, dignity and efficiency of the celebrations, as well as by the contrast with the lifestyle of the Abyssinians outside the Palace and in the country.

The Emperors' invitation to the Press ensured that for the first time wide coverage was given to Ethiopia in the European and American Press and if Evelyn Waugh's books were not much appreciated in Ethiopia they at least added to the international interest. The internal impression was more mixed: the Ethiopians had always been distrustful of foreigners and many in the Court and among the Rases suspected that the Emperor's increasing use of foreign advisers, experts and loans was intended to reduce their own power.

For a young and very junior member of the consular service this was heady stuff. Quite apart from the official British delegation to the Coronation, Chapman-Andrews was able to mix with interesting visitors to the country, as well as the many unusual figures who were to be found in Ethiopia at the time. Friendships were made with men such as Thesiger, Sandford and Cheesman, whose names appear repeatedly in this story and which continued until the end of their lives. Rather less close, and slightly improbable, was his friendship with Evelyn Waugh,who was at the coronation representing *The Times* and whose writings, both fictional and descriptive, in the Press and his books, helped to make Ethiopia a familiar, if rather alarming, name in Britain. Both at the time and even more through his subsequent books, Waugh did not make himself popular in Ethiopia or among those whom he met there during his brief vists, but Chapman-Andrews escapes his caustic tongue which was applied particularly sharply to the Legation and to the Minister himself, who was always suspected – quite wrongly, Waugh always said- of being the model of the vague Sir Sampson Courtney and his daughter, Esme (later to become the wife of George Steer), of Prudence in *Black Mischief*. Waugh's Diary records: 'November 15th: Train left Addis. Carriage with Chapman-Andrews, Major Cheesman, Plowman. Agreeable journey,' which is as close to approval as his diary records anywhere. 'Lunched Sandford, unsuccessful farmer, general middle-man for *Daily Mail*' is more typical. The publication of his *Remote People* in 1931 and, more importantly, *Black Mischief* in 1932 brought Ethiopia a wider public, albeit in highly coloured caricature.

For Chapman-Andrews there was also plenty of hard work; the first three months had involved almost continuous study of Amharic under the supervision of Tafara Worq, the Amharic clerk in the Legation who will appear later as Haile Selassie's eminence grise, 'who did his best to teach me Amharic,' and the Consul 'Hajji' Bullard (later Sir Reader Bullard) and the multilingual Zaphiro, the Oriental Secretary. He acquired sufficient spoken and written knowledge to satisfy the Minister, little realizing how much use of it he would have to make later on.

Fortunately, he had already met Barton when the latter was en route from Shanghai to Addis Ababa earlier in 1929 and obviously made an impresssion on him. He had been summoned from Suez, where he was acting Vice-Consul, to Cairo by Lord Lloyd, the High Commissioner in Egypt, who introduced him to Barton, whom he was briefing.

'I accompanied Sir Sidney Barton by road to Suez the following day across the desert and saw him safely on board the *Messageries Maritime* ship, which took him to Djibouti; so I felt that I had something like a privileged position near the inside of the bend when I was moved to Addis from Cairo in December of that year.

We all realized that the Italians were to be carefully watched. They controlled all radio services from Ethiopia to Europe, and from Eritrea they were in the best position to make a nuisance of themselves if they wished. Barton used to invite me often to dinner when he was entertaining Ethiopians, as one of my main targets was to learn Ethiopian. He kept a close eye on my progress, as he had previously done on probationer vice-consuls in China. He believed in people speaking local languages, and he kept a close scrutiny on my notes in Court as a judge of the Consular Court. Here, however, I had the good fortune to be under Bullard, which was especially important when we went together to Mixed Courts. Bullard and Barton were not birds of a feather, but I will say no more of that, though both confided to me their private opinions of one another.

'Sir Sidney Barton was a man of spare build and he made a special point of keeping himself physically fit by regular exercise. Without being an ascetic, he was not given to indulgence of any kind, but he liked to see other people eating, drinking and smoking to their full enjoyment and he was a perfect host. His main career had been in the China Consular Service and he was a distinguished Chinese linguist. There was a lot in common between that Service and the Levant Consular Service to which I belonged, for members of both had to be practical oriental linguists, serving a period of probation for five years, their confirmation in the Service, at the age of 27 or 28, depending upon their passing a language exam and getting a good report for their general work at the end of each probational year. Marriage was discouraged and certainly not taken into account where posting or allowances were concerned and until the end of probation one was covered by a money bond, forfeited on resignation. Moreover, both services covered countries where Britain enjoyed extra-territorial rights: i.e. maintained Consular Courts. Sir Sidney Barton was a member of the English Bar and a real stickler for the proper conduct in detail of Court work. He had been brought up very strictly, his people being Plymouth Brethren. Himself an Ulsterman, there was no compromise on matters which he regarded as of principle. He had a quick temper which was not altogether a bad thing at times, though he did his best to keep it under control, especially when dealing with foreigners. During the Italian/Ethiopians War his complete devotion to the Ethiopian cause earned him not only the gratitude but the implicit trust of all Ethiopians from the Emperor down-wards. Lady Barton's tireless activity on behalf of Ethiopian womanhood and, during the War, Save The Children Fund, endeared her to all.'

Apart from the delegation to the Coronation and all the preparations involved for a small Legation, there was plenty of time for picnics, shooting expeditions and riding. Chapman-Andrews lived in small bungalow in the Legation's park-like grounds and acquired his own horse – a new experience for a young man with an urban Exeter background.

He was able to compete in the Coronation show-jumping competition at the race course and was lucky enough to get second place in the Open Contest which 'gave me a lot of pleasure especially as the Italians had some crack cavalry men competing. The Duke of Gloucester presented me with my prize.'

However, ill health had been a problem, following a bad case of Blackwater fever in Suez the year before, and at the end of December1930 he had to leave to return to London for medical treatment, during which he worked in the Consular Section of the Foreign Office. This put his future career at risk as he was still a probationer, but his good reports from Egypt and Ethiopia carried the day. Although his medical condition caused complications throughout his life, never again would it interfere with his career. He was confirmed in the Service and in November 1931 married Sadie Nixon, the daughter of a successful engineer, whom he had met in his early days at University College.

In 1932 he was posted to Iraq as Vice Consul, in the north of the country, based on Kirkuk, Suleimaniya and Rowanduz. Following the British Iraq Treaty of 1931 Britain had ceased to be the occupying power under the Mandate and had to establish normal diplomatic and consular relations; hence the new consular post. This process was not accomplished without considerable insecurity and instability and Chapman-Andrews gained useful experience dealing with the problems of local minorities such as Kurds and the Christian Assyrians and protecting them from the new Arab-dominated government in Baghdad. Sir Robert Vansittart, Permanent Secretary at the Foriegn Office, wrote to him in 1934 over an incident where Chapman-Andrews averted another Assyrian massacre: 'We were fortunate to have on the spot when the danger threatened an officer possessing your presence of mind and resourcefulness who did not hesitate to assume responsibility and take independent action in circumstances of peculiar difficulty.' As in 2005, Iraq was a challenging post; not least for a young married couple, soon to have their first child. Three years later he completed his posting with high commendations from the British Minister, Sir Francis Humphrys, and the Foreign Office.

Chapter Two

The Italian Invasion

Meanwhile Ethiopia had not stood still. The new Emperor was determined to modernize his country and made much use of foreign help, whenever offered, although this was not popular amongst the older noblemen; the Ethiopians were proverbially distrustful of foreigners. The central administration of this still very disparate land was greatly strengthened and the power of the local nobles eroded. A new Army was being trained by a Belgian Military Mission and armed largely by foreigners. Ethiopian legations abroad were opened in leading countries. Communications were improved with new roads, telephones and an embryo airforce. By 1935 the effects of five years of stability were already very evident and the Emperor and the Ethiopians noticeably more self-confident, not that diffidence was ever an Ethiopian characteristic; all observers commented on the fact that they, and particularly the Amhara people, were always convinced that they were in the right and had nothing to learn from any other nation.

However, there was one particular cloud – the Italians, who were far from happy that a much stronger Ethiopia was emerging between their colony of Eritrea in the north and of Italian Somaliland in the south, neither of which borders had been formally defined. It was the border incident at WalWal in November 1934 in the Ogaden, adjacent to the borders with British and Italian Somaliland, which gave rise to the international crisis which dominated the world headlines during the next twelve months and made Ethiopia a household name throughout the world. This was not because Ethiopia had any great strategic importance in the eyes of any of the Great Powers, but because a

11

clearly colonial invasion threatened the integrity of the League of the Nations, to whom the far-sighted Emperor inevitably appealed. Arguments continue as why Italy decided on war; their defeat at Adowa, almost 40 years before, seemed hardly an issue and it more likely that the very absence of opportunities for domestic triumphs by the mid-1930s may have made Mussolini respond to the otherwise minor WalWal incident as he did. What is clear is that he rapidly started military preparations in both Eritrea and Somalia and a stream of troopships and supplies began passing through the Suez Canal, closely observed by the British in Egypt.

The British Government concluded from an urgent report commissioned in 1935 from Sir John Maffey, the Governor-General of the Sudan, that there were: 'No vital British interests in Abyssinia or adjoining countries such as to necessitate British resistance to an Italian conquest of Abyssinia. In general it is a matter of indifference whether Abyssinia remains independent or is absorbed by Italy. From a standpoint of Imperial defence, an Independent Abyssinia would be preferable to an Italian one, but the threat to British interests appears distant and would depend only on a war against Italy which for the moment appears improbable.' In many ways British interests in Lake Tana and the Nile waters might be better advanced with the Italians than with the Emperor, who continued to resist all attempts to pin him down on the subject – and would continue to do so. Unfortunately, no sooner had the report had been submitted than it emerged on the desk of the Italian government through the notoriously leaky British Embassy in Rome, as were most of their communications with London.

The main concern of Britain and, especially, of France was to try and maintain their Great War alliance with Italy and to prevent Mussolini's Fascist Government siding with the newly emerging Nazi Germany of Hitler. Thus the early reaction of the newly elected French Prime Minister, Laval,and the new British Foreign Secretary, Sir Samuel Hoare, was to come to a secret agreement with Italy which appeared to be giving Italy *carte blanche* over Ethiopia to Italy. When this emerged in December 1935 British public opinion was appalled and Hoare had to resign, to be succeeded by the very differently minded Anthony Eden. The decision of the League of Nations to apply sanctions on Italy rapidly escalated the crisis to a potential War situation. A special

12

'Abyssinian Department' was created in the Foreign Office. International volunteers from twenty-eight countries under medical or Red Cross auspices poured into Ethiopia, as well a number of mercenaries and adventurers, and a number of black American 'Rastafarians' anxious to support their spiritual 'leader', an early sign of that remarkable social phenomenon. The world Press followed and by October there were over 100 journalists in Ethiopia.

Consul in Harar

So it was not surprising that the Foreign Office decided to reinforce their small Legation in Addis Ababa and the Consulate at Harar, the gateway to the Ogaden and the link with British Somaliland, and likely to be in the front line of an Ethiopian/Italian conflict. Chapman-Andrews, who had just been appointed Vice Consul at Smyrna, was transferred from Iraq as Acting Consul at Harar, a post previously staffed by the Colonial service from nearby British Somaliland. With his previous experience under Barton and his growing reputation for being a good man in difficult situations, he was an obvious choice.

Chapman-Andrews and his wife and 3-year-old son took a fortnight to reach Harar, filling up several passport pages to do so: car and train to Baghdad; flight to Damascus; car to Haifa via Beirut; train to Port Said; boat to Djibouti; train to Diredawa; car to Harar, where they arrived at last on 17 April. One major improvement was the new road from Diredawa; the 35-mile journey which Chapman-Andrews had described in 1930 as taking a day and a night by foot and mule now took only a few hours.

He found the Consulate unchanged. It was located in a small estate outside Harar and belonged to the Emperor, who had spent many happy days in his childhood there. Chapman-Andrews wrote: 'It was lovely house in those days with a lovely garden, surrounded by the Emperor's coffee plantations. The Emperor and the Empress twice honoured us by coming to tea and inviting us to meals with them. Chrysanthemums bloomed with the bougainvillea and apple with the peach.' Waugh described it as 'a large attractive house, three storeys, large drawing room, thick pillars, good garden, glass in windows, Bronco in lavatory.' Given the dramatic events which it was to witness over the next twelve months, it was fortunate that it was well outside the town and the compound had sufficient space to accommodate the many visitors and refugees who periodically descended on it, as well as of the protective force of British Somali Guards which were brought in once the war began. At almost 6,000 feet above sea level, the climate was pleasant and quite healthy compared with the steamy heat of Diredawa and the sweltering coast beyond.

Harar itself was a very un-Ethiopian city. Until its capture by the Emperor Menelik, it had been an independent emirate and the centre of a thriving trading and slaving market with close links with the Arab merchants in Aden and Berbera. Sir Richard Burton had visited it in the 1850s, the first European to do so, and described it as 'a mean city only a mile long and half a mile wide, its narrow streets strewn with gigantic rubbish heaps'. Subsequently the Egyptians had claimed it and the British had toyed with acquisition. Whilst under Ethiopian control from the 1890s, it had fallen under the influence of Menelik's French allies from Djibouti during the brief period when the latter had hoped to link up with Marchand in the Southern Sudan and French West Africa, and had established a French Mission and Hospital there under the remarkable Monseigneur Jarosseau, who was still in charge. In 1930 it still retained its ancient city walls with the gates closed at night and it had remained the largely Moslem city which had attracted Rimbaud in the early part of the century. However, even by 1935 it was already changing, partly as a result of the new road from Diredawa but more from the big influx of Amhara people in the administration and army and the departure of many native Hararis. There were new buildings and it was well on its way to becoming a Christian and Ethiopian city – to Evelyn Waugh's disapproval.

The War Starts

An early British visitor was Geoffrey Harmsworth, a member of the Northcliffe/Rothermere family and later 3rd Baronet who had arranged for the *Daily Mail* to send him to Ethiopia as their correspondent well in advance of the expected war. His very readable *Abyssinian Adventures* was published later in 1935 and makes several references to the Chapman-Andrews.

'The new English Vice-Consul and his wife and small son had

recently arrived and were unpacking blankets when we made ourselves known at the Consulate. The garden is full of English flowers and every day while the Court is in Harar, Mrs Chapman-Andrews sends large bunches of roses at the Emperor's request to the Palace.'

Harmsworth was invited with the Chapman-Andrews to a formal dinner with the Emperor attended by a number of local notables including the Governor, Lorenzo Taezes, Monseigneur Jarosseau, the Emperor's old mentor, 'with his long flowing hair and beard looking like a primitive Italian saint', and the Italian Consul, who spent most of the dinner discussing the uncontroversial subject of the local price of cattle rather than the current crisis. 'Chapman-Andrews turned up looking rather like an Admiral and his decorations included the Star of Ethiopia Third Class which had been distributed wholesale at the Coronation. Mrs Chapman-Andrews was bemoaning the non-arrival of a parcel from Paris which had been held up at Djibouti, but nevertheless contrived to look the best dressed woman at the dinner.'

Harmsworth was surprised to find how apparently unconcerned everyone was about the Italian war threat: 'Even Chapman-Andrews seemed outwardly more concerned about his puppet Empire than the question of what he might do about his wife and small son in the event of war.' When he reached Addis Ababa he called on Barton who was equally calm and told him; 'We cannot believe that Italy would wantonly endanger the peace of Europe because of a minor colonial incident such as WalWal. Here our relationship with Italy is so friendly. My eldest daughter is married to Baron Muzzi, the Italian consul at Debra Markos. The British Minister looked tired and far from strong; the altitude affects his heart.' Given Harmsworth's press role and previous experience with those who were to publish their Ethiopian experiences, it seems likely that both Barton and Chapman-Andrews were suitably guarded and diplomatic in their responses. The staff at the Legation were quoted as saying that: 'We hope that you will say nicer things about us than Evelyn Waugh.' All agreed that Miss Esme Barton was the most attractive girl in all Addis Ababa.

Chapman-Andrews was able to take his wife and son to Addis Ababa in August for brief holiday, after making a number of official visits to the Ogaden. This gave rise to a melodramatic article in an American newspaper since in their train carriage was a rather humourless reporter from the *North American News* who was obviously impressed by 'Bronzed Young Englishman Busy Among Border Tribes. The spirit of Lawrence of Arabia works in Ethiopia'. Quizzed about his visits to the Ogaden and WalWal, Chapman-Andrews had replied: 'Just my official visits. Nothing extrardinary except that we were stopped when a troop of some thousand baboons marched across the road.' Reporter: 'That is interesting but hasn't a great deal to do with the WalWal incident.' Reply: 'Neither had I, old chap.'

War began on 3 October once the rainy season had come to an end. It was widely expected that the Ogaden, and thus Harar, would be one of the main areas of battle, which proved not to be the case. Two days after the war began the Italians under General Graziani, Governor of Somalia, defeated an Ethiopian force in the Ogaden near WalWal and killed their leader, but failed to follow through their success and the front on the ground was quiet for the next six months. The Emperor visited the front in November and decided to reinforce his armies in the south. Those in Harar and Jijiga were under the command of the Governor, Nasibu, supported by the Turkish military mission under Wahib Pasha, an experienced but elderly General who had fought at Gallipoli and had been sent by his government to show solidarity against Italy. Steer described him as an 'elderly stout short man in off-white trousers and gym shoes', but he respected his strategic advice, which recognized the need for a strong defensive line in the Marda Pass which lay on the road from the Ogaden to Harar.

To the south, between the Kenyan border and the Ogaden, the Emperor sent his strongest armies under his son-in-law Ras Desta Damtew, the latter's brother Dejazmatch Abebe Damtew and Ras Makonnen Endalkatchew, with the intention that they would be in a position to resist the Italians and invade Somalia. However, Graziani held them in check and early in January rebuffed the Ethiopian offensive near the Kenyan border.

From then on the main concern was the widely expected Italian bombing raids. This brought a large number of journalists to Harar. First to come in August, even before the war began, was George Steer for *The Times*, who was also reporting back to the Emperor on the preparedness of his forces in the Ogaden. Hence the fact that he was allowed down towards WalWal and reported that he got back with difficulty 'to be revived with Chapman-

Andrews' porridge'. In November rumours came of mustard gas injuries in the Ogaden and this brought a new invasion including Evelyn Waugh, who had returned, this time for the *Daily Mail*, Pat Balfour (Lord Kinross), Tovey, the photographer, the Americans Genock (Associated Press) and Knickerbocker (Hearst Press and a possible model for Pappenhacker in *Scoop*), together with William Deedes (Lord Deedes) for *The Daily Telegraph*. After visiting the Hospital to see those wounded in gas and other attacks, there was often little for them to do. They all camped in the Consulate grounds and sent telegrams covering often imaginary events, which Chapman-Andrews said usually resulted in him being instructed by the Foreign Office to investigate. The Somali guards were photographed practising bayonet and gas drill. Waugh tried to persuade Chapman-Andrews' wife, Sadie, to sell him her 'story', which she properly declined. Then the journalists all disappeared, either to Addis to go north where the war was hotting up, or back home.

The Italians denied that they had used mustard gas but there was clear evidence of its use in December by air bombing both on the northern front and to the south-east of Harar. Chapman-Andrews arranged for evidence to be collected and the Military Attaché R.J.R. ('Firkin' from his figure) Taylor came down and sent samples to Porton Down. The tests proved positive and the Foreign Secretary was briefed and later, with some reluctance, the League was informed.

Meanwhile Chapman-Andrews' diary was filled with minor consular matters often concerning the various movements of European Red Cross and other volunteers and missionaries and hearings at the Consular Court. Typical was the arrival of a high-profile British Red Cross mission led by the charasmatic Dr John Melly, who was to be killed in the sack of Addis Ababa in May. They had driven up with their ambulances from British Somaliland:

'We proceeded at once to the British Consulate which in its lovely garden stands on a slope overlooking the town. Here the Consul, Mr Chapman-Andrews, was more than hospitable. He gave us tea in the great pillared room of the consulate and then took us to see the site where he suggested we put up our camp.' Dr Macfie, one of the Mission, added rather wistfully: 'Harar is said to be famous for its beautiful women. I cannot honestly say that unaided we would have discovered that.'

However, Chapman-Andrews' brief diary shows that there were often empty days while they were waiting for the war to move closer: 'Sunday, March 8th. Typical wet Sunday. read Crime Club book all day. Sadie busy making chair covers.'

'Dinner with Lij Gabre Mariam, his wife, her sister and mother. Arrived home 11.45 too full for words'; 'Arrest of the French Comte de Roquefeuille as an Italian spy'. He had a mysterious visit from the notorious French smuggler and suspected arms and drug dealer, Henri de Monfried, bringing him '9.9 livres d'actualites'; de Monfried, of whose Egyptian Police record Chapman-Andrews was aware, was the author of several thrillers describing his exploits on the Red Sea and, later in 1936, of his polemic *Le Masque d'Or* denouncing Haile Selassie and the British for their conspiracy against French interests.

Soon afterwards a smallpox epidemic broke out, which filled the hospitals. One of the Somali guards fell ill and subsequently died, and all of them had to be placed in quarantine. Chapman-Andrews sent his wife and son down to Hargeisa in British Somaliland, where, after an alarming journey over flooded rivers, they had to camp in a still dry riverbed with interesting snakes. Chapman-Andrews went down to the Ogaden to try and get some accurate information of the state of the war there and at the end of March drove down to collect the family from Hargeisa, together with a wireless and an RAF operator which greatly improved communications.

In the north the war, after some initial Italian successes aided by the desertion to the Italians of the embittered Haile Selassie Gugsa, the Governor of Eastern Tigre and son of Ras Gugsa who had been killed in 1929 and who had been married to the Emperor's second daughter who had died, was becalmed. In November Mussolini, who was anxious for quick victories to forestall the League's pressure for damaging oil sanctions, replaced General De Bono by the more ruthless Marshal Badoglio. Badoglio moved his Headquarters south from Asmara, while the Emperor moved his north to Dessie. Over the next four months the armies battled it out, with considerable loss of life on both sides. However, there was little doubt that Italian weaponry, air superiority, training and the use of mustard gas would win. The Italian ability to listen in to Ethiopian wireless communications was also a big advantage. The armies of Ras Kassa, Ras Seyum, Ras Imru and General Mulugueta fought hard but seldom side by side and on 29 March the Emperor led his forces into battle at Mai Chew near Lake Ashangi and was defeated. There followed a confused month in which the Italians advanced in fits and starts against continued opposition and through difficult country, but their supply lines had become stretched and it was not until early in May that they were able to make their final breakthrough towards Addis Ababa. The Emperor and the surviving Rases and their disintegrating forces moved slowly towards the capital, the Emperor stopping to pray for three days at Lalibela Monastery.

In the south Dejazmatches Abebe Damtew and Makonnen with 10,000 men took the offensive in the Ogaden south-east of Jijiga, but after three days of fierce fighting had to withdraw on 14 April towards Harar, where the news of the Ethiopian collapse in both south and north started filtering through and rumours soon abounded. 'It is believed in the town that the hills surrounding Harar are filled with deserters, eager to loot.' Jijiga was bombed on successive nights and Chapman-Andrews, who was able to follow the news with his radio as well as through the Legation, decided to send his family down to Diredawa where the French had a large force of 800 troops protecting the railway. On 29 March (Passion Sunday) the diary says: 'Bugles at 6am as usual. 8am warning by telephone that aircraft were coming up the Fafan valley [towards Harar]. 8.15: guns. 8.50: they arrived. First one then a few waves then 4 then 5 then 3 then 5. They circled widely over the town at an altitude of 6000 ft 3 times and dropped over 300 bombs.'

It was widely believed – correctly – that the Italians were continuing to target foreign and Red Cross Hospitals and buildings to encourage foreigners to leave and thus be unable to witness the coming military offensive. Confirmation of this was therefore carefully recorded and reported to the Legation and thence to London. On 2 April the Foreign Secretary quoted the report of the British Consul to the House of Commons: '18 Italian aircraft flying at 1800 feet bombed the town between 8.45 and 9.30 last Sunday. The machines circled wide three times and nearly 300 bombs fell on the town. 3 fell on the Swedish Mission, 50 on that of the Egyptian Red Cross, 14 on the Roman Catholic Mission, 4 on the French Hospital and 4 on the Harar Red Cross which was showing a ground sign five yards square. The apparatus of the wireless station was destroyed and telephone lines damaged.'

The *News Chronicle* reported: 'BOMBS AND FIRE RUIN HARAR –
Red Cross Units Wiped Out. The entire City, whose inhabitants
number 80,000, was soon in flames,' but Chapman-Andrews was
able to cable his father in Exeter: ' All safe and well. Sadie David
Diredawa Love Ed' A few days later the Exeter papers were able
to report that his wife and son had left Abyssinia and were on their
way home by ship from Djibouti.

The next day ' Everybody standing to from dawn onwards.
About 40 Indians, Greeks and others in our main dugout. All the
Swedish missionaries came up and will shelter with us every
morning.' It was clear that the end was getting close and late in
April Graziani at last launched his offensive from the south and
Chapman-Andrews radioed Barton in Addis Ababa on the 24th:
'Events reported in my last message have been confirmed. Dej
Abebe [Damtew] and Makonnen [Endalkatchew] are now engaged
and Dej Nasibu [the Governor]is now South. Orders have been
issued to officers in charge of outlying districts to bring as many
men as they can muster to Harar as quickly as possible. The
balloon has started to go up at last.'

On 1 May a message came through from Dr Elphick, a doctor
in the Egyptian Red Cross hospital in Jijiga: 'There is no resistance
at all to their advance to Jijiga (or to Harar by direct road)
according to Wahib Pasha and all the way back they were struggling from Daghabar, where three Ethiopian officers who wanted
their men to sit and fight there were shot for their opinions by their
retreat-minded men. There are trenches in the hills round Jijiga but
Wahib doubts if he can find soldiers for them . . . Am now going
to see Wahib again who suggests we go to Harar; he is a great chap
and I shall try and stick to him like a limpet. If you can tell my
people that I am well, I would be forever grateful and would pay
anything. Please write to me by the bearer of this.'

The Emperor Escapes

Meanwhile the Emperor had reached Addis Ababa on Thursday,
30 April, with some of his supporters but not many troops; they
had spent the last few days dodging the Italian advance down the
main route from Dessie and continued to trickle in, exhausted and
disorganized. However, a large number of the Emperor's Council
were still in the capital and a meeting took place that afternoon.

20

There were conflicting arguments; some, led by Blatta Takele, an old confidant of the Emperor, and Lorenzo Taezes, his Secretary, urged resistance north of Addis Ababa and for the Emperor and government to continue the fight from Gore in the west; others, and this included many who had witnessed the fighting and collapse in the north, argued that the fight was effectively over and that the Emperor should leave for Europe to continue the fight at the League. A frantic and bewildering 24 hours followed, during which the Empress pressed strongly that the Emperor and the Imperial family should leave the country for Jerusalem while the rail route to the coast still remained open. The next day, Friday 1 May, Sir Sidney Barton telegraphed the Foreign Office that the Emperor's Secretary had come to the Legation to advise that the Emperor had decided to hand over to the Council of State and was leaving for the coast and asked that a naval ship should come to Djibouti to take him and his family to Palestine. Anthony Eden had immediately contacted the French Ambassador, de Margerie, to ask for his assistance at Djibouti, to be told that the Emperor had made no approach to the French authorities. Eden advised that a British cruiser was now sailing for Djibouti and would be there at 6pm on the 3rd and de Margerie confirmed that the French would be happy to assist. The timing of this suggests that, contrary to the belief that the decision to leave was only taken later that afternoon, the Emperor, or at least Taezes and some of his advisers, had already decided to do so. With the Italians reported only 100 miles north of the city, it was later that day that the Council voted 21 to 3 that the Emperor should leave; only Blatta Tekele and two others argued that he should not desert his country but should fight, if necessary, to the end. What is clear is that, perhaps for the first time in his life, the Emperor, who had seen the defeat of everything he had fought for over the last 20 years, was shattered and unable to make up his mind. He knew that for many Ethiopians the 'Elect of God' was a warrior who must fight to the death in his own country and in flight to the lands of the distrusted foreigners he would be considered to have forfeited his position as Emperor and that the Italians would use it to deride him. It was not only men like Blatta Tekele who would remember this; in 1940 many of the Allied commanders doubted if the Emperor would be accepted again by his subjects.

The Emperor and his staff knew that attempts might well be

21

made to restrain his departure. At 4.20am on Saturday, 2 May he went to the railway station and waved off the train taking the Imperial family and many others to Djibouti, but rather than returning to his Palace he gave the crowds the slip and went secretly to board the train 10 miles down the track.

Late that evening, a stormy night, Chapman-Andrews had a telephone call from the Governor of Harar, Nasibu, 'summoning me to accompany him to Diredawa where the Emperor wished to see me. I took ten of my Somali guards in a truck behind my car and they were extremely useful in pulling my car through several hundred yards of thick mud on the road near Lake Haramiya. As a results of that night's consultations the Emperor reluctantly decided to proceed by train to Djibouti and leave the country rather than fulfil his original intention of raising his standard with a view to resisting the Italians between Harar and Jijiga. The military situation in this locality at that time was quite hopeless. If the Emperor had attempted to continue the fight I do not think that he could have escaped death or capture.'

From this it would appear that the Emperor, racked by doubts, was still undecided. Chapman-Andrews later made it clear that he had advised the Emperor that there was no hope for him to continue resistance from within Ethiopia and that he must leave. He kept the scribbled radio message which he must have sent to Barton on behalf of the Emperor dated 1 am 3 May: 'Regarding the communication of yesterday by Wolde Giorgis on the subject of our joining a British battleship, we beg Y[our] E[xcellency] to communicate with us if he has received a reply to the telegram which he kindly allowed me to send to his government. We shall be grateful to Y.E. if our journey could eventually be made by way of Berbera and that the reply be given either to Aden or the Captain of the Ship'. In the event the French authorities allowed the party to continue to Djibouti where they embarked on the British cruiser HMS *Enterprise* on the 4th, together with some forty other notables, including Governor Nasibu and the Turkish General Wahib, who managed to reach them via Berbera just in time. Another forty had to find their own way out of the country.

Doubtless Chapman-Andrews had been well briefed by wireless from Barton in the Legation that a British warship was awaiting him at Djibouti, but the Emperor never forgot that night and the advice that Chapman-Andrews had given him.

Four days later the High Commissioner in Palestine, Sir Arthur Wauchope, reported the Emperor's safe arrival in Jerusalem, where the Ethiopian Church had an important traditional presence: 'Emperor very frail and under medical supervision'. Leaving his family behind, he was determined to press ahead to England where he arrived under naval protection on 3 June to a big welcome at Victoria station, but with minimal official representation. On 30 June he presented his case in an elegant and prophetic speech, claiming the justice due to his people, at the League of Nations in Geneva. He ended: 'It is not merely a question of the settlement of Italian aggression. It is the very existence of the League of Nations. It is the confidence that each state is to place in international treaties. It is the value of promises to small states that their integrity and independence shall be respected. In a word it is international morality that is at stake. Representatives of the world, I have come to Geneva to discharge in your midst the most painful of the duties of a head of state. What reply shall I have to take back to my people?' As he stepped down he was reported as saying: 'It is us today; it will be you tomorrow'.

But answer came there none. To the leading powers, pre-occupied with the diplomatic manoeuvering following the German reoccupation of the Rhineland on 3 March, Ethiopia was now history and four days later the Assembly voted to lift sanctions against Italy. What HMG and France had feared was to follow shortly: in October Italy and Germany signed an agreement which was to place Italy firmly in the Axis camp. As Vansittart, Permanent Secretary at the Foreign Office, expressed later a view widely held, including by Churchill, 'Because a few *askari* had died by brackish waterholes in an African waste, thus was taken the first step to the second German holocaust'. It was a defeat for the Emperor, which he never forgave, and even more the death knell for the whole concept of the League of Nations itself.

In November 1938 Chamberlain's government, from which Eden had resigned, joined France in recognizing Italy as the *de jure* ruler of Ethiopia.

The Collapse in Harar

As the Emperor left Diredawa for Djibouti on 3 May a well-known figure was observed boarding the train leaving for the capital; it

23

was his old enemy Ras Hailu, whom the Emperor had been taking along under effective 'house arrest', but who had given him the slip and was returning to meet the Italians. In Addis Ababa there had been two days of looting and rioting and law and order had completely broken down, as George Steer's *Caesar in Abyssinia* relates. Some 1400 people were sheltering in the Legation grounds protected by Sikh troops which the far-seeing Barton had reinforced shortly before. The arrival of the Italian army was anxiously awaited, which is probably what they had intended: to appear as saviours of the foreign population from the savagery of the looting Ethiopians. For this it was important that they should give the looters time to do their work.

It was not long before Harar was to see the same tactics. As Chapman-Andrews drove back from Diredawa early in the morning he met the Ethiopian generals leaving Harar and looting was beginning. He immediately gathered all British protected persons, including the Finns, at the Consulate, where the twenty Somali Guards were patrolling the perimeter, and awaited the Italian arrival. In spite of the departure of the Governor, the authorities tried to calm an anxious city with a proclamation on 5 May that everything was under control and that life, including tax-paying, should continue as normal. Jijiga fell to Graziani later that day. It was now only a matter of time and the situation in Harar deteriorated further. It was a matter of '*sauve qui peut*' and there were many requests to the Consul for advice and help. The doctor at the French Leprosy Hospital wrote: '*Monsieur le Consul, que pensez-vous de la situation? Est-ce que vous restez a Ginella? et dans ce cas pourrait-on refugier au Consulat d'Angleterre. Bien sincerement à vous.*' The following day, 6 May, a rough roll call showed 124 at the Consulate: ' British Subjects 43; British Protected Persons 30; Harari 20; Greek 1; Ethiopian 30'. The next day messengers continued to pour in, including an Ethiopian plea for Union Jacks: ' We are very pleased to hear that the British flag is being flown at Harar and Jijiga and as the inhabitants are looting and killing one another and the Somalis are to destroy the country, I request you to send me a flag and two or three if available.' The aged Monseigneur Jarosseau, the head of the French Catholic Mission, wrote very formally to thank the Consul warmly for offers of help '*en ces heures tragiques*', but said that he would stay to protect the Mission. (He survived, but, according to Evelyn

24

Waugh who called on him in August, was expelled but brought back again amidst tears of the populace.

Later that evening the representative of Mohamedally & Co, long-established Indian merchants and thus British Protected Persons, sent a frantic plea for help: 'Humbly we beg to inform you that this morning our doors are attacked by the rioters. Whole of the town is panic-stricken. Every piece of article is looted and men beaten. We are in the utmost danger. Up to now we have saved our life as we have only one gun and four cartridges and now it is the last moment. If the proper aid will not come immediately, we do not know what shall happen to us. For God's sake please send help. Send some armed men as well as guns etc to save our lives., I remain, Yours faithfully.' Chapman-Andrews immediately responded by coming to their rescue, as we know from the British Press and from the speech at a dinner given for him by the Indian merchants on 7 July: 'It is now a joy to express that 7 May was a terrible day for a handful of British Indian merchants who were surrounded by ferocious and excited Abyssinians who were either going to make severe injuries to these people or to kill them. But the timely help of Mr Consul was a God-sent boon to those distressed persons. It was courageous action on the part of Mr Chapman, who paid little heed for the excited well armed mobs whose numbers were five or ten times greater than Mr Consul's party, which rushed forward for the rescue and got our people removed to a safe place.'

The Italian army arrived the next day and Chapman-Andrews' recording of his meeting with General Nasi rather delphically noted: 'once MA London – Bargain', which probably refers to his retention for the time being of his British Somali guards and his wireless. Barton radioed: 'Warmest congratulations to yourself, your staff and your guard on your courageous and successful main-tenance of HBM Consulate,' and on the 12th a further message, probably after telegrams of thanks from other governments for the safety of their subjects, came in to London: 'The Secretary of State desires me to convey to you his warmest congratulations on manner in which you your staff and Somali Police Guard have surmounted a most trying situation and have succeeded in protecting British and other foreign lives'. The British Press was full of headlines: 'British Consul keeps Looters at Bay' (*News Chronicle*); 'British Hero of Looted town' (*Daily Mirror*); 'British to the Rescue again in Abyssinia – Consul with Somaliland Police Saves Foreigners in Looted Harar' (*Daily Sketch*) 'Exonian Consul's Heroism – Mr Chapman-Andrews' Fine Work at Harar – So terrible was the experience that several women who stayed in the town went mad'(*Exeter Express and Echo*); 'British Consul Helping to Keep Order' (more prosaically *The Times*).

On 23 June the award to Chapman-Andrews of the OBE was gazetted, one of the few that bear the signature of Edward VIII.

The next few months were an anticlimax and Chapman-Andrews' diary records little but the serial number of radio messages to and from the Legation in Addis Ababa, now without a Minister as Barton had been withdrawn, and shortly to be reduced to a Consulate General. The Italians gradually restored some order to Harar, but the Consul's position was steadily eroded, since they required no official witnesses to their activities and foreigners were 'encouraged' to leave. Passes were necessary to move within Harar and in June to allow him to visit Jijiga, signed by Nasi. There are notes in the diary saying 'Close wireless' and 'Flag insult'. All the foreign medical and other volunteers – and journalists – left.

In August Evelyn Waugh, who was completing his book *Waugh in Abyssinia*, came to see him and described in his diary: 'August 20th. Arrived consulate about 6. Chapman-Andrews recuperating after bad go of fever. Long talk about situation. Local wops are clearly being extremely amenable but the British peevish – in their language "browned off". During war Wahib Pasha's defence line never used because army already broken before they fell back on them and no one to man them. Nasibu fled with the first. Gas used four or five times on southern front; some blind brought back to hospital. Harar was entirely empty of troops at time of bombardment, but important supply centre and some arms found hidden there later by looters. When town first taken by Italians handed over to savage banda who killed all Christians they found, including three priests within short distance British Consulate. Banda since sent back. Usual complaints of interference with telegraph and posts. Weaver birds opposite my window.' Much of this is clearly from his discussion with Chapman-Andrews.

In *Waugh in Abyssinia* he describes Chapman-Andrews in, for him, uniquely polite terms: 'I spent two nights with my former host at the British Consulate. He is a man who shuns publicity and for that reason alone I have been obliged to omit any detailed descrip-

26

tion of his achievements during the preceding eighteen months. From the attack on WalWal until the time of his departure shortly after my visit, he worked alone in circumstances of constant anxiety aggravated at the end by a grave attack of fever. He dealt with a situation of the utmost delicacy and responsibility, a responsibility out of all proportion to his seniority in the service. [He was only 33.] It is too little to say – but it is all I dare say without antagonising him and betraying his hospitality – that of the honours distributed amongst the various Englishmen who distinguished themselves in Abyssinia during this unhappy period, none was more admirably earned than his.'

On 1 September Mohamedallys gave him a Farewell Address on behalf of the Indian merchants: 'During the time of your tenure of office we have experienced nothing but mercy, kindness, goodwill and true affection from your hands. You have spared no pains in guarding our interests as well as of all British subjects, sick or poor, high or low, in this country at a time most delicate and most dangerous! We wish you a safe journey and a refreshing and enjoyable holiday in England.' On the 9th the Chargé d'Affaires in Addis Ababa reported Chapman-Andrews' departure on leave on an RAF plane via Aden. The next month he received from Sir Robert Vansittart, Permanent Secretary at the Foreign Office, a copy of the Legation's despatch: 'I am directed by Mr Secretary Eden . . . to convey to you the expression of the warm pleasure which which he has read this high and well deserved tribute to your services as Acting British Consul at Harar: A year of exceptionally difficult and exacting conditions culminated in the anxious responsibilities of the days immediately preceding the entry of the Italian troops into Harar early in May when Mr Chapman-Andrews abundantly justified the implicit confidence reposed in him by his intrepidity and by that coolness which has distinguished him throughout . . . In conclusion I would say that Mr Chapman-Andrews has filled his post with a distinction that many an older man might envy and that his transfer will be a substantial loss to British representation in this country.'

Egypt and the Approaching War

Chapman-Andrews wrote long afterwards: 'During the intervening years I did not see the Emperor even once nor did I have any contact other than occasional personal friendly encounters with any Ethiopians. I was not a private individual but an officer in the Foreign Office.' He kept a letter written in August 1937 at Bush House from C.S Collier, who had been the Emperor's financial adviser in Addis Ababa and had followed him into exile, enquiring, 'Would you care to have an audience with the Emperor? He recently spoke of your kindness to him when he was in Harar district' – probably a euphemism for the traumatic meeting at Diredawa station on the night of 2/3 May. One senses from his remarks that Chapman-Andrews was perhaps conscious later of the fact that he had played no part in supporting the Emperor in his dark days of exile. However, he had nothing to reproach himself about; he was an impecunious young consular official with a young family and a career to make in a service which needed to be critical of over-involvement or the taking of sides by its officials. The Emperor's tribulations in exile have been well documented elsewhere as he bided his time, which was not long in coming.

In England Chapman-Andrews was reunited with family, who had returned by boat and, after leave, reported to the Foreign Office in London, where he worked until he was promoted in 1937 to the Post of Assistant Oriental Secretary in the Embassy in Cairo under the formidable Sir Miles Lampson (later Lord Killearn) and his Oriental Secretary, Sir Walter Smart. However, he undoubtedly maintained his interest and sympathy in Ethiopia and persuaded Lampson that he should be allowed discreetly to keep in touch with Ethiopian exiles residing or passing through Egypt.

The Italian/Ethiopian War had helped to persuade the Egyptians in 1936 to sign an Anglo-Egyptian Agreement which included suitable mutual defence arrangemnts, soon to be implemented, and the establishment of mutual diplomatic relations and the conversion of the British representative from High Commissioner to Ambassador. For a brief period relations between the two countries were amicable and Chapman-Andrews was able to throw himself into the official and social life of Cairo and Alexandria. In May 1938 there was a further addition to the family and in May 1939 they returned to England on leave, soon to be interrupted by the gathering war clouds.

He wrote later: 'Whilst I did not foresee exactly the date of the outbreak of war, I believed that it would break out towards the end of that summer. I accordingly took my wife and six-year-old son and his baby sister home from Egypt for an early leave; my wife was expecting our younger daughter to be born in September and I was taking no chances. That summer we bought a small cottage in South Devon and made arrangements against the possible outbreak of war. My leave was nearly up and my cabin trunk had already been consigned to the Port of London for shipment by the P & O s.s. *Rawalpindi*, which I was booked to join a week later in Marseilles.

'Then came a telegram from the Foreign Office: "Report to the Embarkation officer, Victoria Station at 2.00pm." So in that morning's rig, namely hard hat, chamois leather gloves, rolled umbrella, dark suit, stiff white collar, report I did. No time for anything but the purchase of a spare shirt and a small bag to put it in, with my shaving kit. Just as well, as there was no room for luggage. 300 officers reported to Victoria that afternoon and 1000 ratings from the Royal Naval reserve all with muster money in their pockets. Special trains took us to Dover where we embarked, packed like sardines, for a night crossing of the Channel. From Calais next morning special trains conveyed us by slow degrees round Paris towards Marseilles. Most of the muster money had been invested in cases of beer and cheap cognac, so the trip was a rowdy one, marked, at the occasional halt, by a rating or two making a break at a fast pace across country for England, home and beauty. This greatly surprised us at the time. On the outskirts of Paris, we were given a 'runashore' and, as most of us hadn't a clue where we were supposed to be going, it was amusing to learn from the French that we were a naval division en route for the Dardanelles!

'At Marseilles we were packed on board one of HM's ships. Our sparse kit was stowed, we were issued with two blankets apiece and assigned a sleeping space measuring about 6 feet by 2 feet. Mine was a table on the Royal Marines' mess deck, but after a brief reconnaissance I managed to swap for a smaller but more airy billet under the forward gun turret. The ship was battened down and darkened at night and we made full speed for Malta. Meals were served continuously during daylight by the Royal Marines. Their discipline, despatch and bearing, doing a job for which they had not enlisted, under trying conditions, was beyond all praise. The brief run ashore at Malta started with a mad dash for the shops

29

which were cleared of lilos in a few minutes. After a swim – Oh heavenly half hour! – we were back on board. I shared my lilo, sleeping top and toe with the Manager of the Alexandria Water Company. Those still hot moonlight nights, as the ship cut through the opal sea, were broken only by the periodic swing of the gun turret and the flat "clock" of the cartridge as the gunners checked on the electrical firing circuit. We spent our day moving around the turret to keep in the shade, and listening eagerly to the news, of which my outstanding recollection is the strident hysterical voice of Adolf Hitler on radio newsreel. He thought he had us.

'A few days later we were ashore at Alexandria, the voyage over, another world. The war seemed as remote as ever, except in the Embassy. There, we worked all hours, and by chance one afternoon I was in the Chancery when the code word "Plumper" was received and acknowledged. The Ambassador's ADC from the RAF was with me. It meant "War with Germany".

'My cabin trunk, though not securely locked, fetched up in Devon some two years later, everything in apple pie order, my shot gun carefully laid between the shirts. It had been around the Cape of Good Hope to Egypt and, finding me gone, it had made its way home again via the Cape, across the Atlantic and back. Gallant *Rawalpindi* had then long been at the bottom of the North Sea. She was sunk in action by a German cruiser in what was, I think, the first sea fight of the Second World War.'

It was another nine months before Chapman-Andrews was to see his family again and meet his new daughter, born on 11 September. It was a busy time for the Embassy and the impact of the war on the Egyptians and the surrounding countries made for plenty of work, particularly in trying to ensure that King Farouk and the Egyptian Government were committed to the Allied side. There were many Egyptians who were not: one was the future President Anwar Sadat of whom Chapman-Andrews wrote many years later: 'I saw Sadat when he was over here (in London). He remembered me all right. He tried to join the Germans in 1940. I always had more than a sneaking regard for him because he was a genuine patriot; he had a fair amount of guts and from all accounts was straight.'

Cairo was filling up rapidly with the arrival of troops and the expansion of GHQ Middle East under General Wavell. In April 1940 Chapman-Andrews was summoned to London for reasons which are not clear, but may have been in connection with his knowledge of Ethiopia and the Emperor, although he never acknowledged this. With France crumbling and neutral Italy poised to come in with Germany, it must have been a nerve-racking journey; by Khedival Mail line boat to Marseilles and train across France to Calais on 29 April. By that time the French were understandably very nervy and the British thought to be insufficiently supportive and attitudes had become unfriendly as the train moved north and as Denmark and Norway fell.

He spent a few days with the family in Devon: 'Wonderful early summer; cloudless blue skies; bright moonlight nights.' and was due back early in May, but with the German invasion of Belgium and the Netherlands on 10 May and the deteriorating situation in France, he was ordered to 'stay put'. It was clearly no longer possible to reach Marseilles by train as the Germans had already reached the channel at Abbeville. It wasn't until 25 May that he was ordered to Sandbanks to pick up a flying boat at Poole harbour on which a Turkish Military mission was waiting to return. They flew via Bordeaux and Marseilles and were held at Lake Bracciano in Italy before being allowed to proceed to Athens; after a night at the Grande Bretagne, they reached Cairo safely.

A month later Chapman-Andrews would be back in Alexandria on the start of his next Ethiopian adventure.

Chapter Three

With the Emperor at Khartoum

On the morning of 26 June 1940 Chapman-Andrews, then Ist Secretary (Oriental) in the Embassy in Cairo, was summoned to join General Wavell, the Ambassador, Sir Miles Lampson and Colonel Clayton, head of Middle East Intelligence, at GHQ. They had just been signalled from London that Emperor Haile Selassie was due to arrive from England in a flying boat at Alexandria later that day. It is not clear what the Emperor had been told about his ultimate destination, but Wavell and Lampson rapidly decided that he could not stay in Egypt and that he should continue to Khartoum. Chapman-Andrews was given the delicate task of flying at 10 minutes' notice to meet him on arrival in Alexandria and of accompanying him to Khartoum to introduce him to his still unsuspecting future hosts.

The Emperor had spent his years of exile, since arriving in London in 1936, in Bath, surrounded by a small group of devoted staff and supported by a number of British who had felt that HMG had let him down, including Sir Sidney Barton, recently retired from the Legation in Addis Ababa, and Sandford, of whom much hereafter. Money was short and HMG, preoccupied with the darkening diplomatic skies and anxious to give no excuse to Italy to ally itself more closely to Germany, chose to ignore him. This was still the case early in 1940. However, in Cairo Wavell, C-in-C Middle East, fully realized the implications of Ethiopia, at the heart of Italian East Africa, where the Italians had some 300,000 troops. Separated only by the Sudan and Egypt, they had a further 215,000 troops in Libya. In his command in Egypt, Sudan, Palestine, Aden and East Africa, Wavell had some 100,000 troops, a fifth of the Italian forces. He was also looking to the French forces of similar size in Syria and Djibouti, but the French armistice in June 1940 left him suddenly deprived of this support. In his strategic assessment Wavell appreciated the threat of Italy entering the war against the Allies, overrunning the British Territories and taking control of the Mediterranean, the Red Sea and the route to the oilfields and India. In Churchill, now Prime Minister, he found someone who knew the Middle East well and who, whilst he had previously thought of 'Abyssinia' as a dangerous distraction from the real struggle in Europe, now fully appreciated his concerns. With France crumbling, it was clear that Italy would not long delay coming into the War, which they did on 10 June.

With help from his political friends, the Emperor wrote to Lord Halifax, the Foreign Secretary, to propose that he should return to the Middle East as a first step to destabilizing the Italians in Italian East Africa and, in his mind, to recovering his throne. In the War Office a new section, the 'Special Operations Executive' or SOE, had been set up some months before under Major-General Colin Gubbins to organize and support what was to become known as 'Resistance' in Occupied Territories. They had already had been planning how to support resistance to the Italians in Ethiopia and to this end, according to Douglas Dodds-Parker in *Setting Europe Ablaze*, had secured a gift of 10,000 Springfield rifles from the USA through President Roosevelt and permission to arrange the minting of Maria Theresa dollars in Bombay to supply the Ethiopian 'Patriots'. SOE worked very informally and with much secrecy and deliberately kept few records. As a result they hardly appear in the official accounts of the war in Ethiopia, but it is clear that they were both the inspirers and controllers of the Emperor's return, of Mission 101 and, initially, of what was to become Gideon Force. So, while the Emperor was probably unaware of this background, it is no surprise that on 18 June Churchill and the Cabinet agreed to his immediate return to the Middle East. Eden cabled Wavell stressing the need to defend the Sudan and added: 'An insurrection in Ethiopia would greatly assist your task,' of which Wavell was well aware. With the collapse of France, it was important to get him there as quickly as possible and the Emperor and a small party, together with George Steer as his liaison officer from SOE, were spirited secretly out of London to Plymouth where a Sunderland flying boat was waiting for them. Flying over occupied France and

French North Africa, they refuelled in Malta and landed at Alexandria 18 hours later.

Meanwhile Khartoum was unaware of the imminent arrival of their uninvited guest. The administration in the condominium of the Anglo-Egyptian Sudan had always regarded themselves as rather independent, with their prime responsibility to the Sudanese, and did not regard instructions from HMG in London with the awe expected in mere colonies. Headed by the Governor-General, Sir Stewart Symes, they consisted of a small body of the devoted and elite Sudan Political Service, often rather caustically described as 'the Blues ruling the Blacks'. Symes was supported by the Civil Secretary, Sir Douglas Newbold, and the Kaid – the Egyptian title was still used – Major-General Platt, as Head of the Sudan Defence Force. While, at the time, they would have deplored the seizure of Ethiopia by the Italians as being thoroughly 'off side', they had little sympathy with the Ethiopians, whom they tended to regard as bandits and trouble-makers and as traditional enemies of the Sudan; particularly after the arrival in 1938 of the more emollient Duke of Aosta as Italian Viceroy, some of them found that they had many things in common with the Italian colonial administration, who were trying to get to grips with law and order and keeping their shared frontier quiet. There was regular contact since all Italian planes flying to and from Addis Ababa refuelled at Khartoum right up to the declaration of war. Aosta himself was welcome in Khartoum where he visited Symes in July 1939 and invited Douglas Dodds-Parker, then working in the Security department in Khartoum, to visit him in Ethiopia. As late as 25 April 1940 Aosta visited Cairo where Ambassador Lampson, who was married to an Italian wife, found him most sympathetic and equally worried about Italy's warlike intentions. The Sudan Political Service often found their Italian opposite numbers personally agreeable and, in any case, were not thought a threat to be taken seriously. While the British in the Sudan were not at all racist – indeed, very much the contrary – it is not surprising, given the European cultural sympathies of the period, that many of them felt that they had more in common with the Italians than with the notoriously difficult Ethiopians.

Symes, who was waiting to retire, and his team, were fully aware of the vulnerability of the Sudan to the Italian forces. Platt was very conscious that he had at his command only some 7000 men, including three British home counties battalions (2500) and 4000 in the locally enlisted Sudan Defence Force. The RAF had forty planes, of which only nine were fighters, and all but seven were dedicated to keeping the Red Sea clear from Suez to Aden. He and Symes had concluded that he must play for time and that nothing should be done to provoke immediate Italian action. While obedient to Whitehall's *bon voisonage* policy with regard to the Italians, he and Platt had set up in June 1939 a small Ethiopian Intelligence department, under Lieutenant-Colonel Jose Penney, Chief of Sudan Military Intelligence, and asked Cheesman, who had been Consul in Dangila until 1934, to return from retirement in England to join them. At Dangila Cheesman had been responsible to the Sudan government for local intelligence and for promoting Britain's interest in Lake Tana and the Nile waters and a possible road between the two countries. Already in his 60s, Cheesman remained at Khartoum HQ throughout the campaign until posted to the Addis Ababa legation in 1942. In Cairo Clayton, Chief of Middle East Intelligence, had recruited Sandford to join him in Cairo and in October 1939 sent him to Khartoum, but Newbold wrote that 'for certain psychological and other reasons, he is not a suitable person to have here'. He and Platt felt that he was too committed to the Emperor and would be a red rag to the Italians. So Sandford returned to Cairo where he concentrated on building up knowledge of the Ethiopian exiles until the time was ripe. In October 1939 the War Office wrote to Khartoum that any Ethiopian rebel activities should be 'assisted', but Platt limited his response to increasing Intelligence work.

With the Italian declaration of war, any Khartoum reticence ended and Colonel Sandford arrived in Khartoum on 17 June. After service in the Sudan Political Service and in the First World War, Sandford had lived from 1920–35 in Addis Ababa and was well known to the Emperor and, as we have already seen, to all the foreign visitors to Ethiopia during that period. (Harmsworth commented that Sandford's farm was the only source of 'Fresh Farm Eggs' in the town.) At 58 he was remarkably fit, emergetic and self-reliant, as he was to need to be. Having spent his years of 'exile' as Treasurer to the Guildford Cathedral Building Fund, he was longing to get back to the Front Line and to his confiscated home in Ethiopia. Plans were discussed as to how the Ethiopian guerrillas could be supported and liaison with the small and hitherto ignored group of Ethiopian exiles in Khartoum established, presumably in liaison with SOE's Cairo office.

So, against this background, it is not surprising that Wavell's radio message to Khartoum advising of the Emperor's imminent arrival in the Sudan, sent late on 26 June and probably too late to reach Symes that night, was not received with any pleasure; it was a clear provocation to the Italians.

To return to Alexandria, George Steer wrote: 'A boat chuffed out of the harbour between the pale walls of another immobilized French fleet and in it, as it drew abreast, I saw the philosophic face of Clayton, who had enlisted me [as a member of SOE Intelligence] and the sharper features of Chapman-Andrews, whom I had last known when we waited for Graziani in 1936 in his Harar consulate with three American journalist who spent most of their time looking for gin because they could not find stories. In those early days of 1940, I recall with some shame, we eyed each other rather foxily, wondering which was to be the new Lawrence.' (Such an idea would certainly not have been in Chapman-Andrews' thoughts since Lawrence of Arabia was not one of his heroes!) Given the need for secrecy, it was decided that the party should be entertained in the recently seized enemy property of the Italian Sailing Club, where the pictures of Mussolini had to be quickly removed. Clayton had to explain to the Emperor the need for secrecy and the move to Khartoum and Chapman-Andrews' role. The Emperor's party consisted, apart from Steer, of his younger son, Prince Makonnen, who had been brought out in mid-term from Wellington where he was at school, and his private secretaries, Lorenzo Taezes (technically still his Ambassador to the League of Nations) and Wolde Giorgis. Clayton returned to Cairo and the party, with Chapman-Andrews, flew on in the morning for Khartoum.

Shortly after becoming airborne they received a wireless message from the Governor-General ordering them not to proceed to Khartoum but to land at Wadi Halfa, the lonely Sudanese railhead just over the Egyptian frontier. This caused consternation to the Emperor and his party and, writing many years later, the pilot, Group Captain Bevan John, described Chapman-Andrews, with masterly understatement, as being 'somewhat put out'. Describing the alarm in Khartoum, Cheesman wrote, diplomatically: 'The unannounced arrival caused some embarrassment as no suitable accommodation had been arranged and, what was equally important, no precautions had been taken for His Majesty's safety. It was realised that it would be well worth while for the Italians to pay someone a large sum of money for his assassination. The responsibilities which rested on the shoulders of the Governor General were heavy.' While all this was true, it was only part of the story: Symes and Platt were concerned that the news of the arrival of the Emperor in Khartoum would be all that was needed to provoke the Italians to invade the virtually defenceless Sudan. Having despatched the message halting the party at Wadi Halfa, Symes immediately called a meeting at the Palace with Platt, Newbold and Cheesman to decide what to do before Chapman-Andrews, who insisted on flying down to reaffirm HMG and Wavell's orders, could arrive 'to try and clear matters up and to arrange for the Emperor's forward movements'. Quite apart from strategic considerations, considerable doubts were expressed as to whether the Emperor still held any power over his people and would be able to help to destabilize the Italians. Cheesman argued strongly on the basis of his intelligence work and of Colonel Sandford's soundings on the ground that it would make all the difference and could result in a general Ethiopian revolt which would distract the Italians from any warlike intentions with regard to the Sudan.

Chapman-Andrews, still at 36 a comparatively junior diplomat, had a difficult meeting with three such senior men, who much resented the position in which they found themselves. He had to make it clear that there was no way in which the Cabinet's decision could be overturned and the Emperor sent back or elsewhere. Symes asked indignantly why he had not been consulted and Platt talked of Bonnie Prince Charlie and suggested that the Emperor should return to London. After further discussions between themselves, Symes conceded that the Emperor would have to be allowed in and suitable accommodation found, but, requested Mr Chapman-Andrews 'to leave the Emperor under no misapprehension, whatever may have been said by him in London, that practically nothing had or could for some time be prepared to promote a revolt in Ethiopia and that meanwhile His Majesty would have to endure patiently the somewhat restrictive measures necessary to ensure his security'.

The next day Chapman-Andrews, accompanied by Sandford,

flew back to Wadi Halfa to tell the Emperor what had been decided, to explain that virtually no preparations had been made or resources made available to take the offensive in Ethiopia and the reasons for the continued secrecy. The Emperor, who had been led, or chose to believe, that he had received assurances before he left London that full British help would be immediately available to assist him in his planned return to Ethiopia, was most upset. However, Sandford was able to outline his plan, which had received Wavell's blessing, to enter North-Western Ethiopia with small groups of mixed British and Ethiopian soldiers to make contact with and support any 'patriot' forces. It had also been agreed that other exiled Ethiopians could join him in Khartoum. Later that evening the Emperor, with his usual patience, had accepted the situation and Chapman-Andrews flew back in the flying boat to Cairo to brief Wavell and Lampson. Meanwhile the Emperor and his party had to remain incommunicado in the intense heat of desolate Wadi Halfa in a specially screened-off area of the Sudan Railways' Nile Hotel for a further frustrating week. Steer recalled filling in the time with trips on the Nile to visit Christian archaeological sites and drinks of shandy and listening to Charlie Kunz on the radiogram. First, however, a tailor had to be let into the secret and allowed in to make some clothes, since the Emperor and his party had had to reduce their baggage to bare necessities.

The Emperor Finally Arrives in Khartoum

Meanwhile decisions were reached in Khartoum that the Emperor, or 'Mr Smith' as General Platt had decreed he should be described, should be housed in a secluded house belonging to the old Sudanese family of Sherif Yousif El Hindi some two miles upstream from town on the Blue Nile in the recently commandeered British Military Compound. Because of the colour of its distemper it was always known as the 'Pink Palace'. (Some other sources described it incorrectly as being at the Jebel Aulia dam on the White Nile some 20 miles up-country, although this was used for some of the other Ethiopian exiles from Jerusalem who arrived suspiciously conveniently later that week, which suggests that the Emperor had already envisaged Khartoum as his base for return to his country, whatever HMG or Wavell might have been thinking.

Cheesman met them at the station and said, in his dry way, that as 'mile upon mile of lonely desert rolled past, they evinced some nervousness as to their fate'.)

Amidst everincreasing secrecy, including the arrest of likely Italian spies and undesirable elements, plans were made for the Emperor's actual arrival. Cheesman wrote: 'The special train from Wadi Halfa was timed to arrive at Khartoum North Railway station a few miles north of town after dark at 8.30pm on July 3rd. The question of how to maintain secrecy if taxi drivers had been hired was settled by Mr Edward Attiyah of the Public Security Department, and one of Khartoum's well known citizens, Mr Gabs Kfouri, who offered to disguise themselves as Sudanese taxi drivers and use their own cars. Having arrived at the Pink Palace and thrown off their motley attire they joined in the reception party. General Platt met the Emperor at the train with some of the Ethiopian exiles who had already arrived and they all accompanied the Emperor to the Pink Palace. There Sir Stewart Symes and Major Cheesman were waiting to welcome His Majesty. Prince Makonnen, also Wolde Giorgis, Lorenzo Taezes and Captain Steer, had come by the same train. There was a short reception ceremony when good luck to the great venture and the future was drunk in champagne. Sir Stewart, speaking in French, then informed His Majesty that he was instructing Major Cheesman to take personal charge of him and that he was to consider him as a liaison officer between himself and the Governor General.'

The next day Sir Stewart's worst fears were confirmed when the Italians invaded and occupied Kassala on Sudan's Eritrean border. Cheesman had to explain to the Emperor the continued need for secrecy and that he must remain out of sight with strict control on all access to him. 'It amounted to keeping him as a prisoner, but we were not sure who were our friends and who our enemies. [This will have applied particularly to visitors from Ethiopia.] His Majesty replied with his usual charm that he quite understood. As the months passed and the political and military situation improved we were able to relax these irksome restrictions.' There were moments of farce: the next morning the Emperor asked to see a bank manager and Cheesman telephoned his bank to try and explain that 'Mr Smith' would like an interview. The bank manager said that 'Mr Smith' should come and see him as he didn't usually go out and see clients. What was his Christian name? He had many different Smiths on his books. Why can't he come? Is he ill? After endless reiteration by Cheesman that this was *THE* Mr Smith, it dawned on the manager who it was and he duly called. Cheesman proudly states that it took the Italians in Ethiopia twenty days before they learnt of the Emperor's whereabouts, and then it was from Rome! (The allies were greatly aided by the fact that the Italian codes had already been broken and thus Intelligence in Khartoum was able to monitor their messages.)

While the Emperor was disappointed that the British forces were so stretched and so little able to support his ambitions to recover his throne, he was proverbially patient and he needed to be; some six months were to pass before the situation could move from the defensive. Confidentially briefing Richard Dimbleby and other journalists, Platt told them, 'Gentlemen, I think you should know the exact facts of the situation. I am facing an Italian Army which could walk right through the Sudan tomorrow if it wanted to. It doesn't want to because I'm bluffing it with all my available forces.' Although the Italians had immediately crossed the frontier and seized Kassala and Gallabat and began rather tentative air raids on the nearer Sudanese towns, they took no further steps to advance into the Sudan. The main Italian thrust was to take place from Libya across the Egyptian frontier and the Duke of Aosta, who was a member of the Royal family and not a fascist, and whose heart was not really in the war, was more concerned at now being cut off from access to Italy and to his supply lines of fuel and equipment. He restricted his main effort to seizing British Somaliland which was evacuated on 16 August after giving the Italian forces rather more trouble than they had expected.

Wavell visited Khartoum on 14 July en route to East Africa to assess the situation, bringing Chapman-Andrews with him. The latter, from his desk in the Embassy in Cairo, had continued to be involved in Ethiopia and had been interviewing local exiles of which he had engaged over 100 to join Sandford's Mission 101; these had included a jockey and a monk. Wavell saw Haile Selassie, who submitted a long list of complaints, prepared probably with the help of Sandford, urging that the Sudanese authorities should make greater efforts to arm the 'Patriots' in Ethiopia, that his position as Emperor should be formally recognized, that exiles in Kenya and elsewhere should be brought in to form an Ethiopian

Army and that the Crown Prince should be brought out to help. If more was not done, he threatened to form his own Government in exile and enter Ethiopia within a month. This was partly bluff, and after further discussion with the monosyllabic but impressive Wavell, who was able to update him on the current situation in the Middle East where the emergence of the Vichy Government had deprived the Allies of important forces in Syria and, more importantly, in Djibouti, where the warlike General Le Gentilhomme, who had been responsible for the defence of British Somaliland and the control of the rail link to Addis Ababa, had been superseded by the Vichy Government, the Emperor accepted the need for delay. However, Wavell accepted most of the Emperor's points; he later put across strongly to the Kaid and the Sudan Authorities the need for more active support.

Wavell found the Emperor an attractive personality, 'though not always easy to deal with' and always treated him with great courtesy, although he was well aware that the Emperor always had his own agenda. Given his great responsibilities and Churchill's endless pressure for action in North Africa in what was by the second half of 1940 the only active war front, the Emperor was only a secondary player. Writing to Chapman-Andrews in 1949, Wavell recalled 'your tactful handling of our "White Elephant", the Lion of Judah'.

Plans Take Shape

With the realization that the Italians seemed to have little appetite to take the offensive, at least until later in the year after the end of the rainy season in Ethiopia, the Kaid and the Sudan Government were encouraged by SOE to accelerate their plans.

Firstly, Major Boustead, an ex-soldier and now District Commissioner, Darfur, was seconded to the Sudan Defence Force as Lieutenant-Colonel to form the 'Frontier battalion' with British officers recruited from Sudan Political Service or local British civilians. Boustead was a remarkable character who had deserted from the Royal Navy in the First World War to fight in France where he had won an MC and been pardoned, served in the Caucasus with the White Russians, captained the British Olympic Pentathlon team and been a member of the 4th Everest Expedition. He was just the man to take on an unusual adventure and clearly enjoyed the challenge. With the assistance of GHQ in Cairo, recruits were sought from Allied forces in the Middle East for what were later to be called 'Operational Centres', consisting of one or two officers and three or four NCOs. It was intended that, accompanied by Ethiopian soldiers, these should escort arms and money into Ethiopia to hand over to 'Patriot' forces, as the guerrilla bands were called, and later to undertake active operations within the country.

Secondly, Colonel Sandford, given the alias 'Fikre Mariam' to confuse the Italians, pressed ahead with the preparation for his 'Mission 101', named after the standard British percussion fuse which went off with an unexpectedly nasty bang. Mission 101 was designed to enter the nearby Gojjam province and establish links with the Ethiopian Patriot forces and report back on their capabilities. He had built up a small and rather motley group of old Ethiopian hands including Major Count Bentinck, who had served in Ethiopia in the 1920s, and the ex-Australian Senator Arnold Weinholt. Weinholt, now in his 60s and a long-time enthusiast for the Emperor, met his death in September at the hands of Ethiopian tribesmen when delivering rifles to the Patriots, which underlined the risks of operating in lawless Gojjam. Sandford moved across the Ethiopian border from Sudan into nearby Gojjam on 6 August and Bentinck took his group into Beghemder to the north on 9 September. Although the rainy season made travel and communication difficult, it brought the benefit of surprise. Their and the Emperor's expectations were quickly confirmed by the comparative ease with which they and the Patriots were able to move round the country without interference from the Italians, who remained defensively in their forts.

Thirdly, George Steer, seconded from SOE, with his knowledge of Ethiopia from reporting on the Italian Invasion and his subsequent experiences as a correspondent in Spain, realized the important role of propaganda in the game of bluff that was to be played in frightening the Italians and persuading the Patriots to change gear in their guerrilla war in support of the Emperor and his British allies. With Cheesman's help, he persuaded the Emperor and Platt, after one or two bruising encounters, to support him in an innovative propaganda exercise, which served as a model for those used later in the war. Already, following the Italian declaration of war, messages with offers of help had gone to a large number of Patriots, but Steer now started a systematic propaganda offensive. Amharic printing presses were found in Cairo and brought to Khartoum and large numbers of leaflets were printed and dropped by the few and rather caustic RAF pilots over Ethiopia and Eritrea.

A regular newssheet called *Banderachin* (Our Flag) was initiated and also distributed to rally the morale of the increasing number of Ethiopians who were beginning to converge on Khartoum where they had to be accommodated in training camps nearby at Soba. In all twenty-eight issues of the *Banderachin* appeared, all headed with the Lion of Judah and the Imperial Title. Appropriate banners with a huge replica of the Imperial seal were prepared for the Allied Offficers to introduce themselves to the often suspicious Patriots in the interior. They were also used by the Emperor himself, since Steer rightly thought that, whilst the face of the Emperor would be largely unknown, the Imperial Seal would be wholly familiar, even in the wildest areas. Later on Allied forces were accompanied by loud-hailers encouraging the Italians' locally recruited Ethiopian and Somali troops to desert. These innovative techniques proved effective and later were widely copied on other fronts.

Since few people in Khartoum read Amharic and there was often no opportunity of clearing editions with the Emperor's staff, it was Steer who was usually alone responsible for the contents, which, for instance, included an Ethiopian claim to the Italian colony of Eritrea and other contentious policy statements.

Fourthly, Sandford and Cheesman pressed GHQ for help in building up numbers of trainable exiles, since the numbers of suitable Ethiopian leaders and potential soldiers were still inadequate. They rightly considered that it was important that the Emperor was seen to be building up his own army and supporters to reinforce the rallying call which was going out across the frontier. On Wavell's orders Chapman-Andrews visited Jerusalem early in August to convey the Emperor's summons for certain Ethiopian noblemen, who had perhaps been hanging back waiting to see if the British were really supporting him, to join him in Khartoum: 'These letters were received and read aloud to assembled Ethiopian notables in exile with every sign of respect and dispelled fears expressed in some quarters that the Emperor could not even count upon the support of many of his former statesmen who had accompanied or followed him into exile.'

Fifthly, SOE set up what they called a 'GR' office in Khartoum HQ under Lieutenant-Colonel (later Lieutenant-General Sir Terence) Airey and Captain Dodds-Parker to control the Ethiopian activities in liaison with General Platt. Dodds-Parker had served in the Sudan Political Service both as a District Commissioner on the Ethiopian Frontier and in Security, but had left because he had wanted to be involved in the imminent World War. He was later to play a major part in SOE's European work and after the War became an MP and junior Government minister. Given SOE's 'invisibility', neither appear in any of the accounts of the subsequent Ethiopian campaign.

Lastly, to meet the need to keep the Emperor on side, Wavell arranged with Lampson and the Foreign Office that Chapman-Andrews should be seconded from the Embassy in Cairo to Haile Selassie as liaison officer between the two of them, with the military rank of Major. (For reasons of local convenience his appointment was gazetted in the Royal Sussex Regiment for which appropriate badges could be swiftly obtained; his military identity card was carefully marked 'No pay or allowances from Army Funds.') His reporting line was to be direct to Wavell as C-in-C Middle East with a copy to the Ambassador but not to HQ Sudan and General Platt. He and Platt remained mutually suspicious. Newbold described Platt as 'courageous and works like a hero, but is testy and not very approachable'. Writing to Chapman-Andrews two years later, Newbold said: 'Your letter arrived two days ago and on top of it William Platt blew in by air from Nairobi on his way to the UK and spent the night with me. I did not show him your letter . . . he blenched slightly at your name, but I rallied him. He has mellowed a good deal but still dislikes Jews, Journalists and Diplomats.'

Preparations in Khartoum

Khartoum, where Chapman-Andrews was to spend the next four months, was still on a pre-war footing. Alan Moorehead, correspondent and later author of *The Blue Nile*, described it as a well-run Empire country club. Richard Dimbleby, flying in from often dangerous war fronts, was surprised to find that the normal round of cocktail parties, dressing for dinner, tennis parties, river sailing and picnics continued to be the order of the day. Chapman-Andrews was invited to stay with the Civil Secretary, Newbold, an agreeable bachelor devoted to the Sudan and the Sudanese and much loved by them, in his handsome, if rather austere, Government house near the river, with its big lawns shaded by acacia and neem trees. It was, no doubt, as convenient for him to be able to keep up to date on the Emperor's activities through his guest as it was for Chapman-Andrews to ensure that he maintained close liaison with the Sudan Political Service. Now that the Emperor's presence no longer needed to be kept so secret he was able to meet Government figures and leading Sudanese such as the Mahdi, whose father had been a scourge of Ethiopia in the 1880s and with whom he was to maintain good relations after his return to Addis Ababa.

As the war entered a more aggressive phase, more active use was made of the Emperor. On 6 September Steer arranged for him to go down to Gedaref near the border to meet a number of Patriot leaders alerted by Sandford and to undertake an important 'photo opportunity' complete with Imperial umbrella and regalia. Later in the month he celebrated the religious feast of Maskal with a formal parade and service which impressed the Sudan Political Service, including Newbold, who wrote on 27 September describing the ceremony and adding: ' Tomorrow I'm having dinner with the Emperor again. I have a great admiration for him. Some of his followers may be barbaric but so were King Alfred's but it was their land . . . I hope he gets it back and we'll do our best for him.' (The Emperor's generally low-key diplomatic policy was clearly winning him friends.) While General Platt retained overall responsibility for military operations, there was much activity at the Pink Palace to co-ordinate the activities of Sandford, Boustead, Steer and the increasing number of Ethiopian 'forces'. New followers continued to arrive from exile and on 7 October the Emperor was happy when the Crown Prince arrived together with several other senior Ethiopians from Jerusalem.

At the end of October Anthony Eden, now Secretary of State for War, visited the Middle East to reinforce Churchill's desire for some immediate military activities. He called a conference at Khartoum with Wavell, Sir Hubert Huddleston, who had just taken over as Governor-General from Symes, who finally retired, and General Platt, together with General Smuts, now leader of South Africa, and General Cunningham who was taking over as C-in-C East Africa. To answer Platt's fears about Sudan's defencelessness, Wavell had posted in the 5th Indian Division under General Heath and they had just arrived, although Platt continued to be very cautious: 'That same evening [29 October] Mr Eden and General Wavell, accompanied by Major Chapman-Andrews, were received by the Emperor and His Majesty left the Secretary of State in no doubt about the bitterness of his feeling in regard to the small number and to the quality of the rifles issued to patriots, the manner of distribution and the tardiness of the measures taken to train his bodyguard. He also pressed for an immediate Treaty of Alliance confirming the recognition of his position as Ruler. As a result, though on the eve of his departure, Mr Eden and the C-in-C convened a further meeting with General Platt and Brigadier Scobie. The meeting was somewhat stormy . . . and Mr Eden and the C-in-C strongly impressed upon all present the high importance which they and HMG attached both from the military and political point of view to backing up the Emperor and the gallant efforts of Colonel Sandford and Mission 101 and to make the most of the Ethiopian revolt now smouldering in Gojjam.'

Eden puts it in his memoirs rather more robustly: 'Haile Selassie was engaged on a war of liberation and I was determined that we must help him without stint. Between tea and dinner Wavell and I called on the Negus. It is no less clear that there is some lack of coordination and I gather to some extent perhaps of interest on the part of the military here. Wavell was not satisfied either. As a result we had a meeting of all concerned after dinner which was at times a stormy affair. Wavell began the indictment and I followed it up. I fear that they must all have regarded me as intolerable, but there are times when it does little good to sit down to a pleasant evening party and I deliberately wanted to stir our folks up.' In this he certainly succeeded and one suspects that Platt did not enjoy it, or the fact that Chapman-Andrews was there to witness his discomfiture! Eden added, 'Khartoum was still hot, even in the lofty rooms of the Palace. We were glad to be able to sleep on the roof and to be wakened by the sun rising over the desert.'

The question of a Treaty was side-stepped. Chapman-Andrews wrote a few years later perhaps rather too diplomatically: 'HMG did not wish to conclude a Treaty with the Emperor until HM should have established himself in Ethiopia itself. This was less from doubt about the attitude the mass of Ethiopians in the interior would adopt towards His Majesty than from the reluctance to conclude an advantageous agreement in circumstances that might later appear to have been under duress. Another factor already taking shape in the mind of GHQ (but which was not brought to the Emperor's notice until the middle of February 1941 when H.M. was already in Ethiopia) was the idea of creating an "Occupied Enemy Territories Adminstration" i.e. a British Military Government organization under the supreme authority of the British Military commander, to deal with all civil matters in territory freed from Italian control.' Whilst both points may have been valid, undoubtedly at that critical and lonely stage of the war, the last priority for HMG was to negotiate a Treaty with an exile who not everyone was convinced would, or should, be able to re-establish himself as ruler.

Eden himself knew that there were many, both in London, Cairo and in the Army, who still doubted the importance of Ethiopia and of the Emperor in the Allied strategy. He asked Chapman-Andrews to prepare a confidential 'Note on Abyssinia' which the latter must have rushed to produce and to give it to him before he left for Cairo and home on 1 November. [In view of Eden's experience of the 'Abyssinian' Crisis of 1936, it was headed 'Abyssinia' rather than 'Ethiopia' which was now standard British usage.]

Chapman-Andrews wrote: '1. The situation on the outbreak of war with Italy was that some twenty Abyssinian chiefs were still unsubdued. They were grouped in four main areas namely north, south and east of Lake Tana and round Ankober, north-east of Addis Ababa. The most powerful of them, Ababa Arragai, (trained as a regular officer at St Cyr) was in the last-named area and in communication with the French in Djibouti, from whom he was to obtain arms and supplies in the event of war. We know that the French supplied him with rifles and ammunition in June but since the departure of General LeGentilhomme, we have had no news of him. Efforts are being made to re-establish contact. Just before entering the war, the Italians made great efforts to bring Ababa Arragai to terms. General Nasi, Deputy Viceroy, took command of operations involving 24 battalions but failed to subdue him. On this occasion the one and only Italian regular division in Italian East Africa was, for short time, taken off garrison duty in Addis Ababa and employed in the operations. Since the outbreak of war Ababa Arragai's pressure in Eastern Ankober has no doubt accounted for the rigid maintenance of the number of Italian garrisons in the area and around the not distant capital.

'2. The three areas around Lake Tana were to be our concern, *but for reasons of high policy,* preparations to help the insurgents had not gone beyond the accumulation of a comparatively small quantity of rifles and ammunition and Maria Theresa thalers in Khartoum, the creation of a small military mission called Mission 101 under the command of Colonel Sandford, and the raising of a 'Frontier battalion' of the Sudan Defence Force. The Mission's task was to stimulate and coordinate revolt inside Abyssinia and to keep the military authorities in the Sudan informed of the situation there. The Frontier battalion was to establish supply dumps along the Abyssinian frontier and to escort convoys for the interior across the frontier.

'3. Colonel Sandford crossed into Abyssinia on 12 August with a small caravan of arms, thalers, supplies and a W/T set, escorted by 100 Abyssinian riflemen. He established wireless contact with the Sudan about a month later and is now at Feresboit, about 70 miles S.S.E. of Lake Tana. Altogether the Mission has six British officers and two or three non-commissioned officers established in Abyssinia. One small dump near the frontier was destroyed by enemy air action and one British officer with party of Abyssinian riflemen was intercepted by a strong enemy patrol which inflicted casualties on his party but failed to prevent him from escaping and joining up with another Mission party. [If this was Weinholt, this was incorrect, as it later became clear that Weinholt had been killed.]

'4. The work of the Mission is being successfully accomplished despite the many difficulties. There is no doubt that the Italians are very worried about the situation in the area where Colonel Sandford is working. They are aware of the presence of British officers there but do not appear to know either their identity or exact locality. Throughout the area where Colonel Sandford is working the enemy cannot patrol except in strength. For example, a high Italian civilian official who was sent in the early part of this month to appease the rebels in this district had to

48

travel with an escort of two companies. We intercepted the daily reports which he sent to his headquarters by field wireless. They confirm to a great extent our own knowledge of the situation formed from Colonel Sandford's reports, from normal intelligence sources, from Abyssinian chiefs who have come in to pay homage to the Emperor Haile Selassie and from deserters from the Italian Colonial army. Over some stretches of the road the official would not move until the area had been reconnoitred by aircraft and close air support made available in case he was attacked. A noteworthy feature of intercepted reports generally is their blatant falsity. Imaginary encounters with Abyssinan 'rebels' are claimed as victories and among the 'dead' are individuals actually with us in the Sudan or who appear later. Deserters from the Italian Colonial army complain of the lack of food, shortage of ammunition and long marches. Their rifles are badly neglected. They are in a far worse state than the native troops I saw in Harar in 1936. Many are ill with malaria. The number of deserters is increasing.

'5. The Emperor, although unable as yet to re-enter his country, has helped greatly with the revolt, by encouraging those loyal to him to fight on and those who had submitted to the Italians or were now wavering to look to their old allegiance. His Proclamation dropped by aircraft and circulated by Mission 101 has had a widespread effect. All the deserters had read it and all said that it had made them resolve to join him. Colonel Sandford has reported that chiefs in those areas east of Lake Tana asked on seeing the Proclamation that the Emperor should send his representatives to govern them, meaning that they were prepared to respect his authority. The Emperor has also sent his representatives armed with letters of authority under his seal and sign manual, with Colonel Sandford and other members of the Mission and has given similar letters to Captain Whalley who, although not part of Mission 101, has been organizing revolt from the Boma Plateau on the south-east frontier of Abyssinia. The Emperor, in the opinion of Colonel Sandford and of all others with whom I have discussed the matter and certainly in my opinion, is our trump card. I am sure that this will be proved beyond all doubt when British forces finally enter Italian East Africa. To have him on our side is an inestimable advantage.

'6. What is wanted to make the revolt succeed completely is:

(a) a constant supply of whatever quantity can be spared of rifles, ammunition, light machine guns, Mills bombs and demolition material; (b) a victory on the frontier of British forces, especially the recapture of lost frontier towns; (c) more air support for the insurgents.

'7. Since the first two of the above desiderata cannot in present circumstances be guaranteed, the importance of the third is greatly increased. The Royal Air Force have done all in their power to assist the revolt and the recent bombing of Italian strongholds south of Lake Tana has, according to Colonel Sandford's latest report, "made a great impression". According to one of his earlier reports, "There is no doubt that lack of aircraft and machine guns is weighing heavily against the Abyssinians". Aircraft are also required for dropping supplies for Colonel Sandford and others by parachute. In my considered opinion, formed after discussion with others whose knowledge of the situation I respect, the ideal solution would be the allocation of a squadron (or whatever can be spared) of long-distance bombers *for the sole purpose of the revolt*. They should come out with a label on them so that they cannot be diverted for other purposes. They should be, in the air, what Mission 101 is on the ground. Constant bombing day after day or, at full moon, night after night, of Italian forts and bridges in the 'rebel' areas would give the rebels what they do much need, namely encouragement at seeing the enemy getting some of their own medicine, in regular daily doses, and opportunities to attack small forts that have been damaged by bombs, snipe those engaged on repairs and harass such enemy movements as repairs, evacuation of wounded and replacing casualties would produce. Such bombing, accompanied by the right type of propaganda, which fortunately is in the very able hands of Captain G.L. Steer, would also cause wholesale desertions among native troops.

I earnestly beg that this suggestion be given such sympathetic consideration as the supply position allows.

(sd) E.A.Chapman-Andrews, Major, Political Liaison Officer 31.10.40.'

Eden's order to Chapman-Andrews to produce this note clearly put the latter in an awkward position vis-à-vis his own reporting line and, after a suitable interval, he wrote from 'War Ofice, Khartoum' on 4 November to Sir Miles Lampson in Cairo: 'I am sending the enclosed "Note" on Abyssinia to you personally because the Secretary of State for War asked me, privately, to write it for him. He gave me an idea of what the sort of thing he wanted and this is the result. He asked me to put in the sentence about native troops in Harar in 1936, otherwise I should not have brought up my past. It is not an *official* report for it has not been through the usual staff channels. It is a dangerous document because it mentions Mission 101, who, what and where they are and it talks of "intercepts". I have sent a copy to Clayton [Head of Middle East Intelligence] but would be grateful if you would give the enclosed copies to the Commander-in-Chief [Wavell] . . . Yours sincerely . . .'

This was a heavily loaded document, as Eden, whose hand can clearly be seen, intended it to be. Knowing himself, as Secretary of State for War, of the acute pressure on the RAF's limited resources and the unlikelihood that they would either be able or be prepared to accede to the idea of a dedicated 'Squadron 101', it made sense to put the idea into the hands of an evidently enthusiastic young diplomat. Indeed, no action was taken on this and the lack of air support for what to become Gideon Force was a recurrent theme of the next six months.

As to the Note's Clause 6 (b) certainly Eden, and possibly Chapman-Andrews, was aware of General Platt's imminent intentions to respond to Eden and Wavell's demand for action by retaking Gallabat on the Ethiopian/Sudan border, with some of his newly arrived British and Indian troops. Brigadier Slim's 10th Indian Brigade, including the Essex Regiment, a squadron of six Matilda tanks and a regiment of Artillery were given the task of capturing the strongly held Frontier post. For once the small RAF contingent would provide maximum bomber and fighter support. On 6 November Slim attacked and quickly captured the Gallabat fort. However, the tanks broke down and the Italians regrouped and called down their Air Force support which bombed the Fort and shot down most of the RAF fighters with the loss of the pilots [including Jack Hayward, the author's eighteen-year-old cousin]. They then counter-attacked and retook the Fort and Slim met the remnants of the Essex Regiment rapidly retreating later that afternoon. It was a minor disaster and Slim and the Essex Regiment were transferred from the Sudan. Slim never forgot the painful experience.

This setback shook the confidence of GHQ Khartoum and of the Emperor's supporters and confirmed Platt in his doubts about minor actions by small bodies of troops. The Italians would need to be attacked in force and the Allied troops led by commanders of experience and quality.

Chapter Four

Wingate Takes Charge

Wavell and Eden realized that the operations inside Ethiopia and the Emperor's return required an unusual and unconventional professional soldier who understood guerrilla warfare. They and SOE's Colonel Airey had little confidence that Platt would be able to provide such a man, whilst Sandford, although greatly respected and a veteran of WWI, was no longer a professional soldier. Wavell's response was to post Major Orde Wingate, DSO, who had just arrived in Cairo, to Khartoum as a staff officer to Haile Selassie with the intention that he should take over plans for the Emperor to enter Ethiopia. Much has been written about Wingate's subsequent career, but in 1940 at 37 he was a not very successful Royal Artillery Major who had won the DSO and bar in Palestine, but made enemies both in the civil Government and in GHQ. Already very much a 'loner', he had built up close relations with the Zionists, of whom he became a passionate supporter, and with the Jewish defenders of the Kibbutzim, who he had armed, encouraged and often led against the Arab Palestinian guerillas who were the Civil Government's principal problem in the late 1930s, at a time when Wavell had been General Officer Commanding in Palestine. In the end his commitment to the Zionist side and his cutting of military corners meant that he had had to be transferred back to England.

Wavell's own experience of Wingate as an imaginative and unusual fighter in Palestine suggested that he might be what was required for Ethiopia. Moreover, the name 'Wingate' meant much in the Sudan where his cousin Sir Reginald ('Rex') Wingate had been Governor General for many years following Kitchener. The fact that Wingate had served as an officer in the Sudan Defence Force some 10 years before and was fluent in Arabic was also seen as an advantage, although he had not been always appreciated by colleagues in the Sudan Defence Force. Rather surprisingly, Wingate had established good connections with some influential politicians and came with a reputation of having supporters 'in high places', including in the recently established and still mysterious Special Operations Executive.

After initial doubts in Cairo as to whether this was a task suitable for his talents and ambitions, Wingate had concluded that this was a mission indeed worthy of him and immediately requested that Major Tony Simonds, MBE, who had served with him in Palestine should join him as GSO2, together with Avram Akavia, a Jewish accountant with whom he had also worked in Palestine. Akavia, who bore no official rank, became Wingate's factotum, secretary and de facto Second-in-Command. In her book *To War With Whittaker* Lady Ranfurly claimed that on 3 November in Cairo a 'short stocky officer with a rather large head like an ant-hill and quick eyes under a heavy brow' burst in on herself and her husband and explained that he was Orde Wingate and was going to Ethiopia to raise a revolt and wanted her to come as his Secretary. The fact that her diary was two months wrong in dating his attempted suicide in 1942 casts doubt on this improbable 'offer'. In the event, she had sensibly declined it: the history of Gideon Force might have been even more unusual.

Wingate arrived in Khartoum on 6 November, to work under Colonel Airey at SOE. His first meeting with General Platt immediately on arrival confirmed his belief that the British were failing to support the Emperor and he made his views clear in terms unusual from a Major to a General. After he left, Platt commented that 'the curse of this war is the Lawrence of the last'. Immediately afterwards, Wingate went to the Pink Palace to see the Emperor. Beforehand he was briefed by Chapman-Andrews and insisted on guidance on the complicated court protocol. After entering into Haile Selassie's presence and bowing appropriately, he made a formal address. Recalling many years later Wingate's typically Messianic language, Chapman-Andrews wrote: 'I well remember his first audience with the Emperor, when he opened: "Now that the lot has fallen to me in a fair ground, I will with God's help be an instrument to set right a great wrong. I pledge my life to restore

Your Majesty to your rightful throne and ask only in return that you trust and support me absolutely". This speech, coming from a mere Major of Artillery, singled Wingate out at once; and the Emperor, who had heard many wordy declarations of loyalty, realized from that moment that here was a man who meant every word he uttered and would spare neither himself nor others to gain his ends.' While Haile Selassie was probably taken aback by Wingate's rather unmilitary appearance, there is no doubt that he was impressed by the intensity with which Wingate spoke and his ambitions, which were music to his ears.

Wingate immediately took command. His first assessment was that there were still not enough of the right sort of Ethiopian soldiers to support the Emperor's entry into his country. Chapman-Andrews and Lorenzo Taezes flew to Kenya and Tanganyika on 11 November to test the feasibility of recruiting both Ethiopians and Eritreans who had taken refuge there after the Italian occupation. There were several thousands of these in Kenya, but recruitment had been restricted to forming one battalion under Major Boyle, later the 2nd Ethiopian Battalion, with whom Chapman-Andrews made contact and later arranged for them to join Gideon Force in December. As many of the other exiles had been living ever since 1936 in refugee camps, it was thought that their loyalty to the Emperor was dubious. Some of them were employed as a labour battalion building roads through the bush in the Northern Province to enable General Cunningham's forces to attack Italian Somaliland. The exiles were enthusiastic, but they were not enjoying building roads. In the event it was too late for them to be trained ready to join Gideon Force. Chapman-Andrews saw General Cunningham in Nairobi and arrangements were made for a number of British or South African officers to be seconded to train them into an Ethiopian battalion and to bring them to Khartoum where they joined the other 'soldiers' in training at the 'Military College' under Colonel Athill at nearby Soba.

One aspect of his visit which he did not mention was the need to ensure that a close watch was kept on any Ethiopian 'dissidents'. Early on in Khartoum the Emperor has received a visit from a well-known resistance leader, Blatta Takele Wolde Hawariat, who had been very close to him before the Italian invasion but had been one of the three members of the Council who had voted against the

Emperor leaving the country on 1 May 1936. As a result he had become a republican and had warned the Emperor in Khartoum of the dangers of returning on the coat tails of the British. He had then gone off to Kenya to raise a separate force with Dejazmatch Abebe Damtew, the brother of the Emperor's son-in-law, last seen trying to defend Harar in 1936. Duly warned, the Kenyan authorities took good care to keep Blatta Tekele in Kenya until after the restoration of the Emperor, who was always able to ensure that all potential opposition was frustrated.

The financial arrangements were also of great importance, since it was clear that substantial sums would be needed to open the offensive in Ethiopia itself. Funding was from the SOE budget in London: the Emperor was paid in Sterling via the Governor-General for his own and his household expenses – for the last two months of 1940 these totalled £9700, but inevitably there were always requests for more. More importantly, Gideon Force was funded in Maria Theresa dollars (£1=MT$8) minted in India and flown in to Khartoum. Between May 1940 and Fenruary 1941 these totalled MT$5million (£404,000). While shortages of almost everything else continued to be a major headache for Wingate, henceforward money was not.

Meanwhile, Wingate's next priority was to make contact with Sandford who had been working in the interior of Gojjam since August and had had no direct contact with Khartoum. In view of the fact that he had had for much of the time to maintain wireless silence, in order not to alert the Italians, only occasional messages had been reaching Khartoum, often with traditional runners with cleft sticks. On 19 November Wingate flew with one of the Emperor's staff, Makonnen Desta, in a small aeroplane into enemy-occupied Gojjam where an airstrip had been cleared and spent two days with Sandford discussing possible plans for action. The airstrip was barely long enough to take off and they needed two runs before they were airborne. On the return flight they had managed to dodge Italian interceptors so as to overfly the area of Mount Belaya which Sandford and Cheesman had identified as the best and safest base inside Gojjam from which the expedition could develop their penetration of Central Ethiopia. Wingate and Sandford disagreed on many things but they were united that only the early return of the Emperor would enable the insurrection to take fire and that it was important that a sufficient number of 'his' staff and troops should accompany him to make it clear that this was not simply a British expeditionary force. Wingate was dismissive of Sandford's policy of arming, and paying, the Ethiopian rebels, since he considered that this was scarce money and equipment largely wasted. He also considered that both Sandford and Bentinck, who was operating rather less successfuly in Beghemder, to the north-west of Lake Tana, were overoptimistic in their assessment of what they had and would achieve. So far, while they had been able to move relatively freely about the country, they had had little impact on the Italians, secure in their strong points along the main lines of communications. Wingate was clear that only organized troops would be able to shake the Italians out of their forts with the help of the Operations Centres, each consisting of a small nucleus of Allied troops and NCOs, supported by a representative of the Emperor, together with a small number of hand-picked soldiers, who had been gathering at Khartoum. With the support of suitable Patriot bands, where these existed, these would keep the Italians on the defensive and enable his main force to deal with their bases one by one. This would both enable him to penetrate the interior and hold down the maximum number of Italian troops while the main thrust would come from the Allied armies attacking from the north from Sudan and the south from Kenya.

At the end of November Wingate flew to Cairo with Generals Platt and Cunningham to join Wavell's Planning Conference. While the main purpose of the conference was the Libyan situation where Graziani had been held at Sidi Barrani, and a planned Allied response, they also discussed the need to eliminate the potentially more powerful threat from Italian East Africa. It was agreed that, as soon as troops were available, a three-pronged attack should take place: General Platt in the north would retake Kassala and attack Eritrea; in the south General Cunningham with South African, Rhodesian and East and West African forces would invade Somalia and seize Kismayu while harassing Ethiopia across the Kenyan border, while the Emperor, with Wingate, would cross the border, join up with Mission 101, raise the rebellion and make for Addis Ababa, supported by Sandford's and Bentinck's Missions, who would destabilize and shake the morale of the Italian garrisons in the centre of the country. It was a tribute to Wingate's professionalism, as well as to General Platt and the others, that the force of his arguments, as a 'mere' major, were stronger than the offensive way in which he presented them. One point which was not covered and which was to lead to trouble in the future was Wingate's line of command. While he was clear that he was in command of all operations in his field in Ethiopia, both Sandford and Bentinck considered that they were individually responsible direct to General Platt.

Gideon Force

Wingate returned to Khartoum and immediately prepared to implement his plans. He decided, with his familiarity with the Old Testament, to name 'his' force after Gideon, whom God had directed to use a small force of 300 to overwhelm the hordes of the Midianites, using tactics very similar to Wingate's. Quite apart from the completion of the melding of the officers and men into coherent units, the transport and equipment requirements were daunting. Wingate realized that he must plan for a six-month campaign and rightly doubted Sandford's belief that it would be possible to find enough of the standard Ethiopian beast of burden, the mule, and decided that camels were the only answer. In the space of the next six weeks some 15,000 camels were gathered from all over the Sudan at a cost of £3Egyptian each and 5,000 camelmen recruited. Equipment and soldiers were in short supply and Platt was adamant that priority must be given to his major campaign in the north. In the end the 'Emperor's Army' was to comprise fifty British Officers, twenty NCOs, 800 Frontier Battalion of the Sudan Defence Force men and 800 Ethiopian troops being formed into the '2nd Ethiopian Battalion'. Apart from rifles and a few machine guns, they also had four 3" mortar guns, ingeniously forged in the Khartoum workshops, and twenty lorries, all of which broke down within 30 miles of the frontier in the impossible terrain.

Within a week of Wingate's return the military situation had changed dramatically for the better with the defeat of the Italians at Sidi Barrani and the advance of the 8th Army into Libya, which had boosted Allied morale throughout the Middle East, as well as in No 10 Downing Street, and with a reverse effect on the Italians in Italian East Africa. With Churchill and Eden pressing Wavell strongly, he decided to switch the 4th Indian Division from

Libya to the Sudan where they would join with the 5th Division to invade Eritrea under General Platt. This, together with Cunningham's attack (planned for early February) and the Emperor's entry, were planned for mid-January with a view to rapid completion before the Ethiopian rainy season, since Wavell was taking a gamble in tying up so many of his scarce resources and in diverting them from Libya and the rest of the Middle East and the Balkans. He left everyone in no doubt of his need to recover them as soon as possible.

On the Gojjam front, however, the Italians had at last woken up to the presence of British and Patriot infiltrators. The failure of the attack on Gallabat and of 101 Mission to have any significant military effect on the Italian forces, together with the fact that the Emperor had not yet appeared, produced some improvement in their morale and the relations with the local Ethiopians. The Italians decided to restore one of the great nobles, Ras Hailu, with whom they had enjoyed a rather uneasy relationship, as Ruler of Gojjam, based on its capital, Debra Markos, and with the brief of taking the offensive against 101 Mission and the Patriots. At the same time they stepped up their propaganda campaign against the Emperor, painting him as a lackey of the British. This reinforced the Emperor and his supporters in the Pink Palace in their strong view that in entering his country as the 'sign' his people demanded before rising in open revolt against the Italians he must be seen to be an independent, sovereign allied power, able, with British advice and help to recover his country, rather than as a somewhat subordinate, if useful, accessory to a British campaign. Wingate and Sandford very much took this on board.

Meanwhile on 29 November Wingate sent a small reconnaisance force of the Frontier battalion under Captain Acland with 150 camels and MT$72000 100 miles into Gojjam to prepare a base near Mount Belaya for Gideon Force and the Emperor and to construct a rough landing ground.

Chapman-Andrews found himself with the responsibility for the Emperor's party which, apart from a growing number of important supporters, included the printing presses of George Steer's Propaganda Unit, all of which would require transport and supplies for several months. One distraction which he could have done without was the Brocklehurst affair. Unimportant in itself, it achieved a high profile and illustrated the Emperor's doubts about the British intentions as well as the extent to which such items had to be dealt with not only by Wavell but by Churchill himself.

When in Nairobi Chapman-Andrews had been told by General Cunningham about an initiative which he was planning of sending a similar force to Sandford's to be called 'Mission 106' into Southern Ethiopia under an ex-Sudan Defence Force retired game warden, Lieutenant-Colonel Courtney Brocklehurst, together with Major Erskine, who had been Sudan's Vice Consul in Gore before the Italian invasion. As soon as the Emperor learned of this he immediately, through Chapman-Andrews, cabled Churchill, since he had previous knowledge of these two men whom he believed were pro-Italian and too sympathetic to his own enemies in the Galla area. [The Galla were a large Hamitic tribe which had on occasions in the past ruled Ethiopia until they were finally conquered by the Emperor Menelik. The Italians had made good use of the Galla's ambivalent relations with the Amhara.] Wingate must have formed a similar view since he had cabled Simonds in Cairo in November: 'On encountering Lieutenant-Colonel Brocklehurst, you will shoot him'!

Chapman-Andrews went to Cairo on business at Christmas and returned in time for Wavell's visit to Khartoum on 5 January, at which the C-in-C wished to finalize the plans for the planned three-pronged attack. Chapman-Andrews' papers includes a note he made of the meeting with Wavell, Platt and the Emperor about the Brocklehurst affair. Wavell was in favour of any action to destabilize the Italians in Ethiopia and the Emperor agreed, but remained adamant in his refusal to accept these names and to divulge his evidence. Wavell, knowing Churchill's conclusion from the Emperor's telegram that Brocklehurst, who had been married to a cousin of Mrs Churchill, was a red herring and that the Emperor's view must be accepted, 'after emphasizing that he considered the position unsatisfactory and leaving the Emperor with the view that he resented his unsubstantiated accusation against Colonel Brocklehurst, said that he did not wish to force upon His Majesty any officer to whom objection was taken'. He then saw Brocklehurst and explained the situation to him. The Emperor then indicated that, subject to General Platt's approval, he might accept another name, a Major Neville, who was known to him. However, Neville, when interviewed by the Emperor, said that he would regret the absence of Brocklehurst whom he decribed as 'an adventurous type of commander and an expert hunter'. This remark precipitated complete silence which reigned uncomfortably until Major Chapman-Andrews asked His Majesty whether he would not after all change his mind about Colonel Brocklehurst. To this the reply was a simple 'No'. It is clear that Chapman-Andrews needed all his skill as a diplomat in this and many other situations in his liaison role with the Emperor, even more in the trying months ahead. Dodds-Parker wrote later that 'Chapman-Andrews was to bear the brunt of the negotiations between Ethiopians and British and Sudanese authorities. The eyes of the world were on the return of the Emperor and many difficulties were delicately resolved by Andrews.'

With departure now fixed for 19 January, the Emperor was making his farewells. On the 14th he held a reception at the Pink Palace for 200 British and Ethiopian guests. The next day Ras Kassa, his oldest supporter and cousin, arrived from Jerusalem. That night General Platt gave a private dinner for the Emperor during which he accepted that the Crown Prince, Prince Makonnen, and Ras Kassa's son, Asrate Kassa [his other three brothers had been murdered by the Italians in 1936] should remain in Khartoum in Cheesman's charge to continue their military education at the Ethiopian Officers Training College and that a British tutor should be engaged to continue their interrupted education. It was clear to the British that the risk of the whole of the Imperial family falling into Italian hands must be avoided; this was accepted reluctantly by the Emperor on the understanding that they would follow once the military situation in Gojjam became clearer.

Newbold wrote: 'The Emperor left here for Abyssinia today [19 January]. I hope he doesn't get blotted; I've come rather to like him. He is a dignified little man and has borne his exile with patience.' Platt told Chapman-Andrews to make sure that he kept the Emperor alive and to dig a slit trench for him whenever they camped. Chapman-Andrews took the first point very seriously, but any enthusiasm for trench-digging evaporated in the stony ground of Ethiopia.

Chapter Five

Gideon Force Sets Forth

When the Emperor, Wingate and Gideon Force crossed the Ethiopian border on 20 January 1941 they would have been well aware of the considerable risks they faced. With comparatively few experienced troops and officers, and having to carry all their own supplies, they were entering a very difficult terrain, nominally under the control of a large Italian army, who had had four years to familiarize themselves with it, and inhabited by various Ethiopian tribes some of whom were in the pay of the Italians, some 'Patriots', but mostly '*shifta*', who were little more than bandits. Many in Khartoum had little confidence in the success or, indeed, survival of what they regarded very much as a side-show. It was the confidence and leadership of Wingate, Sandford and of the Emperor himself in their mission and its strategy which proved to be key to its success.

Wavell's plan was based on the need to break the Italian army in Eritrea in the the north and it was here that he concentrated his main force of the 4th and 5th Indian Divisions led by General Platt. On the same day that the Emperor's party crossed the border Platt retook the Sudanese frontier town of Kassala and started his Eritean offensive. Cunningham in Kenya was still trying to create an effective fighting force from his motley army of South Africas, Rhodesians, Kenyans and West Africans and his initial and rather tentative attacks in January on the Italians on the Ethiopian/ Kenyan border proved unsuccessful, as did the attempts to join up with Ethiopian patriots in the south-west. Elsewhere small initiatives were taking place along the Ethiopian borders with Sudan and with Kenya, all aimed at trying to chase out the Italians and hoping to link up with Patriot forces. Typical of these were Curle's Irregulars in Kenya, led by Chapman-Andrews' old friend Sandy Curle, who had escaped from British Somaliland. Most of these fizzled out: the Italians proved unexpectedly resistant and the Patriots often failed to materialize.

The March to Belaya

Wingate's plan was to advance towards Addis Ababa in stages, the first of which was to establish a secure base in Gojjam at Mount Belaya where supplies and troops could be built up and from which the Emperor could rally the Patriots and the Italian forces be tested. This involved opening up effective lines of transport and communications from Roseires in the Sudan across a wasteland which tsetse fly had made almost uninhabitable and it was here that Wingate's obstinacy encountered its first check. Thereafter Wingate intended in Stage 2 to climb the escarpment and join the new Italian road from Lake Tana, with the help of the Patriots, and in Stage 3 progressively clear the road towards Addis Ababa, some 400 miles away. Wingate was under strict instructions to protect the Emperor and only to allow him to move up when he and HQ considered it was safe for him to do so, but both he and the Emperor were determined to reach Addis Ababa and re-establish the Emperor on this throne, if possible, before the main Allied forces could get there.

The Sudanese base was to be at Roseires on the Blue Nile some 70 miles from the Ethiopian frontier and at the end of the Sudanese rail and road links. The build-up started under Major Donald Nott in November and at the end of the month Captain Acland and some 300 of Frontier Battalion troops set off to the frontier at Um Idla on the 150-mile march to Belaya to set up the base camp there. Wingate himself moved to Roseires on 24 December to be joined later by the 2nd Ethiopian Battalion and progressively by the rest of his troops. Parties of these were sent up to Belaya, whilst Wingate waited for the Emperor to arrive. As soon as he did so, Wingate set off for Belaya.

Chapman-Andrews' diary provides what would appear to be the only daily record of the march as seen from the view of the Emperor's party, not of the military aspects. (Various contemporary accounts exist of the military events, which are also admirably covered in Shirreff's *Barefoot and Bandoliers*.) The Letts 'India and Colonial Diary – 1941' had been acquired before the expedition left Khartoum and contains an account, usually written up by candlelight after the day's march, of things that he wanted to record during the march to Addis, since Chapman-Andrews realized it was going to be a unique and extraordinary experience in his life. It was very much for his own private use and was clearly not designed for eventual publication. Diaries were not allowed in a war zone, not least since loss or capture might have revealed information to the enemy. As a result it is often disappointingly discreet or obscure and rather overloaded with names of Ethiopian leaders – and places – and Allied leaders and officers. [Appendix 1 gives brief biographies of British Leaders, Appendix 2 of Ethiopians and Appendix 3 of the Allied Officers involved in the expedition.]

Monday 20th January. Today I flew with the Emperor from Khartoum to Um Idla in a Valencia. Ras Kassa and the Itcheguey [or Echege] were with the Emperor, also Abba Hanna.* Edward Genock [Paramount News] was also on the plane, having arrived in Khartoum the day before. He took many shots, still and cine-matograph, all the way along including inside the aircraft. We landed for an hour at Sennar where by mistake Ras Kassa, the Itcheguey and Abba Hanna were taken to breakfast at a railway bungalow where the good man and his wife were expecting visitors for breakfast, but not Ethiopian ones! They played up, however, and later found the Ethiopians getting down good and proper to a regular English breakfast while the Emperor and I had a biscuit and some coffee with the D.C., whose name I forget, not very attractive, very dark, rather swarthy, a Scottish name and rather a smelly house.

We landed safely at Um Idla where it was as dry and as hot as hell. After the usual photographs the Emperor drove to the river bed where the Itcheguey at Wingate's wish and somewhat to the Emperor's amusement offered his prayer. Wingate wanted the Emperor to be formally blessed but this the Emperor refused to allow. I read the Kaid's message. Wing Commmander Venn read the AOC's [Air Officer Commanding]. Cameras clicked and the

* See Appendix 2.

64

Emperor replied in Amharic. There had been no time to translate the Amharic despite the best efforts by Lorenzo summoned as soon as his aircraft landed, so none of the journalists were much the wiser. Perry Fellowes was also there but his propaganda unit hamla was behind on the road from Roseires. Major Boyle (2nd Ethiopian Bn), Captain Smith and other officers of the 2nd Ethiopians, Bimbashi Bagge (son of Picton Bagge of the DOT) now o/c Admin and Stores Centre at Um Idla, Bimbashi Hancock [DC Roseires], War Correspondent Matthews (*Daily Herald*) Kenneth Anderson (Reuters) were also among those present. Having hoisted the Ethiopian flag in the riverbed and taken the salute as the company of the 2nd Ethiopian Battalion marched past, the Emperor returned to a chosen spot where, in the absence of the champagne which Wingate telegraphed me to bring, Fellowes' supply of beer (one case) was drunk by all and sundry. Hancock was kicked badly near his elbow by Wingate's horse. We re-entered the cars (Khartoum taxis hired by Robin Tuckey and me two days before) and drove to "Affidavit" camp on the Dinder [river some 25 miles away]. The journalists except Palmer, the official WO photographer [and Anderson], Princes Asfa Wossen and Makonnen and the Wing Commander returned by Valencia to Khartoum and we heard later that it barely took off the ground.

One of Boyle's men manning Anti Aircraft machine gun post nearest Emperor's tent goes off without permission. Downey also out after game and gives coup de grace to fine Roan Antelope shot by absentee, who gets 20 on the bottom as punishment.

An aircraft, thought to be Italian, and the answering roar of a lion in the bush nearby was taken as a good omen of the coming triumph of the Conquering Lion of Judah.

Before leaving Um Idla the Emperor had sent a message via Khartoum to King George VI thanking him for his hospitality during his four years in Britain 'on setting my feet once again on the sacred soil of my ancestors after my painful exile'. While the Emperor certainly didn't intend any sarcasm, he would not have forgotten that one painful aspect was the refusal of the British Government to assist him or to acknowledge his rights as Emperor during that period or to allow the Royal Family to do so.

*   *   *

65

For the next few days the Emperor's party remained in Affidavit camp and Chapman-Andrews wrote up his diary when he reached Belaya so the entries are brief:

Tuesday 21 January. Meeting of officers under Wingate under tree. Bagge turned up.

Wednesday 22 January. Wingate left with Anderson in the morning with 2 trucks for Abu Wendi and forward. Flag hoisted.

Thursday 23 January. Had drinks with doctor. Perry Fellowes passed through with his Propaganda unit Belaya wards

Friday, 24 January. Murasla Mahmoud arrives from Roseires with rest of rations. Wingate left with Anderson in morning by two trucks to Abu Wendi and forward.

Saturday, 25 January. Bimbashi Phillips arrives with Mukria (formerly commander of Imperial Bodyguard at Addis Ababa) and eighty prospective bodyguard. They are camped down 2 miles away from us and are to march on separately and take over from Boyle's guard at Belaya. They are most of the 50 men ex Harar and Somaliland and are more Ethiopian than Boyle's crowd who are mostly Gallas. In my opinion B's are the better lot – more obedient soldiers.

Sunday 26 January. Letter from Wingate saying move on 27th – going very good forward for trucks. He encloses telegram to Kaid saying progress very good, etc, etc.

Monday 27 January. Doc left at 4pm with Stewart (Lt 2nd Ethiopians Quartermaster – Black Watch).

Tuesday 28 January. Left, driving Emperor in Ford truck for Abu Wendi (30 miles) 7am. Arrived about noon [a hummock of hills holding a stagnant pool under hard volcanic rock that radiates heat throughout the day]. Tea with Lt Beard who had a hut of branches made for me. 5pm tea with Doc. Drinks

with Boyle, met Ken Rowe (Lt 2nd Ethiops). Left S/Sgt, Osman and Mahmoud to bring on balance of kit and stores.

Wednesday 29 January. Letter from Wingate: '20 miles from Belaya'. Going looks good ahead, camel men say direct route going bad but possible in 6 days. Doctor left 7pm by camel. Ken Rowe left with rear guard, Emperor to follow next day. Capt Winnie arrived with 1200 camels from north. I tried to settle Lt Binnie's troubles with Roseires road man. S/Sgt arrived minus 4 sacks white flour, 2 of sugar, 50 lbs tea, 2 rice and 1 of dried fruit.

Thursday 30 January. Left 7am GMT up Italian patrol track towards Metemma and off in SE direction through bush. Camped in waterless spot in bush. ['A day going through undergrowth briefly described by Andrews as "Hell"' according to Steer] Two lorries (one driven by Sgt Botha) came in late.

More baggage and all the rations (except 15 days issued at Dinder camp) left behind. S/Sgt Pollitt, Osman to take direct route to Belaya by camel under command of Captain Smith.

Friday 31 January. Up and off at 5am. Reached excellent small spring 20 yards off 'road' and filled our full of bellies and water tanks and water bottles. On through bush to camp at 'pool where the elephants drink' (Wingate letter). Emperor caught about 30 small fish in a mosquito net by dragging the pool. Decided to abandon one truck and put good wheels on others. Botha SDF truck having burst back tire and no spare. Doc and Ken Rowe turned up to dinner which we had with Boyle, sorry to have to leave his trestle table behind at last.

Saturday 1 February. Up and off at 7.30 am. The Emperor decided at Boyle's suggestion to ride a horse, our pace being so slow and the constant trouble crossing *khors* and finding motorable inclines for our *suk* lorries being so tiring in the heat of the day. Half an hour after the Emperor had got out of the lorry (which Sgt Whiffen was driving and I was sitting also) it turned over, on what did not seem to be a very steep slope. I had taken the Emperor's place on the left of Whiffen and Dejaz. Makonnen more on the right. Since the lorry turned over on its right side, Makonnen was underneath but we all got out safely and set the lorry up again and reloaded; it was rather shaky up topside but worked! We stopped for lunch and a rest in a bamboo grove and were off again at 3.30. By 6.00 we had gone about 5 miles further and reached Road's End. Wingate's lorries were planted by a pleasant stream in the charge of Calamambo, a Greek or Cypriot mechanic, who said that Wingate had left 4 days earlier by horse for Belaya which he and Sergeant Dell, his typist, had estimated to be about 10 miles away. Anderson and Sergeant Clarke (2nd Ethiopians) had left the following day without rations on foot. Palmer, who had worked very hard driving the vanguard SDF truck, had lost his watch so I gave him a spare pocket one I had. Boyle and I decided to do a reconnaissance next day early to see if we could find a way on for the trucks.

Sunday 2 February. This we did at crack of dawn on horses. The immediate possibility seemed hopeful but the country looked hopeless for Mount Belaya seemed to me a good 20 miles off as the crow flies. The Emperor thought so too. After breakfast I had a glorious bathe in a deep pool while Boyle went out with Rowe on another recce. After lunch I settled down to supervise ARP trench digging when Wingate turned up, bearded, no buttons on tunic, on horse with Sergeant Clarke. He was in desperate state, haggard and, of course, unshaven, hungry and gaunt, his uniform in tatters under his usual headgear of a Wolseley helmet unadorned with regimental or other badges. He at once criticized Boyle's selection of a camping site for the Emperor and alleged inefficiency in posting sentries but fortunately for me when he came up to the camp I (who with an Ethiopian had been quietly hacking out a hole under the tree for the Emperor to nip into in case of air attack) heard something coming through the forest and laid doggo, rifle cocked ready, to see what it was. I let him come up to about six feet before quietly calling to him. This took him completely by surprise for he did not know until then that he was near our camp.

'The first thing,' Wingate said, 'is good' [It would not have appeared so to his audience.] I took him straight to the Emperor (for we were just outside his tent) who gave him rice, *wat* and cheese. 'Belaya,' said Wingate, 'is about 50 miles away.' We leave tomorrow by horse and mule (of which he had bought three) and march fast. Beard, Winnie, Smith and others turned up that same day and reported that the caravan by the main route from Abu Wendi was 2 miles away or less and that S/Sgt Pollitt was feeling the hardships of the journey badly.

The clue to the impression of muddle, and even irritation, in the descriptions of their route lies in Wingate's obstinate belief, on the basis of his brief flight over the area in November, that the best route to Belaya for motor transport and camels lay in a direct compass route across country to the northern side of the mountain. This was in spite of the fact that Acland's advance guard had reconnoitred the ground in December on their way to establish the base camp and all local experts, including Boustead, had advised against it. Wingate held that it was always preferable to rely on maps rather than local experts and guides; this might have been right in Palestine but was certainly not so in the largely uncharted Ethiopia. As can be seen, Wingate's route did not prove possible for vehicles and the Shankalla wastes, described by Lieutenant-Colonel Boustead as 'hot stony ridges and shrubland burnt black by honey hunters' and by Major Harris as '200 miles of thick bush, water uncertain and tracks non-existent- almost uninhabitable', with few water places and the little grazing were bad for the camels, many of whom died, as the frequent references throughout the march to their stinking remains bears witness. Laurens van der Post described rather more lyrically 'the chorus of insects which quickened with the rising of the sun and reaching until noon, the day vibrated like a tuning fork with their singing.' Boustead took three days and nights on a horse to reach Belaya on the 150 odd miles from the Frontier on the southern route, while Wingate and the Emperor's party took fourteen days. Wingate had the slightly ill-grace to acknowledge, when they finally arrived at Belaya, that Boustead had been right, but the friction between the various leading members of the expedition continued until the end and is clearly visible through this otherwise discreet diary. It says much for Wingate's force of character that, in spite of his occasional obstinate wrongheadedness, his decisions were accepted, but his manner certainly did not make for a happy ship.

The next day the Emperor and his party set off on the tough 50 miles which Wingate had promised would bring them to Mount Belaya, which they could now see in the distance.

Monday 3 February. Most of the Emperor's baggage left by camel about noon. Ras Kassa, Dejaz Amda and Dejaz Atenpressen were left at Road End until mules could be sent for them. Wingate, the Emperor, the Itcheguey, Boyle, Dejaz Makonnen and the doctor on his donkey (randy) bringing up the rear rode off at 4pm in bad order, Wolde Giorgis, Asfaw, Abba Hanna, and others on foot. We camped in Bamboo on water at 6.30pm.

Tuesday 4 February. Off at 5am leaving Palmer behind. Stop at 10am on water. Wingate has an " orderly room" for which Boyle and I have to stand, he wearing his hat and I my boots. Wingate tries my murasla Mahmoud and Boyle's camel man for he suspects that their late departure (4.30am) was due to a plot on somebody's part to delay the march. We march again at 4pm and camp in a village, the first we have seen since leaving the Sudan at 9pm. The road is terrible. I passed 47 dead camels. The hills are stony and precipitous. Both my food box and bed are down on the road but Lorenzo kindly insists on lending me blankets and the Emperor sent bread and eggs. Sergeant Clarke produces a tin of bully and the doctor a swig of whisky. We buy more *ingerra* and decide not to leave till the evening; no salt or *dhoti* or mattress; offer honey and bread. Bush fires getting nearer.

Friday 5 February. On the evening of 5/2 we camped in bamboo, marching from 4.00 to 8.30 pm. Passed Palmer [official photographer] on road looked after by my boy Nasser only two miles from our camp. Wingate sends out a horse before dawn the next morning to bring him so that he may photograph the arrival at Belaya.

Saturday 6 February. We leave at 7.00 am. At 11 we reach good water and I push on with Palmer and Sergeant Clarke to herald the Emperor's approach. Meet Donald Nott and Sandford who looks well but is sore in foot and spirit. He hurried down 10 days ago in response to tel. that Emperor was *awaiting* him at Belaya. I decided to stay with Phillips who has taken on King's guard with Mukria's men. He has a good tent and provides most welcome orange juice (and a little whisky).

At Camp at Belaya

From 6 to the 26 February the diary is silent. The Emperor's party with Chapman-Andrews remained in camp at Belaya while the camp was built up as a base for the further advance. The mountain was some 9000ft high and on its western slopes formed a large tree-covered bowl suitable for concealing the camp and its growing number of inhabitants and equipment from the air. It was well watered by streams that came down from the mountain. There was a continuous build-up of supplies from the Sudan by camel and the southern route was slowly improved and opened up to lorries. From his grass-roofed 'palace' the Emperor started to receive local Ethiopian patriots and chiefs. The most important of these was Fitaurari Taffere Zelleka who was the local chief of the Belaya area. Although the Italians knew that something was going on, there was little real challenge from the Italian army on the ground, but life was restricted by the need to avoid contact with the enemy. A rough landing strip was constructed with difficulty but it wasn't until 11 February that it was in use. A dummy camp was constructed which successfully distracted the Italian planes which regularly overflew and bombed the area.

There were three important developments during this period, both of which would have taken up much of Chapman-Andrews' time. Firstly, on 8 February a wireless signal was received from the Kaid, General Platt, to advise that it had been decided that Wingate was to be in sole command of Gideon Force and that Sandford was to be appointed Chief Political Adviser with the Emperor on Political and Military matters, with Chapman-Andrews as his Deputy. This was no doubt in answer to the stream of wireless message complaints and requests from Wingate, and the realization in HQ that the divided command structure was not working. Nonetheless it came out of the blue and a number of noses were

71

put out of joint, principally Sandford's, who had been running his own show in the wilds of Ethiopia since August. This was the first time since then that he had seen the Emperor and since November that he had had contact with Wingate, whom he had thought was still subordinate to him. There is little doubt that this was a correct recognition of the strengths of the two men: Sandford, a civilian since 1918, aged 58, with intimate knowledge of Ethiopia, and Wingate, the experienced regular soldier of 38.

Taking advantage of the new landing strip, both men were flown back to Khartoum on 11 February to discuss the new relationship and tactics with the Kaid. Wingate was promoted Lieutenant-Colonel. Sandford went on to Cairo and saw Wavell and was promoted Brigadier, which, together with Sandford's role as political adviser, ensured that the friction continued, as the diary reveals.

For Chapman-Andrews it also represented a redefinition of his role. He described Sandford as being 'concerned with the day-to-day political situation actually surrounding the Emperor on the ground in his relations with his own people; whilst I was concerened as a representative of the Foreign Office with the Emperor's future status, his establishment again as a fully effective sovereign of an independent Ethiopia – thus putting the clock right back to status quo anti bellum – that is before the Italians invaded his territory in 1935.'

Secondly, some major political developments had taken place. The sudden change from the defensive to the offensive in North as well as in East Africa and the Emperor's unchallenged entry into Ethiopia made imperative a decision on what should be the respective roles of the Emperor and the Allied Military Forces with regard to the administration of a liberated country. The Emperor's view and that of most Ethiopians was clear: the removal of the Italian invaders would restore the country to the status quo ante 1935 as an independent state under the Emperor and that should include Eritrea, captured by the Italians in the 1880s.

The British Government saw many practical problems. While, in spite of many Ethiopian suspicions, they had no desire to colonize Ethiopia and Wavell was anxious to recover as quickly as possible his scarce battalions for use in North Africa, Greece and the Middle East, they considered that the re-establishment of law and order and an Ethiopian administration would take time and risk holding down the Allied forces as the sole provider of all services in what they hoped would be the three liberated countries of Somalia, Eritrea and Ethiopia. It was by no means clear in many British eyes, and particularly in the neighbouring British-run countries, that the Emperor would be able quickly, if at all, to reunify the whole of his disparate Empire and rally all his subjects behind him, many of whom had been obliged to transfer their loyalties to the Italian occupying forces. There was also the potential problem of Italian prisoners of war and the many thousands of Italian civilians – over 100,000 – which the Ethiopians considered would be a matter from them to handle. At that early stage of the war and with the experience of the Italian collapse in Cyrenaica behind them, the British Military in Cairo saw this in terms of the Geneva Convention and the treatment of fellow white combatants and non-combatants in an African country. Remarkably, the Emperor's clear Proclamations were obeyed and there were virtually no cases of prisoners and civilians being treated improperly by the Ethiopians.

On 4 February the Foreign Secretary, Anthony Eden made a carefully worded statement to the House of Commons that: 'HMG will welcome the reappearance of an independent Ethiopian state and will recognize the claim of the Emperor to the throne. HMG reaffirms that they have themselves no territorial ambitions in Abyssinia.' He stated that an Occupied Enemy Territories Administration (OETA)would be set up under Sir Philip Mitchell [appointed Major-General] with Brigadier Maurice Lush as his Deputy. [Mitchell was Governor of Uganda and Lush of Sudan's northern province, which fuelled Ethiopian suspicions of British colonial ambitions. Wavell wrote to the Emperor to this effect and reminded the Emperor of Lush's experience in the British Legation in the 1920s.]

Sandford and Lush, who was also his brother-in-law, flew back to Belaya on 17 February with Wavell's letter to consult with the Emperor, which they proceeded to do over the next three days with Chapman-Andrews taking the notes. At the end the Emperor reluctantly agreed to OETA but only as a strictly temporary measure and that it must be he who issued proclamations and made his own appointments in respect of Ethiopia. With this Lush flew back to Cairo via Khartoum on the 22nd, taking with him the Emperor's formal reply which include a number of other points.

Thirdly, events were moving on the main fronts. By 2 February, General Platt had captured Agordat in the north and occupied the Eritrean lowlands in preparation for an attack up the escarpment and the Keren Pass. Initial attacks began on the 10th, but encountered strong Italian resistance from their dominating position on the high ground. It was to be another month and after heavy casualties on both sides before the battle was won. In the south General Cunningham, after some unsuccessful attempts to cross the Ethiopian/Kenyan border, decided to attack the main Italian forces in Somalia. He crossed the frontier at the Tana River on the 11th and, encountering little resistance, captured the important port of Kismayu and was now pressing ahead to Mogadishu, the capital of Italian Somaliland.

These moves had an immediate effect on the nervous Italians with implications for Wingate's plans. Following his return by air from Khartoum on the 14th, he assembled his force at the foot of the escarpment at Metekal on the 17th and addressed his new officers, now at last officially under his command: 'The comforts which we now lack and the supplies we need are in the possession of our enemies. It is my intention to wrest them from them by a bold stroke.' He struck a less happy note in a message to the Patriots when he urged them to 'rouse themselves and put an end to your bickerings and disputes which have disgraced your Ethiopian name among future generations.'

Mission 101 troops were now fanning out into Gojjam and linking up with Patriot forces. Towards the east, Boustead's troops were testing the Italian defences on the escarpment which rose like a wall some 25 miles east of Belaya with a view to establishing the best route up for Gideon Force to take. They were able to identify a climbable route near Metekal (for camels as well as men) some way to the west of the Italian fort at Engiabara which was one of a series of strong points along the road which linked Lake Tana in the north to Debra Markos in the east and eventually to Addis Ababa.

However, before Wingate could move came the good news on 16 February that the Italian High Command had decided to shorten its defensive position by withdrawing from Engiabara and from Dangila further to the north, which would greatly facilitate Gideon Force's advance into the Highlands. This was a major mistake on the Italians' part and was undoubted caused by the moves of Gideon Force and Mission 101, which they believed to much bigger than it was, by Platt's moves from Sudan at Kassala which had been recaptured in January and by Cunningham's successes in Somalia. Local patriots, with Mission 101 support, swiftly occupied Engiabara and Dangila. Leaving a notice 'The way to the Promised Land' at the foot, Wingate brought his force of some 100 men and camels up the escarpment and reached Engiabara on 18 February. The rest of the force followed. Meanwhile, Wingate went on into the interior to Faguta to meet and give fresh orders to the rest of Mission 101, now under Major Simonds. Akavia, his clerk/staff officer, in a rare touch of humour (he was aware of the Don Quixote/Sancho Panza parallel) described Wingate on his mule with the Ethiopian colours on his topi and, totally unarmed, raising his hat now and then and saying in his only words of Amharic 'English' and 'Health may God give you'. At Faguta he despatched Simonds to cut off the Italians' escape route to Lake Tana and the north where Bentinck was also operating. While this further reduced his force, he considered it essential to keep the pressure up on the still considerable Italian force in the north and to prevent them returning down the main road to cut him off from his base and to put the Emperor at risk. (Understandably Bentinck and the northern officers do not figure much in the diary or in the main accounts of the campaign, which fail to give full credit to the important role that they and other initiatives in Beghemder in the north had in holding down large Italian forces, who were thus not available to the Italian High Command to reinforce their other fronts.)

The occupation of Engiabara was a big step forward, but it also involved a change from the strategy agreed with Platt and Sandford to hold down as many of their forces as possible in Gojjam by destablizing the entire area and to avoid them switching troops to the major fronts in the north and south and to avoid a major confrontation with an enemy which had such overwhelming superiority in numbers. Wingate decided to press ahead towards Addis Ababa and to take the Italian fort at Burye to consolidate his position before attacking the main Italian forces at Debra Markos, the capital of Gojjam. Until this was effected, the Emperor and his party would have to delay moving up the escarpment, where he hoped that the Emperor's appearance would result in a widespread uprising and hasten the collapse of the Italians.

Meanwhile supplies and reinforcements continued to arrrive at Belaya and, in particular, the British officers and NCO volunteers from other Middle East forces whom Wingate had requested to form his ten small 'Op.Centres'. He intended that these should be used, supported by groups of Ethiopian troops, to move tactically about in Gojjam to link up with Patriot forces and to try and give them some direction in a way that he considered that Mission 101 had so far found difficulty in doing. Owing to the need to bring Gideon Force across the border quickly, many of them had not arrived in Khartoum before the crossing on 20 January. Although most of them had had some training and some were professional soldiers, both officers and NCOs tended to be strong characters who had volunteered for Gideon Force because they were bored with their garrison duties in Palestine and elsewhere and wanted to see some action. Among them were two unusual men, Bill Allen and Laurens van der Post, who had already had colourful lives and both of whom left records of their Ethiopia experiences. Allen was an Ulsterman who, reputedly, had left Eton to take part in the uprisings in the Caucasus in 1918. He had subsequently run a successful business, been active in the Rif wars in Morocco, become an MP as a member of Mosley's fascist party, married three times and served in MI5, probably throughout the inter-war years. His *Guerilla War in Abyssinia* by 'W.E.D. Allen sometime Captain in His Majesty's Army' was published by Penguin in 1943 and is the best, if rather idiosyncratic, account of Gideon Force and its remarkable collection of characters.

Laurens van der Post, at 33, had already published a number of books and made a certain name for himself in London literary circles, although it was only in the 1960s that he became famous. Allen was, like many, impressed by van der Post's descriptions of his adventures and the latter was equally impressed by Allen. Allen described him as 'rosy-cheeked, mild-voiced and rather plump, with wide blue eyes; he is a Boer with a love of England. No mean poet, his intellectual attainments include a translation of Baudelaire into Africaans.' After their night marches, they sat and talked endlessly of 'Baudelaire, Dostoevsky, D.H. Lawrence and the Sitwells in the light of the fire with the pale necks of the munching camels all around'. Van der Post took exception to Allen's description of him and complained that 'Allen was so oblivious of his beautiful surroundings that he could only talk

Dostoevsky to me. These blasted intellectuals.' but also that Allen was 'tall, good-looking, self-centred, lovable and mad', and they clearly enjoyed each other's company. Chapman-Andrews quickly recognized that the Emperor would find them interesting. Van der Post never wrote an account of his part but brief, highly colourful and, as J.D.F. Jones points out in his *Storyteller,* often imaginary references to his role appear in two of his later books.

Up the Escarpment

Van der Post described how they saw 'the great escarpment of Ethiopia itself, a darker blue within the blue and there began to appear with increasing frequency around us pillars of broken hills, columns of rocks and walls of stone like the ruins of great cities (a table-land eroded by wind and water with a deep labyrinthine system of canyons and river cuts, rivalled only by the Grand Canyon. A land flowing with milk and honey.' The Sudanese welcomed the scenery and temperature change and marvelled at the fat cattle, very different the skinny beasts at home. Everyone was relieved to be free of the Shankalla wastelands, but the further from the Sudan the more difficult became the problem of supplies and henceforth Gideon Force and the Emperor had mainly to live off the land; this was precarious and they were often short of food.

As the Emperor's camp starts to follow up the escarpment, Chapman-Andrews resumes his diary:

> **Wednesday 26 February.** Reveille 5.30. Pack kit. Decide to leave Mahmoud and Osman with rations and what 7 mules allotted cannot bring. Said mules are for my kit, S/Sgts and office. Jock Maxwell helps or rather directs roping up of boxes and manufacture of pack saddles from the old sacks stuffed with grass. He shares with me most welcome bottle of beer bought by aircraft sent to pick up F/Os Johnston and Duncan [who had been rescued after their plane had been shot down].
> Leave at 4.00 and march till 8.30 arriving in utter darkness. Stinking camels and burnt-out smouldering forest all the way. Bush fires all around. Arrive to find none of my mules up but all but 2 arrive during night. Donald [Nott] gives welcome

drink and dinner. Bush fires v near – 200 yards and almost choked by smoke. Fire break across *khor* saves us.

Thursday 27th February. Reveille 4.30. My *hamla* [camel caravan made up of a number of camels and their herds] up and off 5.45 but I pass them on the road. We stop at 9.15 by water and I have breakfast with Donald. My *hamla* arrives at 10.00 and I tell them must move at 1.00 Short *shid* [camel march] and prepare drink for Donald and Doctor. I have bath in stream, very welcome. Doctor loses mule – dead but load taken by one of the Emperor's mules. March with Mangistu and reach Balas [river camp] after dark to find Staff/Sergeant flat out but excellent dinner [Nott wrote: 'Andrews broke open one of the Emperor's boxes and we finished a bottle of John Haig in no time. Andrew provided a rattling good dinner.'] and bed all in order by Nasser. Saw unidentified aircraft at midday very high.

Friday 28 February. We leave Balas at dawn. The *hamla* gets away before dawn (reveille at 4.30am) but I delay departure with the doctor until 6.30 so as not to arrive before *hamla*. Staff Sergeant Pollitt leaves with my *hamla* at 5.30. The road crosses the Dinder at a picturesque spot, the river rushing in a torrent: difficult to coax the animals especially the camels of the Emperor's 'radio hamla' across. On the far side is an abandoned Sudan Defence Force truck, one of LeBlanc's 10. [LeBlanc, the Transport Officer, was a French-Canadian engineer. He was determined to open up the road up the escarpment so that trucks could get through from the Sudan, in which he was eventually successful.] The road is uphill and hard going, leading through recently burnt-out bush, most of it still smoking. Stinking camels. I pass Pollitt half way. I walk most of the way, arriving at hill top 11.15 just as my *hamla* is in. Wretched hot burnt-out halting place. Animals very tired. Question:. stop for the night? Donald and I again leave with my *hamla* at 1.30 (Emperor sends goat) expect 6 hour *shid* but surprised to reach foot of Metekal 4.15 Pass Hayes checking rations boxes and Riley's *hamla* on road and find Allen at river crossing. I bathe at night. Right foot *black* and sore toe. Excellent dinner *ful sudani,* mixed grill, goat's liver and blancmange and cigar. Two last mules arrive today before nightfall.

Saturday 1 March. We arrived here yesterday at the foot of Metekal, a group of hills leading up to the Gojjam plateau and I am writing this page beside a shady pool of cool deep water. Donald Nott (Major MC Worcestershire Rgt) and I found it and would like to move our camp here to get away from the crowd but since we shall in any case be moving up the hill soon and since any move would attract people to the pool, we shall keep it secret like schoolboys and pass what part of the day we can here, hidden away. The river here runs through a gorge over a bed of granite-like rock, polished smooth by the flood. The rock of the river bed gives way up to steeply sloping grass and tree-covered banks to a height of perhaps 100 foot above. Our pool is filled by two waterfalls breaking over a ten-foot drop and the overflow passes gently down over a shallow where it is narrow enough to step across without effort. Our pool must be a good 15 yards wide and long. It might well be as deep too. We plunged in off a low top rock. After the toil and filth and sweat of the march it is wonderful.

Van der Post (Operational Centre No 5- Captain: South African: Gentleman: brought 100 camels from Roseires without losing one) came in this morning from the top of the hill with a letter from Macdonald (Sudan Defence Force, formerly Sudan Political Service). No news from forward but Sandford has gone towards Engiabara to meet Wingate. Sandford spent last night with Zallaka Birru, lord of Metekal, formerly commander of 600 local Italian *banda*, all of whom have submitted with him to the Emperor.

Shankalla negroes kept arriving this morning to greet the Emperor, playing their tuneful if monotonous joyful music on bamboo pipes of various sizes. The Emperor got his radio set up and we heard news of the entry of Bulgaria into the Axis pact and of Eden's agreement with the Turks. Officers present at a conference this morning were Nott, van der Post, Lieutenant Allen (ex MP), Lieutenant Welsh (Buffs), Bathgate(Lieutenant, King's Own), Naylor (Lieutenant), Bimbashi Hayes, Captain Mackay, Bimbashi Riley, Bimbashi Phillips, Bimbashi Hunt (Medical).

I was rather unkind to Phillips today. He has been growing a sort of imperial beard which I think wrong for a soldier. Seeing him shaving, I asked him if he was going to shave his beard. He said, 'No'. Sergeant Rees then said to him, 'What are you doing to yourself Sir?' I spoke up, 'He's trying to make himself look like a French poodle'. The poor fellow shaved it straight off. Many of the officers (and NCOs) are growing or have already grown beards. I suppose it's all right: they are like pioneers, cut off from brushes and soap, but not shaving is one thing and half-shaving quite another. When on the march I don't shave, unless we get in early. Lately we have got in after dark and got the mules off next morning again before dawn. I meet Lieutenant Haggar(RAMC) who wears Star of Ethiopia and claims to know the Emperor and me. He says he is personal physician to Emperor. Less said about him the better. [The rather mysterious Haggar, a Syrian doctor, may have been one of the doctors who Wingate requested from Palestine. Allen describes him as 'a mine of anecdotes on the gynaecological history of different royal families of the Middle East'. Apparently he must have been in Ethiopia at one time.] The Sudani *hamlagia* are selling a *raz* of sugar for 50pt and 10 Woodbines for MT$1(8½pt)

Sunday 2 March. I creep off and spend morning writing up back parts of my diary with doctor at the pool. I see Emperor at 12.45 and listen to radio. He is *not* impressed with Haggar and awaits Sandford's return to speak about it. Donald left at 5am to climb Metekal and hopes to return tonight. A lazy day and I feel, more than yesterday, rather fed up with the human race. It is now 4.20 and Nasser is to bring me tea here at the pool at 4.30. When I arrived this afternoon I found *Golga* (wild boar)and the Shankalla buglers bathing just above the waterfall inlet to the pool and grass cutters keep passing up and down getting fodder for the animals. I slipped clambering down to the pool and again near the waterfall and got my shorts wet. Think I have cold and shall turn in early after have presented some of the officers to the Emperor at 6.30. This trekking is hard on footwear. Everybody's boots going, including my new shoes and shooting boots.

I present Captain van der Post, Lieutenant Allen and 2 Lieutenant Welsh to the Emperor. They stayed one hour and evidently much enjoyed their conversation. VDP and Allen speak very good French and have travelled widely and thoughtfully. The Emperor was interested in Chinese food (VDP and his story of eating a live monkey's brain and Morocco where Allen was *Morning Post* correspondent during the Rif wars). [Allen describes the scene: 'The heir of the House of Solomon was sitting under a tree at a camp table, covered with a red plush cloth and lit by a single candle-lamp. A common brown Kurdish rug was on the ground. We were regaled with sufficient whisky, Turkish Delight and pistachio nuts. The Emperor looked frail and rather tired'.]

Welsh of the Buffs operational centre afterwards complained about Sergeant Schreider of Rhodesia – not a Buff, inclined to argue, a square peg in a round hole. I told him I would inform Donald Nott on his return. Donald returned at 8.30 pm with no news from forward except that he had some excellent *ingerra* and boiled eggs and *tej* for lunch. Lorenzo came after dinner and said that British Imperial forces [Cunningham from Kenya] had taken Mogadishu according to the Emperors' wireless

Monday 3 March. Doctor moved camp to site I suggested for him down towards bathing pool. Emperor's baggage moves today and we to follow tomorrow. News is that enemy made sortie from Burye and were beaten back by the Patriots. I awoke with a wretched cold. Sat by pool and wrote letter to Sadie [his wife].

The Ethiopians have now done one week of their foolish 45 days fast. No meat, eggs, milk, butter or fowl. Only fish and vegetable products. Weakens them and complicates supply problem.

Tuesday 4 March. Bad cold all day. Delayed signal from Kaid orders 'no move forward till Burye has fallen', but Emperor orders move am 5/3. 2/Lt Mark Pilkington (Life Guards) and 2/Lt McLean(The Scots Greys) of Operational Centre dined. In the morning we shifted camp to the pool. The mules had a rough passage but we arrived in time to hear Emperor's decision to move next day! Visited Emperor in evening with Donald Nott. Burye still holding: attempts to evacuate garrison repelled by Patriots. 2nd Ethiopians said to be cutting Engiabara and Burye road and Frontier battalion Engiabara/Debra Markos Road.

Wednesday 5 March. Emperor moved at 7 am. My *hamla* got off at 1pm and I had pink gins with Doctor and then dined. I left at 2pm. A very steep climb – too steep for mule to do comfortably with me up. Took 50 minutes to get to top, then 3 hours across rolling, treed grassy plains. Signs of cultivation and small but healthy herds of cattle. No dead camels now though the climb up was made hideous by their stinking corpses every ten yards. This with the deep fine dust of the track and the burnt-out bush round about made the climb grim. The change on top was all the more pleasant. Camp in the bed of a stream under branches growing in the bank. Donald 'next door'. Our camp is like a series of rooms with willow trees for ceilings and the bath 'laid on'. Dura River camp [where they remained until 10 March waiting for Wingate's OK for the move to Burye].

Thursday 6 March. Long lie in. Laze all day. Saw Emperor in evening and heard of the fall of Burye on London radio (Emperor's). Emperor rather annoyed Sandford not here and no direct news of Burye.

The capture of Burye had not been easy. As Allen wrote, 'The hundred miles of upland between Engiabara and the Blue Nile canyon at Safartak is not ideal for guerrilla war. It is an open landscape swept by strong dusty winds and, even in the dry season, by occasional violent storms. Every dozen miles or so the ravines of streams falling to the Blue Nile offer cover with their belts of thick undergrowth and woods. But over the plateau there is no cover except for occasional coppices of trees round the scattered villages.' Burye was too strongly held for a frontal attack: the experienced Colonel Natale had some 6000 troops under his command, excluding the Ethiopian *banda* of Lij Mammo, Ras Hailu's nephew. For the first time Wingate was facing serious opposition and of his 1300 men only the Sudanese Defence Force

Frontier battalion's 600 could be described as professionally commanded.

Wingate used his usual tactics of playing on the Italians' nerves in order to force them to evacuate down the road where he could ambush them. Night attacks were used and propaganda by leaflet and loudspeaker encouraged their Ethiopian troops to join the patriots of Dejazmatch Negash Bezahbu. By day the Italians had command of the air which meant most troop movements had to be by night, with camels camouflaged with mud. Inevitably, this led to confusion and much irritation to Wingate. A number of skirmishes occurred, but the Patriot forces proved reluctant to join in with Wingate's local plans for attack, which confirmed his belief that they were of little tactical value. On the 28th, for once, the RAF were able to provide support and the bombing of Burye helped to shake the morale of Natale's troops and to persuade Lij Mammo and his *banda* of some 1500 men to desert the Italians and withdraw. On 3 March Wingate received a radio message from HQ Khartoum, who had intercepted Colonel Natale's request to General Nasi, his superior in Gondar, for permission to evacuate, which was given. However, Wingate's troops were by now widely dispersed and communications, except by cleft stick, had broken down. So when the garrison started their retreat on 4 March along the road towards Debra Markos, Boustead's small force, to Wingate's fury, were unable to intercept their greatly superior numbers. Boyle's 2nd Ethiopians, who had been sent off several days before to move down to cut off the road towards Debra Markos and knew nothing of the evacuation of Burye, were camped further along the road by the bridge over the Charaka River and were taken by surprise by the Italian vanguard, who were equally surprised. Whilst Boyle's troops did well and most were able to withdraw, the bulk of the Italians were able to continue their retreat, followed closely by Boustead's troops who quickly occupied the next two forts of Dembecha and Fort Emmanuel. Much of the blame for the failure to trap the Italians lay with Wingate who had difficulty in keeping effective control and communication with his disparate troops, but he was free in his blame of both officers. In the heat of the moment he accused Boustead, totally undeservedly, of cowardice, which was not forgotten.

A furious General Nasi flew down to Debra Markos to relieve

Colonel Natale of his command and replace with him the more belligerent Colonel Maraventano, with instructions to rally his troops and counterattack. Wingate knew that Debra Markos was going to be a much tougher nut to crack and that he would need time to reorganize his troops and establish his new base at Burye before the Emperor would be able to join him.

1. The Emperor and the Empress at his Coronation, November 1930, with a Ras in the centre.

2. The Emperor greets the Duke of Gloucester at Addis Ababa railway station. (Sir John Maffey, Governor-General of the Sudan, is on the right).

3. The British Party which attended the Coronation on the steps of the British Legation, Addis Ababa. *Front row left to right*: Sir Harold Kittermaster, Governor, Somaliland; Sir Sidney Barton, H.B.M. Minister; H.R.H. The Duke of Gloucester; Sir John Maffey, Governor-General, Sudan; Rear-Admiral Fullerton C.B., D.S.O. *Others*: Sir Stewart Symes, Political Resident, Aden *(2nd row left)*, followed by The Earl of Airlie A.D.C.; R. Cheesman, Consul Dangila, *(3rd row, second from left)*, Wilfred Thesiger *(4th row, third from left in top hat)*; E. A. Chapman-Andrews *(5th row on left)*.

4. The British Consulate at Harar in 1935.

5. Somali guards in gas-masks defending the British Consulate, Harar, 1936.

6. The aftermath of disorder in Harar.

7. The staff of the British Consulate with their Somali guards on 8 May, 1936, the day after the Italian occupation of Harar. *Seated left to right:* Indian clerk; Mackie, R.A.F. Wireless Operator; Chapman-Andrews; Dr Elphick, Red Cross Doctor who had sought refuge; Ethiopian clerk.

8. The Emperor with his sons, the Crown Prince and the Duke of Harar at Khartoum; Christmas Card, 1940.

9. Anthony Eden (British Minister for War), with arms folded, General Sir Archibald Wavell, *far right,* and Major General W. Platt, (G.O.C. Sudan Forces), *second from left,* watching a march-past of troops in Khartoum. *(Imperial War Museum - E1129).*

10. The Emperor returns to his country as Gideon Force crosses the border at Um Idla on 20 January 1941. Chapman-Andrews is on the right.

11. The Emperor returning to camp after making a tour of inspection of the surrounding countryside, 1941.   *(Imperial War Museum - E2073).*

12. Ethiopian troops displaying the Emperor's Banner, 1941. The Banner was regularly used by the Emperor and by Mission 101 to rally Ethiopians to the flag.

(Imperial War Museum - E2088).

13. Unloading camels on arrival at a camp.   *(Imperial War Museum - E2077).*

14. At a camp during the march through Gojjam, 1941.   *(Imperial War Museum - E2084)*

15. Wingate and the Emperor discussing the campaign, 1941.

(Imperial War Museum - MH6006)

16. Brigadier Sandford on trek with Mission 101, 1941. *(Imperial War Museum - E2092)*

17. Hauling transport up the Escarpment, 1941. *(Imperial War Museum - E2445)*

18. Ras Hailu, robed and in the foreground, prepares to submit to the Emperor at Debra Markos, 1941.

19. Ras Hailu's army submits to the Emperor at Debra Markos, 1941.

XXXVII BATTAGLIONE AMARA "S. GIORGIO

ባሕሬር፡ እግስ ቅ ዎኝ

Condudo, giugno - luglio 1936 == Cercer, 1-10-1936 - 15-12-1936 ==
Arussi, 15-12-1936 == Galla - Sidama, 1-4-1937 - 6-6-1937
Ancoberino, 7-6-1938 - 31-12-1938

ON ACTIVE SERVICE.

This magnificent picture shows what the Italians thought their Ethiopian troops looked like. But when it came to fighting, most of them deserted & tried to join our side. I found this post card in a village not far from Harar where you used to live. Do you remember E'sa who used to make bows & arrows for you? He is with me as I write this. He remembers you & recognised your photograph playing cricket on the sands, immediately. Love from Daddy.

1941.

YA

David Chapman-Andrew
Norwood School
Pennsylvania
Exeter
Devon
England.

20. A postcard sent by Chapman-Andrews from Harar in April, 1941 to his son David, aged 8, at school in England. The Italians produced large numbers of triumphalist postcards for their troops and settlers to send home to Italy. Allied troops were happy to send them home to the UK after the 'Liberation'.

21. The Emperor en route to Addis Ababa, which he entered on 5 May, 1941.

(Imperial War Museum - E3064).

22. The road to Jimma. Typical of central Ethiopia.

23. Chapman-Andrews *(front right)* hosts a luncheon party for General Nuri Al Sa'id *(front centre)*, Prime Minister and strongman of Iraq, during the latter's private visit in August 1949 to Alexandria. Donald Maclean is at the back, partially concealed; his wife Melinda at the front next to Nuri Al Sa'id.

24. Chapman-Andrews with Ernest Bevin, then the British Foreign Minister, on a sight-seeing tour of Cairo in 1950.

25. King Farouk's farewell party for the British Ambassador Sir Ralph Campbell, at the Koubbeh Palace 17 May, 1950. *Left to right:* Nahas Pasha, Prime Minister; Chapman-Andrews; King Farouk; Sir Ralph Campbell.

26. The Emperor and Chapman-Andrews during his visit to Addis Ababa in 1956.

23. Chapman-Andrews *(front right)* hosts a luncheon party for General Nuri Al Sa'id *(front centre)*, Prime Minister and strongman of Iraq, during the latter's private visit in August 1949 to Alexandria. Donald Maclean is at the back, partially concealed; his wife Melinda at the front next to Nuri Al Sa'id.

24. Chapman-Andrews with Ernest Bevin, then the British Foreign Minister, on a sight-seeing tour of Cairo in 1950.

25. King Farouk's farewell party for the British Ambassador Sir Ralph Campbell, at the Koubbeh Palace 17 May, 1950. *Left to right:* Nahas Pasha, Prime Minister; Chapman-Andrews; King Farouk; Sir Ralph Campbell.

26. The Emperor and Chapman-Andrews during his visit to Addis Ababa in 1956.

27. Wilfred Thesiger in
    Lebanon in March 1953,
    while staying with
    Chapman-Andrews.

28. Sir Hugh Boustead *(below
    left)*, Resident Advisor,
    Agent Mukalla, Aden
    Protectorate in the 1950's.
    (Bodleian Library)

29. Sayed Sir Abdel Rahman
    El Mahdi *(below right)*,
    arriving at the Foreign
    Office for talks with Mr
    Eden, 11 October 1952.
    *(Illustrated London News
    Picture Archive)*

30. Sir Edwin Chapman-Andrews, KCMG, OBE, on retirement in London.

Chapter Six

The Taking of Debra Markos

The situation of Gideon Force had been transformed with the capture of Burye. Wingate ordered the move of his base up from Belaya, where it would be much closer to the front. While the Italians still had air supremacy, the Italian landing grounds at Engiabara and Burye allowed much easier air access from Khartoum for supplies, messages and movement of wounded and officers compared to the long-drawn-out route by camel, mule and truck from Roseires, although this was to improve when LeBlanc managed to open a route for vehicles up the escarpment. Major supplies, particularly of foodstuff and petrol, had been captured, as well as of Chianti and some vehicles. Local supplies of vegetables were now becoming available from the many local markets – a big change after the virtually uninhabited wastes below Belaya – and there was now no shortage of water for men or beasts. A good road allowed faster communication between Mission 101 forces to the north of Dangila, through Engiabara and Burye and up to the new front before Debra Markos, once the risk of mines had been cleared. The Allied successes were at last encouraging the Patriots to come in and swear loyalty to the Emperor and waverers, including *banda* who had hitherto supported the Italians, were now arriving. One less beneficial aspect of this was that they were now more concerned with gaining advantage for themselves and their men than attacking the Italians. 'Let the real soldiers get on with that!' As soon as Dangila, Engiabara and Burye had been evacuated, the local patriot leaders had rapidly moved in, with plenty of opportunity for looting, which was another problem for Gideon Force.

However, Wingate now faced a strong Italian-trained force of some 14,000, at least ten times stronger than his, still supported by fighter planes and Ras Hailu's own force of 6000 *banda*. While the capture of Mogadishu had shaken the Italians, they were still successfully holding General Platt at Keren with vastly superior forces in the north. Wingate's own forces were now widely dispersed, with many of his best officers in the ten Operations Centres scattered through Gojjam, largely without communication with him. With the 2nd Ethiopians having suffered losses, not least of confidence, after the Charaka Bridge battle, he was really dependent now on Boustead's Frontier Battalion. Both he and the Emperor were impatient to break through to Addis Ababa, now only 200 miles away by road, but he was well aware how vulnerable they were to Colonel Maraventano's forces just down the road.

He decide to repeat his tactics at Burye: a small force under Captains Foley and Thesiger would be sent to cut off the road at the vital Safartak bridge in the gorge over the Abbai [Blue Nile] some 50 miles beyond Debra Markos; the Patriots, supported by small groups of British officers and the Propaganda Unit, would be encouraged to skirmish round the Italian forts around Debra Markos, while Wingate and his main force would try and make contact with Ras Hailu and 'encourage' him to change sides. The Emperor would be brought up as soon as it was safe to do so to rally the waverers. Meanwhile he would increasingly be able to act as an Emperor in holding *fukara* [rallies] and receiving homage from local dignitaries.

In the event it proved a frustrating three weeks and in the Emperor's camp near Engiabara there much impatience until they were able to move up to Burye on 14 March.

Thursday 6 March. Went out with Donald to site landing ground and found very good place. Walked over it with van der Post and Naylor who are to burn it tomorrow. Saw Emperor with Donald about 5.45. He very anxious to press on but feels tied until Sandford arrives. During the day letters from Carroll Leahy, Dangila, enclosing Simonds' report of conditions to me. [They were in the northern section of Mission 101 operating near Lake Tana]

Friday 7 March. I still have heavy cold in the head and some signs of dysentery. Emperor sent me a good strong black mule

86

last night as a gift. I saw him at 5.45 and thanked him. Distributed rations to Asfaw this afternoon and had dinner with Donald (and Phillips). We now have chicken and meat (goat and cow) in fair abundance (because the Ethiopians are fasting); also spinach-like green vegetable, gourds, eggs and fresh milk and chillies. Everything is very dear; 6 eggs for MT$1; chicken, however, costs only MT$1. [The Maria Theresa dollar was the traditional currency in much of the Horn of Africa and Gideon Force was supplied from Khartoum with fresh mintings from India.] $1 for a pint of milk. A *raz* of sugar (1/6 in the Sudan) is now worth £E1 here, I'm told [£1= £1 Egyptian]. So we had a regular royal dinner, finishing up with suet pudding and honey. Among other local products now available are *injerra*, *tej*, Ethiopian coffee and honey.

Saturday 8 March. Tummy rather bad. Been on run all day until the evening when walked to landing ground site with Donald. We took our guns. He got 2 pigeons and a quail. I got a guinea fowl and a gyppy goose (in 15 seconds). Just had time to reload to get goose. We missed other guinea fowl and both missed a beautiful wedge of teal and walked back to camp through bush fire. [Writing to Chapman-Andrews from prison camp in Italy, following his capture in the Western desert in 1943, Nott recalled their time together in Gojjam: 'Do you remember our day's shooting together on the top of the plateau? What fun it all was. I wonder how Orde (Wingate) and George (Steer) are getting on (in Burma); Johnson and Boswell now? Had some exciting times in the desert; wish that you had been with me.']

The fire lighted to clear the landing ground spread 'like wild fire' and disclosed a better site than that originally chosen nearby. I turn in on a diet of cornflour with a little medicinal whisky, hot, and decide not to eat solid food until my diarrhoea is better.

Sunday 9 March. No lunch. During the evening I walked to new landing ground where the entire pack camel force of two operational centres (about 200 animals) were marching about in long lines over the burnt grass to roll it. The men were in very good heart after so long a journey from the Sudan and sang as they swept along behind their leaders who bore, like the Dervishes of old, tattered, improvised banners aloft on sticks so that those behind might know the direction of the march. No luck shooting. Allen got a gyppy goose (on the ground) and Donald another (in the air). Also got a guinea fowl. On our return we heard that the Emperor is moving the next day [in stages to Burye] at 7am!

Monday 10 March. Gave *hamlagia* [camel team of ten men] MT$10 each for month's rations plus MT$5 extra for Sheikh Mohamed Juma. The Emperor and party moved at 8am. At last moment I found that my seven mules were all we had to move all my stuff, the S/sgt's, servants', office and Phillips' personal stuff. No provision whatever had been made for moving the rations. Altogether about sixty mules were needed and we had seven. Four were produced for Phillips without saddles or ropes and 20 for the rations with poor ropes and poorer men. The Ethiopian mules (twenty) objected to being loaded even lightly and twice stampeded. They stampeded every mule in the place; packs fell off, mules fell, several galloped about half a mile madly through the long elephant grass and it took an hour or more to collect them. One mule broke its leg and had to be shot. I gave Mahmoud MT$10 in lieu of flour till end of the month. I got off hot, tired and angry at 1.30 My tummy seemed better a little. Got to camp at 6.pm passing Allen and Bathgate nearby out visiting a Coptic church perched on a little hill among tall trees. I passed a lot of ex-*banda* on the road and overtook one who with four armed men had just taken a thaler's worth of *tej* from a village paid with 3 useless Italian cartridges. One of the 3 soldiers with me acted as [judge?] and awarded the $ to the village. The *banda* leader paid with ill grace. Very cold at night.

Tuesday 11 March. I got off early and marched all day near Emperor actually reaching camp before him. Had a hot bath at 4.30pm and felt pretty good. Very cold night. Saw duck flighting; vow to have gun ready for next morning. Gundi River camp.

Wednesday 12 March. Left Gundi River Camp 8 am. Donald and I walked round with guns and got four duck. (I got one and he got two on water with one shot – we were in a hurry.) Pleasant ride to Engiabara. Arrived 9.45 Donald shot five duck (I got one) before lunch 3pm Emperor had a *fukara* of Dejazmatch Mangasha's men, 1500 rifle we reckon. Mangasha rather twittering. I presented Jack to His Majesty. He is vet but o/c Engiabara for past 3 days. Engiabara store contains dozens boxes sardines, tomato paste, jars olive oil and tinned vegetables. Jack accompanied Emperor round town. Donald and I went off shooting and got 11 duck and returned 7pm. Donald got one by moonlight and I ditto but mine was pricked and swimming in a patch of moonlight. Very cold wind, which dropped and gave way to a little rain during night.

Thursday 13 March. Duck: Donald: 2; C-A: 1; Jack: 2. Left Engiabara 8.30am and arrived Fattam River Camp 11.45. Winding hilly road mostly along Italian motor route to Burye. Passed a large crater lake with blue water and steep wooded edges. Road passed over its lip. I met Sandford and Lush near camp in captured Fiat. They and I and Taffara Worq received by Emperor at 3.45 and I dictated minutes of the meeting after. Donald gave me a pipe, one of two brought by Lush. Sandford and I left at 5.15 only to return later (9.00) cold and hungry. We fed then and sent them [Sandford and Lush] off at 10.30 by mule. I went to Mesfin's camp fire with Lorenzo to see them on the road and had a glass of *tej* with Mesfin. Later a messenger came from Sandford with a note saying that a lorry had come from Burye and picked them up. Bed 11.45

Friday 14 March. Vow not to drink *tej*. [Sergeant] Burke is an ex full back from Australia. Mules leave about 7am. I am to go by lorry. Four lorries and two cars to come from Burye and collect us at 9am but somebody blundered. The lorries all but one went on to Engiabara; that *one* took the Emperor's private baggage, S/Sgt Pollitt, my servant, Ras Kassa and Dejazmatch Amda. The Emperor and the rest of us started to walk at about 11.30 and picked up mules etc en route. We reached Burye at 5.00 pm or later just as a thunderstorm that had been threatening all day broke. Although the S/Sgt and his servant had been in since 3.00 and the Brigadier (Sandford) had ordered him to put my tent up they all sat down and had tea. The S/Sgt actually had bully beef! I got soaking putting the tent up and then had no change of clothes, or bedroll or food box. Fellowes helped me erect tent. Phillips, however, got his large tent up. Later my clothes box arrived, he found some good hay fodder for a bed for himself and some for the top of me (my camp bed, but no bedding having arrived) and we slept.

Allen describes Burye Fort as 'a grim and dismal place situated on the crown of the principal of the five hills of Burye. It was made up of stone huts giving on to a barrack yard – the whole surrounded by a wall; trenches, dugouts, wire, dead mules and dung, human and animal, covered the hillside. Flies were myriad. In the afternoon violent dust storms of the hamsin type enveloped the countryside, and when the wind dropped, the dust hung in the air like a fog.' No wonder everyone preferred to camp outside! They remained at the camp outside Burye until 4 April.

Lush had flown in from Khartoum bringing Wavell's formal reply to the Emperor's letter of 22 February expressing concern about the proposed arrangements for the administration of liberated Ethiopia. Lush had to make clear to the Emperor that the immediate implementation of OETA was not negotiable. After lengthy discussions a suitable proclamation was reluctantly agreed by the Emperor telling his people of the 'temporary' arrangements. Together with his complaint that he was not being kept in touch with military developments both throughout Ethiopia and by Wingate and the local commanders, this resulted in a difficult period for the Emperor and thus for Sandford and Chapman-Andrews.

Wavell and Platt had more urgent preoccupations: the major advance on Eritrea had stalled at Keren and, although in the south Cunningham had broken into Somalia, Wavell was fearful of getting bogged down in Italian East Africa which would prevent his planned withdrawal of troops to face the German threat in Greece and Libya. In the event Wavell, with his usual brilliance, played his weak hand masterfully. His visit to the Eritrean front put new energy into Platt's attack on Keren; a force from Aden invaded British Somaliland and recovered Berbera on the 16th to link up with Cunningham's troops advancing from Mogadishu; Sandford and Wingate were asked that the Patriots step up the destabilization of the Italians in Gojjam and prevent them switching reinforcements to their main armies.

Wingate now faced the strong Italian force reinvigorated by its new commander, Maraventano, who had taken over on the 14th and had quickly acted to block to the road to Debra Markos by moving some of his best troops, together with Ras Hailu's *banda*, on to the Gulit Ridge, where they were able to hold up Wingate's advance. Wingate sent messages to Ras Hailu to encourage him to change sides, but to no avail. As always the old fox was waiting to see which way the battle was going before taking action. On 17 March Wingate sent a small force under Foley and Thesiger to bypass Debra Markos and link up with the Patriots under Belai Zelleka in order to cut off any Italian retreat across the Abbai Bridge over the Safartak Gorge. Apart from Boustead's troops near the Gulit Ridge, Wingate's force was now widely dispersed and Maraventano took advantage of this to send two battalions down the Gulit road and recaptured Fort Emmanuel from the platoon of Sudanese troops under Creeden who had to retreat back towards Dembecha after a brief battle. This left the road to Burye danger- ously exposed. Meanwhile LeBlanc had set off from Khartoum with new Ford trucks determined to open up a motorized route to Burye and guided by the trail of dead camels.He wrote that 'the smell is sickening', but obviated the need for guides or maps!

Encamped near Burye

Saturday 15 March. Next day Phillips removed himself and effects to another camp site and I find a good one nearby myself, another for the S/Sgt(2 small tents, one to be used also as an office) and the remainder (or most) of our stuff left at the Durra River camp arriving during the day, put up the outer cover of the other tent as a shelter for the rest of our kit and my servants. Heavy rain again during the afternoon and a long meeting with the Emperor at 11.15 am. I met a little Italian prisoner with an armed Ethiopian guard behind him. He told me there were a Capt and a Lieut also prisoners. He said they were 'bene' more or less but hadn't enough to eat.

Sunday 16 March. A heavy day. 10.00am the Emperor visited Italian prisoners 11.00 am. A terrific *fukara*, of which I took many photographs, though I arrived late and mixed with the crowd, having spent all the morning writing and dictating. Sandford saw the Emperor afterwards and we lunched at 3.00. At 6.00 the Emperor was to receive Lush, but he did not get back from his visit to Burye until 8.00 We had an hour with him. After dinner 9.30 we awaited his second call. He was conferring with all his chiefs and received us at midnight. The meeting ended at 1.30 and I went to bed,cold and tired. A large 3-engined aircraft arrived just before sunset (Junkers – for Lush).

Monday 17 March. Lush left. Up at 5.30 left at 6.00 on mule for aerodrome with Emperor' proclamation regarding British Military Administration. I beat my mule, fairly flogged it to persistent trot all the way and when I was 200 yards away from the aircraft it took off!!! I then went to the Burye post (1½ miles from the aerodrome and 4½ from our camp) with Sandford and had breakfast with him. Donald's foot is very bad from blister acquired out shooting and his leg badly swollen. Ronald Critchley also left by the aeroplane with a poisoned foot. 25 minutes after the Junkers left three 79s and two R42s [Italian planes] appeared. One made off after dropping one bomb and Phillips said later that he thought he had hit it with one of the Emperor's Lewis guns. The other two circled for nearly an hour and dropped bombs on the aerodrome and valleys round Burye. They were obviously looking for the Emperor's camp. The bomb did in fact just drop fairly near the camp. After breakfast I sent a man back for 2 mules to remove flour etc of which there are almost 400 sacks in the Fort. There is also macaroni, jam, olive oil and many sorts of tinned stuff. Then I went to the new aerodrome where the Emperor was encouraging Mangasha's men to clear the ground (but they had no tools) so I asked for 20 men (at Donald's request) to fill in the holes on old aerodrome. The Emperor came himself with a great multitude and we filled 2 holes as big as a house (50 kilo bombs together) and one other. I also stuffed grass twigs and sods on top of 3 unexploded bombs (50 kilos) which had gone 10 feet into the earth. Then I returned to the Fort to pick up

92

the flour etc and just reached the aerodrome at 5pm as three Junkers (3 engines) landed. They brought 5 tons of supplies chiefly ammunition and grenades. The first person I saw get out of the aircraft was George Steer.

Tuesday 18 March. George Steer and Perry Fellowes [who had already set up his Amharic propoganda printing press in Burye] came to breakfast 10.00 am and lunch (2.30) today and we were (5.25pm) with Lorenzo drafting pamphlets. George returns tomorrow at 2pm. He gave me all the news of Saturday's attack on Keren and our progress towards Harar. We are nearly at Harar. Sandford moved his camp here last night and is to go to the Fort every day. I have just had tea of bread made from captured white flour (we were living on unground millet seed 2 weeks ago) captured apricot jam (very good) and captured tea, also very good. Things are undoubtedly looking up!

Wednesday 19 March. George is still here. He is going tomorrow but aircraft arrive every day with supplies, chiefly ammunition. George returns tomorrow. He and Fellowes came to lunch much improved by a crate of fresh vegetables arrived by air from Sandford. We had a bathe in my private bit of the stream before lunch and heard the news on the Emperor's radio at 1pm. We are in Berbera [it fell on the 16th] and have taken the heights (Brigadier's peak) commanding Keren. George thinks Keren will fall soon. Lorenzo gave me a bottle of Italian cognac as a present from Negash. Sandford went to the fort at 11.30 and returned at 5.15. I saw Emperor at 4 pm. He has a beastly cold. Some of George's remarks: 'That monkey could climb almost any tree' about Sir Philip Mitchell CPO, and 'He takes the temperature of the last room he was in' about Maurice Lush DCPO. [Steer was always caustic in hs comments!]

Dr Wohlman (Lieut RAMC) [Wohlman was one of the Jewish doctors requested from Jerusalem by Wingate] arrived after dark with no tent. Fixed him up with us temporarily.

Thursday 20 March. George left this morning for Burye camp hoping to return to Roseires by air at 2 pm. He took a letter to Sadie [Chapman-Andrews' wife in Devon] by bag and one for David [his 8-year-old son] in an Active Service Envelope 'by air'. Spent afternoon dictating and working out establishment. Lieutenant Turrall – said to be a geophysicist, a hell of a talker – arrived at 9.30 pm with 27 cadets from Soba and a letter from Athill [i/c Ethiopian Training Camp, Soba, near Khartoum]. At 10pm approx Sergeant Charley arrived with regrets from Boyle and Bevan that the *Ities* have reoccupied Emmanuel Fort with 1200 troops in 31 MT vehicles at 12 noon yesterday. The radio news is that Jijiga has been occupied by our troops and the heights commanding Keren taken.

Friday 21 March. Signal from Wingate : conflicting story appears to be that enemy entered and retired from Emmanuel Fort on 17th and then retook it on 19th at 1200 hours with 31 MT (1200 troops – Boyle). Wingate not aware of this on the 19th when he sent Sandford telegram (probably later) and letter. None of his messages are 'timed'. Sandford left today by car with Fellowes and Sergeant Burke to clear up the situation. I listened to the radio in evening 6pm with Emperor after presenting Turrall. A new crisis in the Balkans – German threat to Turkey and the *Gneisenau* and *Scharnhorst* in the Atlantic. I am in charge of the Emperor's camp tonight and made a turn round before sunset. Welsh and Bathgate arrived 9.30 and a little later urgent message from Donald for Brigadier. Mackay (Fit Birru's bear leader) has been wounded in the stomach with a bit of shrapnel and Wingate has attacked an Italian post near Debra Markos by surprise at night. This may cause withdrawal of post from Emmanuel.

Saturday 22 March. Sandford back at 6.30 with Fellowes. Emperor went to town [Burye] this afternoon driven by Fellowes to visit Hospital. Dr Hunt arrived 2.30 and stayed to lunch. Azaj Kabada left with 2 letters for Wingate from Brigadier and account of radio news from me. Dr Haggar (SMO Allied Forces in Gojjam – self styled) left with Welsh's unit to operate on Mackay who is to be evacuated by air from Dangila if possible. Doctor Hunt says tail end of his *hamla* was bombed by the two S79s I saw the day before yesterday. He came direct from Metekal.

Sunday 23 March. I went to the Fort this morning. Donald's leg is much better. The Brigadier [Sandford] has now recommended by telegram that I accompany Prince Makonnen to instal him in Harar when it falls. I saw Riley, Hayes and Barlow at the Fort. They are off to rejoin the Frontier battn. Sergeant Burke has already gone to rejoin Lieutenant Brown and Sergeant Botha left with a lorry for Dangila and Bahr Dar [on Lake Tana] this morning. To bed at 2400hrs. Sandford drafting Operations instructions for Beghemder [where Simonds was now operating]. A very gusty evening and night with bad visibility. Have given Mahmoud one stripe. He is instructing the Sudanese muleteers in arms drill to bring them under discipline. Mengasha Abaye and wife, daughter of Dejazmatch Mengesha, formerly Ethiopian Minister in Rome, came to tea. RSM Shaw of 2nd Ethiops also came to camp. He had trouble at Ambiti Ato where during a fracas with camel men a boy of 10 was shot through the head. (Lent Hilaire Belloc *Napoleon* to Sandford.)

Monday 24 March. An aircraft believed enemy passed near camp flying north this morning. Visibility too bad to see it. A warm gusty beastly day. I extracted a jigger flea from ball of right foot this morning. The place is full of them and everyone complaining. Sandford has had two. I have been very careful but think this one got in through my gaping right shoe. A Field Day remodelling the combined Sandford/Political office filing system. [This now consisted of some forty files, listed with true army efficiency.] Barlow very kindly gave me a ration box (and one full for the Brigadier), some soap, three candles, and a tin of marmalade while van der Post gave me a bar of washing soap and a map of Debra Markos. Sent my mule and three pack mules for Blackley (new Col and No 2 to Maurice Lush DCPO OETA (Trevor) and he arrived at 7.00 pm. accompanied by Lionel Gurney of the British Red Cross (BCMS).

Tuesday 25 March. Went to market. About 3000 people buying and selling country produce and rock salt in bars (from Danakil). Blackley tried experiments in small change. He was able to buy lire at 45 to the $ but nobody would *accept* them. I saw women shopping with raw cotton; i.e. they bought a $ worth of raw cotton (4$ the goatskin-full) and traded it against small quantities of chillies, spices, ginger,etc. The raw cotton was purchased carefully by weight, measured on home- made scales. Mark Pilkington came and stayed to luncheon.

Wednesday 26 March. Enrolled about a dozen more *hamlagia* who now number over 20. Mahmoud is teaching them arms drill and doing it very well. Inspected also the beginnings of the escort (20 men) but heard later that the Emperor wants 10 of them! Jack, now mule purchasing and mule transport officer, came and stayed to lunch. One enemy bomber escorted by a fighter came over this afternoon and had a good look round. Matters are getting from bad to worse between Sandford and Wingate and Sandford wants to see Wingate and then go to Khartoum. Wingate complains that he is getting no support of any kind and that all his orders are disobeyed. Dr Hunt looked in this morning. He has diarrhoea like the rest of us. Hunt thinks it is worms!

After the losses to the 2nd Ethiopians following the Charaka Bridge incident, Wingate needed reinforcements and equipment. The use of Burye airfield was enabling supplies to come in by air, but never fast enough for Wingate. His immediate forces had been reduced by the despatch of several of the Operation Centres to rally the Patriots, partly through Sandford's response to General Platt's call to prevent the diversion of Italian forces from Gojjam to the Keren front. Wingate, who tended to strike out when frustrated and when the campaign was not going well, was incensed and stormed back to Burye to have it our with Sandford. All his old complaints about Sandford's belief in the use of Patriots and that equipment should be used to arm them came to the fore. Wingate had little use for Patriots except as a means of frightening the Italians and, with some justification, believed that the new American Springfield rifles arms were more likely to send the Patriots back home than to encourage them to fight. It is interesting to see below that both the very experienced and level-headed Nott and Chapman-Andrews accepted this and sided with him rather than Sandford. A sharp message from General Platt, who was not pleased to be distracted from his battle for Keren, put an end to the argument and Sandford was henceforward responsible only for political liaison and all military matters were to be left to Wingate, who was told to move his HQ to Dembecha nearer his front line.

By now the military situation had changed dramatically for the better. Platt's successes at Keren and the capture of Asmara, followed by the unexpected collapse of the Italians in Somalia and General Cunningham's rapid advance into Ethiopia at Harar, and the reoccupation of British Somaliland now faced the Duke of Aosta and the Italian forces with the likelihood of eventual elimination. However, Aosta still had over 100,000 troops and, with the arrival of the Germans in Libya, his only aim was to play for time. Wingate needed to break the impasse at Debra Markos if he and the Emperor were not going to be left behind.

Boustead was keeping up his night attacks on the Gulit Ridge and Wingate had ordered Boyle and the 2nd Ethiopians to regroup and move forward towards the Italians in Fort Emmanuel. However, they had not really recovered from the Charaka Bridge debacle which had highlighted weakness in Boyle's leadership which Wingate had always suspected. One company mutinied and for the time being they could not be counted on. Wingate, sick with malaria at Dembecha, was furious and sacked Boyle and his adjutant Smith, replacing him temporarily with Major Beard, and asked Khartoum for a replacement as Commanding Officer. With the Emperor's help, the Ethiopians rallied and move forward under their new command.

On 29 March Maraventano was summoned to fly to Addis Ababa, which the Duke of Aosta and the High Command, faced with the imminent collapse of the Italian forces there, were preparing to evacuate. He was ordered to evacuate his forces from Gojjam and to hand over to Ras Hailu, who, it was hoped, would be able to continue to frustrate the advance of Wingate and the Emperor. Wingate knew nothing of this, but over the next few days news filtered out from Debra Markos. The Italians occupying Fort Emmanuel were withdrawn, followed by those on the Gulit Ridge, pursued by Boustead's Sudanese. The various Patriot forces circled 'like vultures' but played no effective part, except by keeping the Italians under pressure. On 3 April Maraventano started to move out from Debra Markos down the road to the Safartak bridge and, although some of Boustead's troops were able to cause some damage to their transport, they were virtually unopposed. Wingate was confident that Foley and Thesiger, with Belai Zelleka's Patriots, would be springing the trap on the bridge.

Thursday 27 March. Keren has fallen. Sandford brought this news to camp from Fort at 10hrs when he went to see Wingate who arrived unannounced from Debra Markos pm today. George Steer writes me letter which arrived same time giving details of action. K had fallen *that morning*. George also sent me all the other things, candles etc, that I had asked for. Good old George. He is one of the best. A true and loyal friend – a rare thing.

Friday 28 March. Wingate and Sandford with the Emperor (Taj W and me) at 11 am. I went to Fort this afternoon and stayed to dinner. Wingate wonders if S 'is more knave than fool'. He will not give way on question of Springfield rifles for formal trips and bodyguard only and is to dash force to Natashtu (?) under Dejazmatch Desta Ishetti. Operations Centre under van der Post. I agree with Wingate. (Hear that Harar has fallen)

Saturday 29 March. Market day. Bought 20 eggs $1, 3 chicken $1, bag of onions $1. Mule prices high, $80 riding mule and $45 pack mules,pack horse $25. Dictated record of meeting yesterday between Wingate, Sandford, Emperor, Taj Worq and me. Brigadier had stormy interview with Emperor this morning. Brigadier upset that Donald 'thinks Wingate is right'.

Sunday 30 March. Borrowed MT $2000 from Mark Pilkington to purchase mules through Kabada and Lij Garrad Isman. Wingate saw Emperor at 6pm. Two Op Centres to be attached to him and bodyguard of 500 of Patriot forces of Mangasha and Negash to invest Debra Markos and so to push across Abbai [Blue Nile]. Hear that Italian garrison at Keren made good retreat to Asmara. Rumours that Debra Markos now occupied by white troops only [untrue]. 12.30 am driven out of bed and tent by red ants.

Monday 31 March. Borrowed $3000 from Fort for Lorenzo who passed it to Kenyas Wardiner(?) for purchasing mules. Wingate left for Dembecha with Donald Nott after seeing the Emperor and issuing marching orders. The news is that according to Italian radio Diredawa has fallen too and that there has been a big battle in the Mediterranean in which three cruisers and two destroyers sunk, certainly two and probably one battleship and one more ship. Our losses two aircraft missing.

The Emperor is fed up and thinks 1) no success in buying mules. 2) Mangasha is not moving forward as ordered. 3) is not 'consulted' by our generals and even by local British officers. 4) not allowed to send representative Prince Makonnen to Harar. 5) not informed of our advances on other fronts in Ethiopia.

Tuesday 1 April. One 2- or 3-engined aircraft, very high, dropped pamphlets and two bombs. narrowly missing bridge. Pamphlets are ours in Banderarchin [written by Steer and his team] and appeal to Italians in Italian to surrender. I pay the staff, taking up practically whole morning. Asmara's fall reported late at night. Preparations to move forward. Hear the Italian prisoner of war Ferdinando Carducci died in Khartoum. He was evacuated by air the night that Blackley left. Emperor still in a very queer mood; almost sullen. He has decided to occupy the Fort at Burye after packing his equipment etc tomorrow. Lieutenant-Colonel Tarleton arrives by air as 'Area Commander' [re 101 Mission]. Hear that he has three Junkers full of personal kit and staff officers.

Wednesday 2 April. Met Lieutenant-Colonel Tarleton, Northumberland Fusiliers, friend of Dodds-Parker. Emperor's kit leaving and I send off ten mules loaded with kit, twelve muleteers, twelve escort under Lieutenant Kabada and Osman and Mahmoud. They leave at almost 11.30 am

LeBlanc, Palmer and USA War Correspondent Stevens arrive with twelve trucks [LeBlanc had at last managed to get the track down the escarpment opened on 27 March] but leave for Dembecha. Junkers [aircraft] leave at 4.30 to land Dembecha. Mule situation. Have loads for 20 mules and have

99

two riding mules and four pack. Emperor in great dudgeon moves to Fort. Sandford goes up to see him at 5pm. I invite Jack (OC Animal transport) to hear my radio which now working and tells of fall of Asmara. Events likely to move quickly. Rumours of evacuation of Debra Markos. Negash reports recapture of Emmanuel.

On to Debra Markos

Thursday 3 April. Emperor moves to Dembecha at 6.30 pm. In afternoon Sandford visits him and returns about 4pm and tells me to clear up various outstanding things with the Emperor. Sandford's new mule throws me, having discovered that it was an English bit and could safely bolt. I return on back of Owen's motor bike and give him dinner. Sandford and S/Sgt Pollitt leave same night with camp for Emmanuel. I entrust radio to LeBlanc. (Jack sent twenty mules with pack saddles, nine over-loaded, and that night I went and fetched from him five pack horses)

Friday 4 April. Up at 5.30 and start loading off at 8.50!! We march all day (till 5.00pm) though I stop and have tea with Cope at about 1pm. He had stopped at the end of his second *shid* [camel march] but I pass him and camp a mile or two beyond Jigga Fort on water. Cope comes up later and camps the other side of the bridge at the end of his 3rd *shid*. We have done ¾ of the way to Dembecha in one *shid*. I sleep under stars with blanket and great coat and turn in early.

Saturday 5 April. Up and off at 6.30 Pass battlefield of 2nd battalion on the way [Charaka bridge]and arrive at Dembecha about 10.00 am. See Wingate, Donald and Mark Pilkington and others in Fort. They leave for Debra Markos which has fallen. All my transport on its last legs. I visit Emperor's camp and find them all packing up. Sandford is just off with Azaj Kabada to Debra Markos but hasn't sent word to Fort to keep me and my mule loads there.

Result: I bring all the loads purposelessly to the camp. Mahmoud badly dragged by one of Kabada's mules. I leave with Emperor 6pm by lorry for Debra Markos.

Sunday 6 April. Emperor camped night of 5/6 on road near Emmanuel. I moved forward at 12.30 midnight with 15 cadets and entered Debra Markos at 2.30 am today. We dodged land mines on road. I find Wingate and Colonel Benson (new commander of 2nd Ethiopians) there. I visit Ras Hailu in morning with Makonnen Desta [the Emperor's liaison officer with the SDF Frontier Battalion]. Boyle and Smith have gone owing to number of desertions from the Battalion due to trouble about burying Italian dead (it is said). Hugh Boustead and Frontier Battalion took and held the Fort.

Emperor arrives pm with Sandford and Ras Hailu makes submission before Ethiopian flag. Sleep night in Resident's dining Bungalow.

Strangely, the diary does not mention the news of the entry into Addis Ababa by Cunningham's South African troops that day, which, together with the fall of Asmara, marked the beginning of the end for the Italians. Meanwhile plenty of problems remained. The evacuation of the Italians from Debra Markos had left a difficult situation. They had left the Emperor's old enemy Ras Hailu in charge with some 4000 of his supporters, vastly outnumbering Wingate's force. For two days Ras Hailu tried to negotiate, but Boustead was firm that he must surrender unconditionally. Chapman-Andrews' visit no doubt reinforced the Emperor's view that immediate submission was required. When the Emperor formally received the homage of the Ethiopian leaders, the old fox, splendidly dressed, arrived late with many of his followers and slowly fell to the ground and three times made obeisance, kissing the Emperor's foot. The Emperor looked on the ground without a motion of acknowledgement. (He kept him in effect under house arrest for the rest of his life).

However, Ras Hailu had his revenge. Wingate had looked to Belai Zelleka, the Patriot leader who had never given in to the Italians and had remained in Gojjam throughout, to intercept and, with a small force of the SDF, stop the Italians crossing the Safartak Bridge over the Blue Nile. Zelleka moved forward, but, to Thesiger's surprise, stalled for two days with various excuses. Thesiger then discovered to his lasting mortification that Zelleka had tricked him and had been bribed by Ras Hailu to let the Italians escape, which they had done before blowing up the vital bridge.

101

The Ras had promised Zelleka, who was of low birth, his daughter in marriage. It is not known if this ever took place but Zelleka rebelled in 1945 and the Emperor had him hung.

Boustead was furious with Thesiger for being taken in, but Wingate was unexpectedly forgiving and, as Thesiger says, gave him a second chance; he won the DSO at Agibar the next month.

Boyle and Smith had been replaced for a different reason; Wingate had never liked them or their man management. At the Charaka Bridge incident the 2nd Ethiopians had suffered severe casualties and the Battalion had subsequently virtually fallen apart and mutinied. This was largely felt to be Boyle and Smith's fault and with the Emperor's full support they were returned to Khartoum.

The capture of his capital also presented the Emperor with a problem: he wanted to to get there quickly. He was aware that all over Ethiopia leading Ethiopians, such as the other great Ras, Seyum, were anxious to come to terms with the British forces and with Lush and OETA, and that these, anxious to conclude the campaign and suspicious of the Emperor's claim of universal support, were not too unhappy with this. He needed all the support from leading Ethiopians that he could get so that he could show that his was the unifying force. Hence, he accepted the submission of Ras Hailu and Zelleka, and later ensured that both, together with Ras Seyum and others of dubious loyalty, formed part of his triumphal entry into Addis Ababa

The next few days were dominated by the Emperor's insistence that he return to his liberated capital as quickly as possible, while the British High Command were equally insistent that he must wait until they got the situation under control. Wingate, who shared the Emperor's concerns but had to obey his orders, was anxious to pursue the retreating Italians, who had escaped his trap, and clear the road to Addis Ababa. Meanwhile the Emperor received his notables and planned for his recovery of power. For Chapman-Andrews, waiting to accompany Prince Makonnen to Harar, there was little to do, other than assist with the surrender of the Italian adminstrators.

Monday 7 April. Move to Dejazmatch Negash's house formerly home of the Resident Dr Elio Lenza. Nasser turns up with kit.

Tuesday 8 April. Had an interview with Dr Elio Lenza formerly Italian Resident. Names of Italians here are, apart from him: Dr Ernesto Giovannone, 2Lt Ernano Mousu, Capt Dr di Gregorio, Din Abramo Trecanni, Sig Carlo Gremo, Sig Giovanni Mucci, Sig Stradiotto, Sig Pietro Guibta, Assistant Mellano Argyri of Dodecanese. Also an Italian wounded soldier called Filippelli.

Wednesday 9 April. I round up Gremo and Mucci in the morning. They have 23 bombs in their house between them. In afternoon visited Mucci's farm and mill and arrested Stradiotto near his mill situated about 2 miles off road 5 miles up Addis Ababa road. Later collected his kit from the town. He had two bombs there.

Thursday 10 April. Prince Asfa Wossen arrived by road from Dembecha am and Prince Makonnen by air from Khartoum with Capt Elles am. Lush also arrived am and returned to Addis Ababa with Sandford. I later saw Wingate and Morrow [Morough] Bernard (Col of bodyguard and to form new Ethopian regular army) re ways and means. Wingate abed for two days with a poisoned foot.

Friday 11 April. Saw Emperor am with Wingate and Morough Bernard. With Elles, commandeered rifles in Gremo's house.

Saturday 12 April. I saw Emperor at 8.20 re saddles etc commandeered yesterday. I saw him again later with Tarleton and Elles and spent a useful 1½ hours thrashing out various question with him. (Wine; Sugar; 'Prizes of War'; Wingate)

Sunday 13 April. Donald Nott (and LeBlanc) took a flip to Addis this morning and back before noon. They say all the houses have polished floors. Saw Emperor at 6pm. Ronald Critchley came in from Bahardar Girgis with a sore foot. He said that Col Torelli was still breathing fire at Bahr Dar but was wounded in one brush with Simonds force. Ronnie [Critchley] called later to say goodbye. He is off tomorrow dawn to Khartoum and hopes to rest for 3 months in Alexandria.

Monday 14 April. Remained in house all day until evening when listened to radio with Lieutenant-Colonel Tarleton, Major Drew and Captain Tim Foley who is just recovering from malaria. Germans claim Sollum but we say our garrisons at Tobruk and Bardia not isolated. Emperor received Belai Zelleka today outside Fort. He is said to have 6000 rifles. He funked attacking Italians near Safartak Bridge. Thesiger, having seen escarpment, thinks BZ could have destroyed Italian force there if he had attacked.

This was the last full diary entry, other than scribbled details of monthly expenses and accounts such as 'pay camelmen MT$x'.

Wingate did not forgive Zelleka and when the Emperor received his submission he stood behind Haile Selaissie with four machine guns trained on Zelleka to make clear what he thought!.

The next three weeks were dominated by the question of the timing of the Emperor's return to his capital, with much toing and froing by air to Addis Ababa by Lush and Sandford. Meanwhile LeBlanc was at work repairing the Safartak Bridge so as to open up the road to Addis Ababa; with his remarkable resourcefulness he was able to make a temporary repair in two days, with oil drums, to enable the 'army' and the Emperor to cross, until the seasonal summer floods swept the drums away.

On 19 April, the Emperor held a big parade at which he promoted his sons to the rank of General, followed by a dinner at which Wingate, in 'captured champagne', toasted the Emperor and the liberation of Ethiopia. On 21 April, accompanied by an intentionally impresssive escort of seven South African airplanes, Chapman-Andrews set off with Prince Makonnen by air to Harar.

With the setbacks that the Allies were now suffering in Libya, it had become increasingly important for the Ethiopian 'sideshow' to be finished.

Chapter Seven

The End of the Campaign

It was essential from the point of view of the Allied forces that the Ethiopian campaign should be brought to a rapid close in line with Wavell's strategy. Rommel, recently arrived in North Africa, had put new heart into the Axis forces and had started their campaign for the recovery of Libya. Greece had been invaded on 7 April and was overrun by the Germans by the end of the month. In Ethiopia the short rains (May and June) would slow down all military movements and the long rains (July to October) would effectively stop them altogether. As planned, Wavell had already withdrawn the 4th Indian Division after Keren and had told Platt and Cunningham that he required the 5th Indian Division and the South African brigade to follow later in April. Meanwhile, three sizeable Italian armies, each of about 40,000 men, still held large parts of the country: the Duke of Aosta at Amba Alagi, General Nasi at Gondar in the north and General Gazzera at Jimma in the south-west. Faced with a big reduction in their forces which left only the West and East African colonial battalions, Cunningham and Platt needed to move fast and, whatever their misgivings, to make full use of the Emperor, the Patriots who were rallying to him and the small British- inspired operations such as Gideon Force, Mission 101 and the half-dozen other irregular task forces to complete Wavell's objectives.

Chapman-Andrews flew down to Harar on 21 April with the 17-year-old Prince Makonnen to assist in his installation as Governor. He had last seen Harar when he had left as Vice Consul in the autumn of 1936 and his knowledge of the town and area was undoubtedly why the Emperor entrusted him with this mission of particular delicacy since General Cunningham had made it his Headquarters and the Emperor wished to underline that he was taking possession of it by the appointment of his son as Governor.

He wrote later: 'Once the Prince was installed at Harar, I remained in and around for a couple of weeks helping to clear the lines of communication with Jijiga. A whole lot of Italian rifles and some mechanical weapons had got into the hands of the local people and were thought to represent a potential threat to the tenuous lines of communication. I went round with a couple of dozen Ethiopians and two bren gun sections of South African troops collecting arms in the villages, hoisting the Ethiopian flag and swearing in villagers to form the nucleus of an organized Ethiopian gendarmerie. I was then recalled to Addis to join the Emperor on his entry into the capital.' He must have arrived there on about 3 May.

Meanwhile, in Debra Markos Sandford was wrestling with the problem of the Emperor's entry into his capital which had been liberated by Allied troops under General Cunningham coming from the south via Somalia, Harar and Diredawa on the day that the Emperor had entered Debra Markos; first the British and, only later, the Ethiopian flag had been raised. The Emperor saw no reason why he should not leave immediately for his capital, but Cunningham and OETA under Mitchell and Lush thought otherwise. Not only was the route between the two towns not yet cleared of Italians, or the broken bridges repaired, but in Addis Ababa itself a small force of Allied troops were faced with disarming some 12,000 Italian troops and civilians who had surrendered and 5000 European women and children for whom Cunningham understandably considered himself responsible. The priority was to disarm the Italians and to start to re-establish law and order and an OETA administration, which required time. There was much negotiation between Lush and Sandford, representing the Emperor, over the Emperor's concerns and the timing of his entry. In Lush's words: 'Pressure to bring him back was intense – from London, from my CPO Mitchell, from the representatives of the Press who had somehow appeared in Addis Ababa and, of course,from the Emperor's HQ, vociferated by Dan [Sandford] quite calmly,and by Wingate loudly and without thought; by British officers who were bored by the inactivity at Debra Markos and wanted "to get shot of the little man and get on with the war".'

Wavell was instructed by the Cabinet on 19 April that the Emperor should return to Addis Ababa as soon as possible.

Meanwhile Wingate had sent part of Gideon Force under Captains Foley, Riley and Thesiger, to be joined by Major Nott, in pursuit of the still sizeable Italian force of 10,000 troops under Colonel Maraventano who had escaped his attempts to stop them crossing the Safartak Bridge and were retreating towards the Duke of Aosta and his army in the north, which he was determined to stop. Colonel Boustead and his remaining forces went north to take the Italian fort at Mota and then on to Lake Tana to join Major Simonds who had now occupied Bahr Dar on the south side of the lake and planned to move against Debra Tabor where he could cut off General Nasi in Gondar from the Duke of Aosta and from Maraventano. Wingate was thus left only with the remnants of the 2nd Ethiopians and a few other troops to keep Ras Hailu in check and to guard the Emperor.

Wingate was as keen as Sandford that the Emperor should return to rule in his capital and was anxious that Ethiopian suspicions of British colonial ambitions should be forestalled by ensuring that this should take place under his control at the earliest possible date and in the right way: i.e. with a large escort of the Emperor's own 'army'. After a stream of wireless messages, Cunningham, Mitchell and Lush agreed that the Emperor's entry should take place early in May. 5 May was the fifth anniversary of the Italian entry into Addis Ababa in 1936 and Sandford and Wingate fixed on this as an auspicious day. The Emperor, Wingate and his 'army' left Debra Markos on 27 April by truck, which managed with difficulty to cross the Blue Nile and to climb the escarpment on the damaged road which LeBlanc was repairing. The 200-mile journey took a week and they stopped at the holy monastery of Debra Libanos for the Emperor and Ras Kassa to pray, as they had done five years before. To provide the Emperor with his 'army', Wingate had to call off most of his forces from their pursuit of the Italians and bring them back to Addis Ababa where on the morning of 5 May an enormously emotional, and brilliantly staged-managed, entry took place. George Steer, now based in Addis Ababa with responsibility for Public and Press Relations, took a large part.

At the Emperor's request Wingate led the march on a white horse, while the Emperor followed in a car, commandeered from

Ras Hailu, with the rest of his escorts, including Sandford, Chapman-Andrews and his 'army' behind, and the Press on the city Fire Engine, down to the Old Gibbi Palace, where General Cunningham and Lush were waiting to receive them. 7000 Patriots under their local leader Abebe Aregai and most of the inhabitants lined the streets. Wave after wave of the Emperor's subjects fell prostrate to the ground, to the amazement of the Allied troops. In the celebrations that followed, they were equally amazed, as were the Italians, that none of the much-feared incidents took place; the Emperor's speech of forgiveness reflected the reality. The disarmed Italians remained safely in their camps and houses throughout the day and no incidents occurred. The whole scene was brilliantly captured in what was one of the Ministry of Information's first films, *The Lion of Judah*. Typically, the formal events in the evening ended in a tropical storm: the rains had begun, a reminder that the main campaigning season was ending.

In spite of this, Wingate and all his available forces immediately left to rejoin Major Nott and the small band of Sudan Defence Force troops and complete his 'unfinished business'- the elimination of Maraventano's forces who were marching north to try and join up with Aosta and the rest of the Italian army. Cunningham repeatedly tried to deflect him, but Wingate, ignoring his radioed orders and deluging HQ with endless coded messages, pressed ahead. After several engagements, in one of which Thesiger redeemed himself in Wingate's and Boustead's eyes by winning the DSO, the Italian morale cracked following weeks of patriot raids and exhaustion and the news on 19 May of the Duke of Aosta's surrender of the main Italian army at Amba Alagi to the 5th Indian Division and the South African Brigade. On 22 May Maraventano finally surrendered to Wingate and Ras Kassa and, to the astonishment of the Italians – a tiny guard of honour of ten Sudanese camel men and a small body of thirty-six Sudanese soldiers. Wingate's bluff had worked again, but he was now faced by a major problem of how his tiny force was to escort some 10,000 prisoners and civilians to safe Allied hands. This he achieved with Ras Kassa's help – they were now in his lands – and arrived on 29 May at Fiche. The Emperor came out to take the salute at the march past of troops escorting the Italian prisoners. Chapman-Andrews later wrote: 'This battle was really Donald Nott's and Ras Kassa's, though Wilfred Thesiger played a crucial role in it and was slightly wounded. Wingate was, of course, in charge of the operation, though just before the battle started he was in Addis Ababa. He dashed back and took command but I really doubt whether this made the slightest difference to the outcome. [This was written long after and was certainly not the view of Nott and Thesiger at the time; the latter said of Wingate's arrival – with Ras Kassa and 3000 reinforcements, 'He was a man whom I think we all disliked but with his arrival the situation was transformed. Now for the first time I really appreciated his greatness.'] He certainly took command at the march past, which I remember the Italian officer prisoners, who numbered a couple of hundred, very much resented. Theirs was not a march but a rabble and, as they passed, they murmured, though they dared not more openly protest.' Chapman-Andrews (whose film of this is now in the Imperial War Museum) and Thesiger then motored back to Addis Ababa where they stayed with Sandford in his old house, now returned to him by the Emperor.

No congratulations were received by Wingate and Gideon Force from General Cunningham, although his immediate commander, Major-General Wetherall, was more generous, but the Emperor put a house at Wingate's and Nott's disposal and invited them, together with all the senior British officers, with Chapman-Andrews and Sandford to dinner to celebrate the successful campaign. There was one sad duty to perform – the burial of Lieutenant Rowe who had died of wounds received whilst chasing Maraventano. As he left the funeral, Wingate received orders to disband Gideon Force, was told that he was relieved of his command and instructed to fly that day to Harar to report to General Cunningham. So he missed the dinner and the chance to take his leave of the Emperor. Cunningham, who found Wingate's wilful disobedience of his orders intolerable, could not get Wingate out of Ethiopia quickly enough and he was immediately flown via Khartoum to Cairo.

At the dinner the Emperor expressed his congratulations and thanks to Colonel Boustead and his officers who recorded their appeciation that, since some of the officers spoke no French, he addressed them for the first time in English.(While his early education by French Fathers at Harar had left him fluent in French which he used with all non-Amharic speakers, he was not confident of his English and was anxious not to be seen to make mistakes or failing to understand.) Boustead and his battalion then left by road for the Sudan via Asmara where they paraded for General Platt who formally congratulated them and shook the hands of every one of the Sudanese soldiers, which was remembered for years afterwards.

Gideon Force in Retrospect

It is necessary to realize that, while to the participants and especially to the Emperor and Wingate, Gideon Force was all-important, to HMG, to the military leaders and to the world it was very much a little-known sideshow and remained so until Steer and later writers told their story. While Platt's battle at Keren and Cunningham's brilliant exploitation of his breakthrough in Somaliland were undoubtedly the decisive events in the collapse of Italian East Africa, the role of Gideon Force and Mission 101 in Gojjam and Beghemder, and the Patriot bands generally, played an important part not only in keeping in check some sixteen Blackshirt battalions and eighteen battalions of colonial troops but also in undermining Italian confidence generally. The Italian collapse was due both to poor leadership and to its dependence on large numbers of Ethiopian and Somali toops and *banda* who in the end often melted away, but above all to the fact that after five years they were still the occupying power in a wild and largely unsubdued country. Given the inadequate support and disparate forces (only some 1800 men) it is remarkable how much Wingate and his men achieved and that his campaign, with all its shortcomings, was so successful. That was due to a large extent to the qualities of leadership of almost all the men involved and the fact that they were united in their objective of eliminating the Italian threat, however much they might have differed over the tactics. To many, including Wingate, Sandford and Chapman-Andrews, this was reinforced by their desire to right a great wrong and re-establish the Emperor on his rightful throne at the head of a liberated, independent Ethiopia. The Emperor played his part here by the respect which he gained from all with whom he came in contact. To the irritation of the Allied Command, he saw his return with Gideon Force as *his* liberation of *his* country which ever after became the 'folk memory' of the annual celebrations of the 'glorious 5th of May ' and which gave little credit to the main Allied campaign.

Their success was all the more remarkable since it was a hotch-potch force mainly of volunteers from different countries and and not a professional army unit. The Sudanese Frontier Battalion had been raised by Boustead from recruitment throughout the Sudan – some from the Nuba mountains had first to be taught Arabic – officered by members of the Sudan Political Service and local British civilians with junior Sudanese Sudan Defence Force officers and NCOs. Most of them had no experience of war or of living at altitudes and in a climate very different from the Sudanese desert, but, in spite of that, they did extraordinarily well. So, too, did the 'camel corps' who looked after the 15,000 camels; both men and camels suffered greatly from the climate and the shortage of appropriate food; only fifty-three camels reached Addis Ababa, where they had to be shot. The Ethiopian troops had been assembled and briefly trained from exiles in Kenya and the Sudan and were officered largely by civilians from British East Africa, Rhodesia and South Africa who had no experience of Ethiopians or Ethiopia, or, in most cases, of fighting. It is not surprising that they were often an unruly lot. The Ethiopian 'Patriots', as Wingate christened them, were often little more than groups of bandits or *shifta* and it is not surprising that they proved difficult allies. Their main role, as Wingate rightly saw, was to frighten the Italian troops, who feared that they had little chance if they fell into their hands, rather than to take part of coordinated attacks.

All of this Chapman-Andrews saw and understood, although his role meant that he saw little of the front line. His discretion as a public servant meant that he was not prepared to expand in his diary on the political implications of his day-to-day work. (This was even true many years later when writers were asking for his recollections: in his book *Haile Selassie's War*, Mockler described being given forty years later 'a somewhat guarded interview'.) He was no doubt conscious of the risk that he, his diary and the Emperor might fall into enemy hands, particularly in the early days in Gojjam. It is clear that, although it was not always possible for him to keep abreast of the daily military developments – and communications were always a weakness of Wingate – there was little else that happened with regard to the Emperor, the local Ethiopians and the interplay with other British staff and policies of which he was not aware and on which he did not have views. The diary makes clear how rough the conditions were and how, to a large extent, every man had to be a jack of all trades: pitching tents, taking minutes, briefing HQ in Khartoum, decoding messages, collecting up Italian civilians, negotiating with Ethiopian leaders, paying camel corps, shooting for the pot, supervising the camel caravan, making sure that the Emperor was properly looked after and guarded and, as far as possible, happy. Apart from his direct reporting lines, Chapman-Andrews had been given military rank and thus with the other officers would have expected to receive all sorts of orders given by his senior officers in the 'exigencies of the service', of which there many in Gojjam.

From other books on the campaign it is clear that Chapman-Andrews was very much accepted by his colleagues, not least for his knowledge of Ethiopia and of Amharic. What is less clear is what he thought of them. With some he remained friends for the rest of their lives. Others he ignores, including Akavia, the Zionist accountant from Palestine whom Wingate had brought in effectively as his Chief of Staff and personal secretary and who remained by his side throughout the campaign. This was reciprocated by Akavia who does not once mention Chapman-Andrews in his Report of the campaign. What he thought of Wingate emerges later in this book. His opinion of Sandford is less clear. While they shared their belief in the Emperor and his cause, one senses that the two men kept a certain distance based on mutual respect rather than very close friendship. Chapman-Andrews was almost twenty years younger and had known Sandford in the 1930s during the latter's rather chequered civilian Ethiopian career. It is noticeable that he never refers in the diary to Sandford by his Christian name but always as 'the Brigadier' or by his surname. Sandford had all the confidence of a well-connected establishment figure, while Chapman-Andrews' career was very much as a self-made public servant and diplomat, so they did not have much in common. One senses that they remained slightly wary of each other, although good relations were maintained until Sandford's death.

The Emperor's British 'Problems'

The next few weeks were dominated for Chapman-Andrews by the problems of the relations between the Emperor and Lush and OETA. Lush wrote that he paid almost daily calls on the Emperor and established, through Sandford, the right of almost instant access. However, relations remained tense and the Emperor was determined to act independently. The positions were irreconcilable: the Allies were faced, after the surrender of the Duke of Aosta and his army, with the military challenge of defeating the still very much larger Italian armies in the north and west of the country; they were determined to play by the book, to exercise immediate and effective control and responsibility for law and order and to evacuate all Italian prisoners and civilians from the country, together with captured military and other equipment considered of importance in the war effort. There was little disagreement over the Allies' right to adminster the occupied Italian colonies of Eritrea and Italian Somaliland, but the Emperor did not consider his Ethiopia as an 'Enemy Territory' and accepted OETA's role in Addis Ababa on sufferance. He considered that many Italian civilians should stay and help in the reconstruction, that the removal of Italian arms and machinery was no better than looting and that he should take immediate steps to take over the administration of the shattered country. However, with no formal forces and only limited funds from Britain, he had little direct power and it would be some months before the British training team would be able to launch a new Ethiopian army. It is clear that Chapman-Andrews agreed with the Emperor and Sandford on the need to hand authority over to the Emperor as soon as possible and relations between him and Lush remained difficult. Elsewhere Lush complained that Chapman-Andrews 'probably never really understood how political problems must give way to military exigencies in time of war'. A 'Most Secret' note sent out in Mitchell's name, but most likely written by Lush or his staff, dated 14 May was kept by Chapman-Andrews and reveals, in its outspoken criticism of Sandford, OETA's strength of feeling and why the Emperor had reason to be suspicious of British intentions, as the following extracts show:

'It appears to be the impression held by Brigadier Sandford and Major Cheesman [previously in charge of Ethiopian intelligence at Khartoum HQ and now joining the Emperor's staff as an adviser], if not by others, that HMG is committed to the forceful restoration of the Emperor Haile Selassie as an uncontrolled autocratic ruler, presumably by Divine Right, over the whole of Ethiopia, irrespective of any other considerations such as the indisputable

113

hereditary position of a man like Ras Seyum. [A powerful noble, he had sided with the Italians and only 'joined' the British and been confirmed in his position after the fall of Asmara]. This is a complete travesty and misinterpretation of the statement of policy made in the House of Commons, the relevant part of which reads:

'HMG would welcome the re-appearance of an independent Ethiopian state and will recognize the claim of the Emperor Haile Selassie to the throne.' No such state has yet reappeared and the Italian army is still in the field in strong force. There is, therefore, no clear idea of what the nature of the throne may be to which the claim of the Emperor *will* be recognized by HMG at the proper time . . .

'I must ask officers to get it once and for all into their heads that what HMG have said they will recognize is the claim of Haile Selassie to the throne of Ethiopia (when the time comes at which there can be said to be such a throne) which is a very different thing to helping him to seize absolute power in Ethiopia by the force of our arms. In the interests of the Emperor himself, and especially of the people of Ethiopia, it must surely be obvious to anyone who takes the trouble to think that the worst thing we could do would be to connive at the establishment of an irresponsible autocracy based on nothing more solid than the personal interest of Haile Selassie and force of arms and that if it is on that foundation that we are party to the reconstruction of Ethiopia, civil war is a certainty in a very short time, in fact immediately our troops are withdrawn. If Ethiopia is to become independent and to be able to stand on its own feet and establish any sort of tolerable government, it must be by genuine collaboration of the leading men in the country . . . Brigadier Sandford truly says that we do not wish to involve ourselves in promoting or taking sides in an Ethiopian civil war. I entirely agree; but no more certain means of doing both could be devised than become a party at this stage to the attempt to reduce people like Ras Seyum to the status of mere salaried officials. There was a ceremony at Runnymede which the over-zealous partisans of irresponsible autocracy might to do well to remember.'

This is strong, if clumsy, stuff, written in the heat of the moment. It says much of the two men that Lush and Sandford managed to remain on good personal relations both then and for the rest of their long lives. The angry tone suggests that the Emperor had some reason to doubt the intentions of OETA and some of the senior Allied people on the ground. Years later one of Chapman-Andrew's old friends, Lieutenant-Colonel 'Sandy' Curle, wrote to him: 'I was with OETA in the senior mess in the Embassy, which had been taken over as our Headquarters with Lush, Blackley and Stafford but I only stuck it for two weeks. So I heard all about their aspirations for a continued British protection of Ethiopia. I was astonished, to put it mildly.' Chapman-Andrews expressed his views strongly in a report which he sent to GHQ in Cairo for onwards transmission to the Foreign Office. He copied it to Mitchell and showed it to Sandford and Steer who said that he would 'get the sack for this'. He didn't and it was no doubt one of the reasons why he was asked to appear before the British Cabinet Committee in November in London. It undoubtedly reflected the view of his ultimate masters in the Foreign Office and the British Government, who were facing far bigger problems in the war in the west and were anxious to finish with what had become a small side-show. On arrival in Cairo in July he submitted what must have been a strongly-worded report to the FO arguing that OETA should be wound up as soon as possible.

However, in hindsight, it could be argued that the country benefited by the temporary imposition of a typical British adminis-tration with all the attention to detail and the devoted work of a small number of experienced civil and military officers. Given the disruption of the old Ethiopian administration, erratic as it was, it is difficult to see how law and order could have returned in any other way.

However, as we shall see, matters were eventually resolved largely to the Emperor's satisfaction, although it reinforced him for the rest of his life in his determination never again to be dependent of any of the Great Powers and in his lasting suspicion of British intentions.

The Captue of Jimma and Return to Cairo

Meanwhile Chapman-Andrews continued to be used for a number of delicate missions which probably he alone was equipped to do. The much-reduced Allied army was still faced by a sizeable Italian army under General Gazzera in the south-west, which Cunning-ham was pursuing with the Ghanaians, Nigerians and the King's African Rifles from Kenya, with the help of Patriots under their leader, Gerassu Duki. The beleaguered General Nasi in his stronghold in Gondar had to be left to be mopped up until after the rains, kept in check by Ras Seyum, local Patriots and the remains of Mission 101 under Simonds and Pilkington and another small British irregular force under Major Ringrose, who had joined them in the north from the Sudan.

Chapman-Andrews was sent down to Jimma to try and conclude their surrender:

'In the early part of June [the diary shows that it was 17 June] General Cunningham sent me on a mission to join the Ethiopian irregular forces surrounding Jimma in order to try and restrain them from entering the town before the commander of the British composite brigade operating in the vicinity was ready. The reason was that General Gazzera had retired across the River Omo with what was thought to be the entire Italian force in that region (over 70,000). He occupied a strong tactical position. Jimma was supposed to have a lot of Italian women and children in the town and the place was hardly defended at all, though there was a whole series of strong points round it still manned by troops with heavy machine guns. General Cunningham naturally felt responsible for these women and children and did not wish to capture the place and deplete his forces by furnishing troops to maintain law and order there before he had settled with Gazzera whom he was calling upon to surrender on the grounds that further resistance would only mean unnecessary loss of life.

'As the matter was urgent, I got the Emperor out of bed sometime after midnight and obtained written instructions signed and sealed to the Patriot Commander outside Jimma. The Emperor had stipulated that when Jimma did eventually fall, his forces should be given the credit for capturing it. This General Cunningham agreed to.

'So with the Emperor's commission in my pocket I set off with half a dozen Ethiopians towards Jimma [about 200 miles southwest of Addis Ababa]. We went all day and laid up at night. Not knowing exactly where Jimma was and thinking it much further away, I inadvertently, at first light, went through the Headquarters camp of the British Brigade Commander [Brigadier Fowkes] and only just missed bumping into a strong Italian armoured car patrol. Some instinct warned me just in time to stop the car and listen. We were off the road and under cover with the car when in no time at all the Italians drove past a couple of hundred yards away to make their routine check on the British position. We lay concealed until they drove back again half an hour later, having meanwhile sent out a few Ethiopians to look for the Patriot Commander Gerassu Duki. He eventually appeared with the British liaison officer, Captain Shaw [detached from 2nd Ethiopians]. Shaw was in bad state with fever and dysentery, but was able to give a good account of the local situation.

'I tried for two or three days to restrain the Ethiopian forces. Part of them I sent off to collect the Italian garrison from a small outlying place, but in the end I could hold out no longer because their supplies were nearly exhausted and their numbers were rapidly diminishing both from this cause and from what they called "camp sickness", i.e. a sort of dysentery acquired by remaining too long in one camp. The camp area was, of course, noisome and swarming with flies. We patrolled about, but in the end I had to tell Brigadier Fowkes that the Ethiopians intended to go in. He therefore arranged a joint entry with them.'

Among Chapman-Andrews' papers was a scribbled note dated 20 June 11.00 a.m. from Brigadier Fowkes' staff officer John Millard [later a Provincial Commissioner, Kenya]: 'Dear Major, The Brig has sent me here to contact my runners and to get a message through to you re the occupation of Jimma tomorrow morning. The Brig has asked me to let you know that he has decided to go in tomorrow morning. Advance brigade party will leave a little before 8.00am and he wants you, the Emperor's representative, and six of Gerassu's bodyguard to meet us at a point about 2 miles from Marna (on the Jimma side). Shaw tells me that a big footpath forms the main road at approximately this point. A lorry will be set aside in the column for Gerassu's party and it will be placed directly behind the Brigadier, or rather discreetly behind your car which I will bring along for you. You and I will travel in your car behind the Brig. Shaw will travel in the lorry behind us with Gerassu and party. The Brig wants me to stress that the Fit [Gerassu Duki] should reduce his personal party to not more than six or seven. It is also important that the party should be ready at the roadside by 8 o'clock. I shall write a separate letter to Gerassu in case you are out of touch or up Agaro way when this arrives. Kinyazmatch Bezzatu's rifle and ammo are safe and will be brought in tomorrow.

All the best – be seeing you tomorrow, yours ever.'

Chapman-Andrews continued: 'The entry on 22 June was, of course, completely unopposed [he recorded that that night he heard that Germany had attacked Russia], our sole anxiety being lest looting, etc. should break out. This, however, did not occur, the Emperor's orders, as always, being most strictly observed by the Ethiopians. Realizing this, Brigadier Fowkes moved with his whole force, such as it was, to the River Omo against Gazzera and I remained in Jimma with my Ethiopians. The next day one of these brought me a lean and ragged messenger with a letter in a traditional cleft stick and addressed to the Ethiopian commander informing him that he should contact the nearest British officer with whom alone the writer of the letter would discuss terms of surrender. This duly took place and the Emperor came down to Jimma to take the surrender parade, and no doubt to ensure that Gerassu was still under his control.'

It has beeen an exhausting week: Chapman-Andrews noted in his diary: 'June 30 No sleep; July 1 Emperor leaves am Sleep. July 2 return Addis Ababa.' General Gazzera rallied his remaining troops and they finally surrendered, with five generals, to a Belgian force which had joined the war from the Congo, near Gambeila on the Sudanese border on 4 July.

On 25 June the Emperor, before setting off for Jimma, had received Wavell, accompanied by Roosevelt's emissary Averell Harriman, then on his way to taking up his new command in India, and expressed his respect and thanks by giving him the order of the Seal of Solomon, only given before to King George V. Sandford had come down with the Emperor with a copy of the order that had been received by wireless for Chapman-Andrews to report back to General Headquarters in Cairo as soon as possible. The next problem was how to achieve this.

Chapman-Andrews continued: 'There was very great difficulty in getting aircraft passages at this stage in the War because all our available aircraft and indeed a great number of our regular troops had been withdrawn for operations elsewhere as the Ethiopian campaign was virtually over. When I got to Addis Ababa I packed as quickly as I could and found that it was impossible to get sufficient priority to get an air passage so I started off in the Fiat with Ward [The Hon Edward Ward] heading for the north. We went by Dessie where I met Derek Riches [a diplomatic colleague, later Sir Derek] who had been established there as Political Officer, and on to Asmara. We slept out on the road overnight as inconspicuously as possible because the whole district was infested with Shifta Brigands. In Asmara, where I spent one night, I reported to Army headquarters and by chance ran into General Platt who was commanding there and he said when he saw me, "Hello, what are you doing here? Haven't you been sacked yet?" I said, "Yes I think that I just about have, but still it is all over in Addis Ababa, so I am off to Cairo to report back." He said, "Well, goodbye then." [Relations between the two men had clearly remained distant!]

'Next day I drove on in the same car to Kassala and the road passed near Keren where the battle had taken place. There were no signs of battle now, the whole road from Addis Ababa right through via Dessie to Asmara and from there down to Kassala on the Sudan frontier had bridges down and bomb holes and derelict cars and shot-up vehicles of all sorts along the sides of the road.

'In Kassala we found a train waiting just about to start for Khartoum as we drove into the station yard. We seized our kit, abandoned the car and jumped into the train. We arrived in Khartoum about 24 hours later. There I reported to the Army headquarters and showed them my instructions and asked for priority passage to Cairo. They said that they had no aircraft available and that I would have to go by train and boat. Where was my Yellow Fever certificate? I said that I had never heard of any such thing, nor had I heard of any Yellow Fever. They said that the train from Kassala had passed through a Yellow Fever area during the night and therefore I had to have a certificate. I told them that the windows of the train had been fitted with a small-gauge wire net, presumably to keep the mosquitoes out and that there had been not so much as a fly in my carriage. They said that did not matter, but that I still had to have an inoculation certificate. So I got myself inoculated immediately but I had to wait another day before I could get started for Cairo, where I arrived early in July.' It was then that he was to meet up again with Wingate in sad and dramatic circumstances.

Chapter Eight

Wingate's Attempted Suicide and the Anglo-Ethiopian Treaty

By the time Chapman-Andrews arrived in Cairo on about 7 July the situation on the Mediteranean Front had changed dramatically, mostly for the worse. The Balkans, Greece and Crete had fallen to the Germans, who had now taken command, under Rommel, in Libya, and driven the Allied forces back to the Egyptian border and were besieging the beleaguered Allied garrison in Tobruk. The Allies had sustained heavy losses of men and equipment in Greece and in Libya. An important convoy of tanks and equipment had managed to reach Alexandria in May and had taken part in the 'Battleaxe' offensive against Rommel on 15 June, where they had been outgunned and largely destroyed, together with Wavell's hopes of regaining the initiative in Libya. On the plus side Rashid Ali's pro-German uprising in Iraq had been defeated; the Vichy French in Syria had been attacked in mid-June and resistance was finally over by 11 July; the War in Italian East Africa was effectively over, bar mopping up the isolated, if large, remaining enemy forces in the north at Gondar. The German invasion of Russia on 22 June brought a powerful new ally into the equation, but the war there was not going well and Wavell was under pressure to protect the vital oil supplies in the Middle East, now vulnerable to the German advance on the Caucasus. Nonetheless, it was already clear that the Axis resources were being stretched by conflicting demands, which was no longer the case for the Allies, and Rommel's supply and communication difficulties had put a stop to his advance. It was at this point that

Wavell, who had done remarkably well over the last 12 months in trying to meet Churchill's conflicting and frequently changing priorities, was superseded by Auchinleck on 1 July and sent as Commander-in-Chief to India.

In Cairo the Egyptians were growing restive. With the outbreak of war the British had taken advantage of the mutual defence clause in the 1936 Anglo-Egyptian Treaty to regain effective control over the country and did not hesitate to give the orders. Although Egypt had not declared war, Germans and Italians had been interned and their assets siezed, but the King and many politicians were by no means committed to the Allied side and some groups were actively pro-Axis. The Egyptian army was considered unreliable and a number of their young officers, like the future Presidents Nasser and Sadat, were anti-British; Sadat himself was involved in an incident with some German spies and dismissed. With Allied troops continuing to pour into the country, particularly from Australia, New Zealand and India, Cairo felt to the Egyptians like an occupied city: by the end of 1941 there were over 140,000 troops in the Cairo area alone. Generals and exiled Balkan Kings and officers sped through the streets in their cars on the way to the races and parties; their soldiers were more likely to be found in the streets late at night enjoying themselves. While the Egyptians were making good money from all this new spending power, they were not enjoying being second citizens in their own country.

This was the city to which Wingate and Chapman-Andrews had returned. Chapman-Andrews wrote later: 'I went straight to my pre-war flat and reoccupied it. I was only too thankful to be able to enjoy again its luxury. [It was a small embassy flat which he had left 12 months before; its 'luxury' was only in comparison with his Ethiopian experiences.] Our old servant and housekeeper, a Greek called Athena, was still there and that was marvellous. Next day I reported to Brigadier Clayton at Headquarters Middle East where he was still head of the Middle East Intelligence Centre. He told me that he had sent for me to give me an employment in Syria as a Political Officer. [As Chapman-Andrews was still seconded with Army rank to GHQ Middle East, his post as Oriental Secretary in the Embassy had been filled. Plans were in course for the occupation of Vichy-held Syria, where Thesiger and a number of his Gideon Force companions were already engaged.] I said that I wasn't very keen on that, so he said that he had it in mind in any case that I should join a Military Mission that was being organized under a Colonel Cotton whom I had never met, and never did meet, whose task it would be to organize Kurdish resistance if the Germans broke through the Caucasus into Northern Iraq in order to occupy the oilfields, outflank Turkey and make a land attack on our Middle East forces from the east. I said that that would suit me very well, especially as I knew much of the country from service in the early 1930s in Kirkuk, Suleimaniya, Rowanduz and the Persian frontier. Clayton said that he had that in mind. In actual fact this Mission never got off the ground because it could not properly be done without arousing all manner of suspicions, by agreement with the Persians and, in particular, the Russians. If the Germans had broken through the Caucasus, which they certainly would have done but for the heroic defence of Stalingrad, they would have burst into Soviet Azerbaijan which merges into the Persian province of Azerbaijan which in turn is plum on the Iraqi frontier – that is to say the Kurdish frontier. As it turned out, as I was told later at GHQ, the Russians from the very first absolutely refused to contemplate or even discuss the possibility of the Germans breaking through the Caucasus. Moreover the Persians under Reza Shah were very wobbly as neutrals and much inclined to side with the Germans whom the Shah thought were winning the war. That was, of course, the reason why, a few months later, we had to intervene militarily in Persia and depose him [in August].

'So while there was nothing specific to do, Clayton gave me a desk and there I was in the Middle East Intelligence Centre and he said I could familiarize myself with the current work and, when I got the form, I could take my turn on the rota and tackle any job that might come along. This suited me very well for the time being as I certainly needed a rest and a change and a steady supply of good food as I had lost a lot of weight and had had dysentery very badly in the march through Gojjam.'

Wingate's Attempted Suicide

Wingate had arrived at GHQ a month before, had spent an unhappy time without a job and had been largely ignored. In the first weeks he had written up his report of Gideon Force, which had been highly critical of just about everyone and particularly of his superiors. As a result he had been carpeted by Wavell and the report had been withdrawn.

Chapman-Andrews wrote: 'Only a few days later George Steer, who was there working closely with Clayton, told me that Wingate was in hospital, the Fifteenth (General) Scottish Hospital, having tried to cut his throat. [This had taken place on 4 July.] We enquired after him and as soon as we were allowed to do so we went to see him. It would have been about 10 July.

'He was sitting up in bed with these eyes of his, which normally in ordinary life as we had known him were half-closed in dark quizzical enquiry, but were now wide open like the eyes of a baby and his skin was quite white, dead white, and he had an enormous bandage round his neck. The nurses were waiting on him as though he was a very special case, which I suppose he was – after all he had got a DSO and Bar which was a rare distinction for anybody at that stage of the War. I said to him, "Well, Orde, how are you?" He said, "I'm all right," and then I said, "Are you going to be all right?" He said, "Yes, but I think I shall have to go back and face an enquiry or a Court Martial or something." I then said to him, "Why did you do it? Have you had trouble with your wife or something of that sort?" because I knew he had married off the cuff on a blind impulse a woman whom he had met on the ship going home from Palestine, where he had been wounded in a night fight with Arab raiders. He said, "Oh no, thank God, there is nothing wrong there," and I said, "Well, look here, why did you do it?" Well then, in actual fact, he didn't tell me the truth. He said, "I don't know; I had had a bit of fever and I was a bit beyond myself. I don't know quite why I did it but at any rate on the spur of the moment I did it." And I could see that he was fencing and foxing in his answers and that it wasn't a true answer. I said to him, "Very well, when you attempt to do something you plan it carefully and succeed in what you try to do. Why didn't you succeed? Why didn't you cut your throat?" He said, "Well, I determined that I was going to kill myself and first of all I thought of my pistol", and then he said something to me which couldn't possibly have been true. "You remember that when I was wounded in Palestine that night and I fell down, I dropped my pistol?" He had had a 45 like everybody else. Of course I wasn't even there, as I was in Egypt at that time. He said, "Well, I remembered after I had been wounded and picked up and taken away that I hadn't cleaned it. I had dropped it in the mud and the barrel must have been full of mud and I had never cleaned it. I knew it was no good using my pistol." [In fact Wingate must have still been very confused and probably drugged at the time. As Akavia confirmed, Wingate had been obliged to leave all his few possessions in Addis Ababa and Akavia brought them, including his pistol, along to Cairo, arriving the day after Wingate's attempted suicide.]

'Then I said, "What else?" and he said, "The knife, I have killed many animals with a knife and the knife is clean and it means death," which is an Arab proverb because the knife or the sword means cleanness and death. He said, "I saw the knife, the knife you gave me." Well this was a knife with a blade about 10 inches long which I had got when I was in Cairo in Christmas 1940. General Wavell had said to me that he wanted to give the Emperor something and asked what I thought he should give him. I suggested a shot gun because the Emperor liked arms and it would be quite useful to have one. "He won't use it himself but we can shoot anything we can for food." He asked if I could get one and I told him that I knew a good gunsmith who would have good second-hand English gun, since I had been shooting in Egypt since 1937. I went off and came back to Wavell and told him that the total bill had come to £47 and he had asked what I would like to do with the change from the £50 he had given me. I told him that I would like to buy something for myself and Wingate and I went off and found these two long knives; they had got a hook that hung on the belt and were useful for cutting up food or even defending yourself if you had to in an emergency. I had got back to Khartoum early in the New Year 1941 and after presenting the gun to the Emperor, I had given one knife to Wingate and kept one myself.

'Wingate continued, "Listen, if you ever want to cut your throat, don't make the mistake I made. Get the knife and make sure it is sharp, tense your arm, bring it up and relax your throat; bring your tense arm with the knife right across the throat and, keeping your throat relaxed, stick the knife right in and pull hard while you still have consciousness. I didn't do that; I forgot to relax my throat sufficiently and before I had completed that stroke I felt the blood going down onto my stomach and I knew that I had not completed the job and I knew that I had failed. That was it and that is why I had failed."

124

He did say later, in the course of general conversation, "Now I see that it was ordained that I should fail in this attempt to kill myself. I know that I am destined to be a great man." This confirmed my realization from the moment that he first mentioned about the pistol in Palestine that he was now, at any rate for a time being, on the narrow razor edge of reason. He also said that he had a black-out. He said nothing whatever about malaria. I mention this because afterwards it was put about and given as the main reason at a medical enquiry for an unbalanced state of mind that he was suffering from malignant malaria and was treating himself and was refusing to retire to bed with it. As to the truth of this I can say nothing. The main reason I am pretty sure for his depression was disappointment – bitter disappointment and frustration to his driving ambition that at the end of his outstandingly successful leadership of the Patriot Campaign in Ethiopia he was virtually ignored by higher authority on his return to Cairo. I have a haunting suspicion that he didn't really mean to kill himself at all but had made this spectacular gesture to draw attention to himself. Here he was unemployed. He knew he had a lot of enemies and wanted his particular case to be drawn to the attention of people in authority in the Government.

As we left the Hospital, I asked George [Steer] what he thought of him. George replied, "Well, he's as mad as a hatter, but his eyes are the eyes of a collie that has been killing sheep." '

Various later accounts exist of Wingate and the background to his collapse, often by writers who were in Cairo at the time. Steer himself, who was later to serve in Burma, where he died, understandably did not include an account of this visit in his book *Sealed and Delivered* or in his official account of the Abyssinian Campaigns for the Ministry of Information, both of which he was then writing in Cairo. Chapman-Andrews' account, however, is unique in its detail. For him it was a most dramatic moment in his very different life as a diplomat and which he never forgot. Here he tries to recall it towards the end of his life, using direct speech more to convey the spirit of the meeting than total accuracy, although he did have an almost photographic memory. His natural discretion meant that only very oblique accounts of his evidence appear in other books.

Wingate, of course, recovered and later made history in Burma, where he died. He and Chapman-Andrews appear to have met briefly for the last time in London, later in the year, when Wingate was trying to rehabilitate himself with the authorities. There was a cryptic note: 'Wingate. His plan. Can I get it typed' in his notes. But Wingate and his extraordinary and contradictory personality haunted Chapman-Andrews as it did many others who had known him, as his retention of a number of relevant letters and papers shows. In the 1970s he joined Sir Bernard Fergusson (Lord Ballantrae) and others in a radio programme. What follows is based on a collation of this and other dictated notes that he made, in which he tries to evaluate Wingate.

What we do not, of course, know is how Wingate regarded Chapman-Andrews, who says that Wingate mistrusted him since Chapman-Andrews 'represented a very important Department of State, the Foreign Office, with whom Wingate was particularly anxious to keep on close terms because their expertise was in an element, namely international relations, technical diplomatic relations, international politics, which, strangely enough he was very unsure about'. One suspects that, although from very different backgrounds, there existed a degree of wary mutual respect between the two men, who were both 37; there is no evidence of any affection, which is not surprising, knowing Wingate's character.

Evaluation of Wingate

Chapman-Andrews wrote much later: 'Wingate enjoyed the exercise of power – absolute power. He made excuses, even sorts of pretexts, for exercising it, but he was very cunning the way he went about it. He was a very odd man indeed. He had to be surround by "Yes" men. But he had a most extraordinary fascination for a number of such men and even women. In saying this, I certainly do not mean that there is any sexual overtone or undertone or whatever it is. Many people were simply drawn to him as if by a magnet. They were people of ability, people who could serve him well but who believed in him as in one inspired. They wanted only to carry out his orders which they would never question and if anything went wrong he immediately searched round for a traitor in his camp. "Surely an enemy hath done this." Then he would ruthlessly dispose of that enemy or obstacle in his path, I often used to think rather as King David disposed of Uriah the Hittite by sending him into the forefront of the battle to his death.'

In his radio interview Chapman-Andrews said: 'Though bold, Wingate did not charge obstructions bull-like and, although single-minded, he was not obstinate or narrow-minded. He was a deep schemer and what he could not break down, whether it was the prejudice of a British General or the walls of an enemy fortress, he quietly and stealthily slipped round. He had a withering contempt for orthodoxy, especially if it meant playing safe. Yet in the many risks he took, whether in the sweep and audacity of his general plan or in hazarding his own life in a particular operation, the chances of success and failure were carefully weighed.

'He owed his military success primarily to his accurate diagnosis of the enemy's state of mind – in Abyssinia the enemy was afraid of being caught on the move between his fortresses, yet terrified of being in isolated garrisons, surrounded by revengeful 'rebels' (as they called the Patriots). Wingate's plan was to surround a garrison and pour fire into it at night, leaving one loophole of escape for the beleaguered defenders. Once on the move, he struck at them through ambushes. Compelled by sheer weight to force a way through, the Italians left casualties on the field and carried terror to the next fortress, the occupants of which were even more eager to clear out while the going was good. Finally the enemy remnants had to abandon even the metalled road and take to the open country, and here,with a ludicrously small force and a lot of bluster, Wingate was able to trick them into throwing down their arms.

'During the year I knew him, it was the man rather than the soldier that constantly held my attention. He appeared to me to be possessed of two personalities. So far I have only spoken of one. The other emerged when plans were going awry. Then his eyes narrowed and glinted. He became morose and spent hours squatting cross- legged, crooning tuneless gibberish, while swaying from side to side. 'I find it restful,' he said. When in this mood he would brood over trifles and imagine enemies from among his best friends. Against such 'enemies' he was ruthless. I have seen him when the timetable was going wrong kick Africans struggling to pull a lorry out of a sandy gully. And I have also seen him tear into shreds his own tent to provide body covering for those same

Africans in the unaccustomed cold and rain of the hills. I have heard, too, of many a muttered threat to 'get him one day'. Some men say he was mad, but, sane or mad, he could at all times command obedience. What I did not see him command was affection. That gentle, human feeling could live, I think, only in the hearts of those who knew him in the times when there were no Emperors to be set on thrones, no enemies to be confounded and no devil to be cast out.'

Chapman-Andrews knew and corresponded with both Mosley and Sykes over their books on Wingate. To Mosley he said little, but there was an interesting exchange with Sykes, whom he had known well in Cairo, to whom he wrote in 1959 from the embassy in Khartoum congratulating him on his book *Orde Wingate*: 'It seems that I knew Orde Wingate during his blackest year. My acquaintance with him covered the period from Autumn 1940 to about Christmas 1941. I believe that his darker moods, even the darkest during which he tried to kill himself, had a greater significance than you attach to them. I think his ambition, if we can call it that, was of a darker nature than your story would have the reader suppose. I do not believe he attached himself to the causes of the oppressed for idealistic and unselfish reasons but rather that he seized upon them as vehicles for his own driving ambition. Your story of his zeal for the Abyssinian cause which he shared with Sylvia Pankhurst in London during the winter of 1941/2 I found particularly interesting as neither then nor when he was in hospital in Cairo did he disclose to me any misgivings whatsoever about the political future of the Emperor and his country. He knew that I was as deeply concerned with this question as anybody. It was in fact the business on which I was employed. If he had spoken about it I would have reassured him. The point was that he did not wish to be reassured. This was all part of his mental make-up which had I believe a much more sombre side that you evidently think. Wilfred Thesiger, who was staying with me the other day, thought that it was an advantage to you in writing your book not to have served with Wingate in the field or to have met him: if you would have done so either you would not have written the book at all or you would have written a different book.'

Sykes replied: 'I have been thinking a lot about what you wrote. Of course, as I was writing with the family's agreement I had to make some concessions to them, and I played down what I knew about Ethiopia, chiefly from Wilfred [Thesiger], but I hope I gave sufficient indication that "the dark period" was very dark indeed. Where I do rather disagree with you, I think, is in regarding Ethiopia as a separate episode in his psychological career. It is quite extraordinary what a different picture you get of him from his Palestine contacts, and from the people he knew in Burma. Bill Allen is the only Gideonite I ever met who really liked him. It seems to me that during the time you knew him he was pretty near to insanity. A fact that I agreed to suppress right at the beginning of this undertaking was that his fear of madness was largely due to the fact that his sister Constance had died in a state of insanity. The psychoanalyst who saw him after his suicide effort recorded that he seemed to be a case of hereditary mental ill-health.

'His ambition is a puzzling business. No one was more skilful at making his career – and more prone to jeopardise it. I think he had a martyr complex. To attain success through espousing Zionism wasn't exciting enough – he wanted to be crucified for it as well. After all, you and I have known plenty of people who were openly pro-Zionist in those years and came into no danger at all of cashiering or rebuke or bad reports. There was a very strong case against HMG from the pro-Zionist point of view, so Wingate's martyrdom seeking espousal of the cause can make sense. But with Ethiopia it was another matter – he had to invent the case against HMG and so the whole thing has an utterly crazy air about it. His whole family (who regard me as one of the supreme denigrators of all time) have an odd tendency towards persecution mania, and a kind of exalted idealistic Puritan egotism that I can easily imagine leading to lunatic martyr-complexes and the like. I started the book as a profound admirer of the Puritan genius; I finished it with serious misgivings about my own Cromwellian ancestry, and with a new sense of how dangerous it is to read the Old Testament rather than the New.'

On a different note Field Marshal Lord Slim wrote to Chapman-Andrews in the late 1950s, 'I fear that in my book [*Unofficial History*], I was too generous to Wingate. As far as I was concerned his effort on the success of the Burma campaign was not worth the resources, lives and efforts that were used on his expeditions. He was at times mentally unstable, a completely self-centred man but he had powers of leadership and a great power of advocacy.'

In trying to sum him up, Chapman-Andrews says: 'I do not want to denigrate anyone, least of all Orde Wingate. A man who gets three DSOs deserves to become a legend; and certainly he has become a legend. But it is important to get the facts right first. It is a fact that Orde Wingate had the power to make men arise and follow him. His intention, when formed, was clear; and he left no one in any doubt about it. His motive was not so discernible. "Motive" is a state of mind and as a Lord Chief Justice of England said long ago, "Who shall judge the mind of man? The devil himself knoweth not the mind of man." He was,indeed, a most remarkable man – a fifty-fifty chance for himself or anybody else was to him fair odds. He believed in his star; he thought he would survive and beat the odds. But I felt in my bones long before he met his death, one day he would come to a sticky end quite un-necessarily, because of his vaulting ambition. And this, I believe, proved to be the case.'

But to the Emperor Wingate was his devoted soldier. On the news of his death in April 1944 he immediately cabled Churchill and Wingate's widow to express his 'intense grief at the disaster which has deprived Ethioipia of one its greatest friends'. It was typical of him that he invited Wingate's son, also a soldier, to the 25th Anniversary celebration of the Liberation and that the Ethiopian Press and historians have accorded to Wingate a special place in Ethiopia's History.

The Anglo-Ethiopian Treaty

Chapman-Andrews spent the next few months in GHQ Middle East Intelligence in Cairo working for Brigadier Clayton, but we have no record of his intelligence work, although he was in contact with men like the Stirlings, involved in movements behind enemy lines. His diary shows that his life was by no means disagreeable and a marked contrast with Britain in 1941, as his family, marooned in wartime Devon, remarked. There were dinner parties, golf and contact with the many interesting people to be found in Cairo at that time.

It is clear that future relations with Ethiopia and the differing views of the Foreign Office and the War Office were continuing to take up much time in London, Cairo and Ethiopia. While Eritrea and Somalia were clearly within OETA's brief as 'Occupied Enemy

Territories', Ethiopia in the Emperor's view was not. The Foreign Office was anxious to normalize relations as quickly as possible with a diplomatic appointment in Addis Ababa and to reduce involvement in Ethiopia's internal affairs to the minimum; the War Office was insistent on the dangers of an unstable Ethiopia to the war in the Middle East and on the need to maintain direct control over the Emperor. It had persuaded the War Cabinet on 9 June to instruct Mitchell to negotiate with the Emperor on an 'Understanding' which would include his undertaking to abide by any 'advice' that the British government and their OETA representatives on the spot gave and an effective control over the adminstration, with a 'sweetener' of an offer of an unspecified but substantial annual payment – they were thinking of £2.5 million a year. This the Emperor could not accept and negotiations continued during the summer. On 14 August 1941 Lampson, who retained political responsibility for Ethiopia, cabled London to say that he had had the opportunity of a discussion with Chapman-Andrews on the question of his possible secondment to Sir Philip Mitchell, Chief Political Officer, OETA, and British Representative in Ethiopia, as Foreign Office Representative in Ethiopia. While naturally replying that, if told to, he would accept, Chapman-Andrews felt that any such 'agent' should be appointed at a more senior level with a view to permanent diplomatic representation. Clearly his 'indiscreet' submission criticizing OETA had struck home and echoed the view of many in the Foreign Office and Downing Street. No more was heard about this idea, nor of the idea for a British High Commissioner in Ethiopia. Lampson added that he found Mitchell very difficult to control. It was clear that he was getting increasingly irritated by London's failure to settle the conflicting views. In Whitehall the battle continued and the files grew larger; the crises of the war had apparently not diminished an endless and typically bureaucratic to and fro. In October the King 'spotted that the latest proposals carried undesirable parallels to Cromer and the British pro-consular role in Egypt'. Eden emphasized that it was important that 'there should be no shadow of tutelage' over relations with Ethiopia.

In late October a cable was received in Cairo asking that Chapman-Andrews return to London by the first available aircraft and report to the Foreign Office. Unexpectedly Sir Philip Mitchell was on board, for reasons which became clear on arrival. The

131

plane stopped at Malta, then in the midst of continuous air attack, and Gibraltar, before landing at Plymouth. In London he learnt that he had been recalled to submit evidence to a Cabinet Committee which had been set up under the Lord President of the Council, Sir John Anderson, with representatives of the Foreign Office, War Office, Colonial Office and Government, 'To examine and present to the War Cabinet the issues for decision in regard to Ethiopia, with particular reference to such safeguards as may be thought necessary to meet the military requirements of the General Staff.' In the next few days they took evidence from 'Lt-General Sir William Platt(GOC East Africa), Sir Philip Mitchell (British Representative in Ethiopia and CPO Occupied Territories, East Africa), Brigadier Sandford (Personal Military and Political Adviser to the Emperor of Ethiopia), Major E.A.Chapman-Andrews (Foreign Office representative to the Middle East Intelligence Centre, Cairo) and Brigadier Lord Rennell of Rodd [OETA's financial chief].' It was a tribute to Chapman-Andrews' growing reputation that he was included in the short and distin-guished list of those required to meet the Committee. It was equally a tribute to Sandford that the Emperor trusted him so completely to represent his interests that he had been sent on his own to London the previous month to continue the negotiations over the future of the country.

The Committee reported to the War Cabinet on 8 November 1941. In general terms the War Office, well aware of the con-tinuing threat from the Axis forces in Libya (and even in Ethiopia Italian forces were still active in Gondar in the north until their final surrender on the 28th), continued to put stress on the strategic importance of Ethiopia in communications in Eastern Africa and the need for stable government there. The Foreign Office, on the other hand, was concerned that the officially stated objective of HMG ' to assist the Emperor to establish an independent Ethiopia' must avoid the country's status appearing 'as indistinguishable from that of a Protectorate' and that the War Office's misgivings could best be met by an independent Ethiopian administration aided by British advisers and a carefully controlled financial grant for the next few years. Chapman-Andrews urged early resumption of diplomatic representation and that HMG 'should not concern itself unduly with how this native state is governed'. The Committee presented the arguments and indicated various areas

132

where a Cabinet decision was required, particularly with regard to financial assistance and diplomatic representation, where they felt Parliament would require an early, and favourable, decision.

The War Cabinet broadly took the Foreign Office view, and was well aware of the need not to enflame US suspicions of Britain's supposed imperial ambitions and instructed Mitchell to complete a Treaty with the Emperor along these lines. Sandford returned to the Emperor well satisfied and he and Mitchell, with increasing mutual respect for each other, worked out the details in the succeeding weeks. Mitchell wrote later in his Memoirs, 'I had sometimes wondered if Brigadier Sandford, in his devotion to the Emperor's interests, was really going to break off relations with Great Britain.' Mitchell, who had a reputation for being a rather forward-thinking colonial servant and was certainly not unduly 'imperialistic' or racist, came to have a 'high respect for the Emperor and recognized his qualities of courage and determination and his considerable wisdom, even when I wished that he had been a little more forthcoming in negotiation'. One suspects that the Emperor was the more wily and successful negotiator.

Chapman-Andrews remained working at the Foreign Office and enjoying some leave with his family until January when he was ordered to travel out to Ethiopia to complete the signing of the Treaty and to support for a time the new British Minister, who was to be appointed. It was during this time that he was contacted briefly by Wingate with a request for help in getting his 'Plan' typed; this was his view of how guerrilla war should be used in a variety of war fronts. Wingate was understandably concerned at rehabilitating himself after his medical problems and had succeeded in bringing his Gideon Force experience to the attention of a number of influential figures including, supposedly, Churchill. Chapman-Andrews was asked at that time by Richard Law, the junior Foreign Officer Minister, 'Who is this Orde Wingate?' for, contrary to some accounts, Wingate was too busy on his own account to have played any part in the Ethiopian negotiations.

While it was agreed that the British should retain responsibility for external communications for a period (the railway to Djibouti, where the Vichy French were still in control) and areas of potential conflict such as the Ogaden, as well as Eritrea and British and Italian Somaliland which were not considered relevant to the restoration of full independence in Ethiopia, the Treaty covered the provision of British advisers, some troops required to train the new Ethiopian army and finance of £2.5million over a three-year period, the re-establishment of the British Legation with a British Minister and the departure of OETA. Any idea of a High Commissioner had been firmly shelved.

In view of the increasingly serious situation in the Mediterranean, Chapman-Andrews was flown out with the Agreement to Ethiopia by flying boat via West Africa. He recalled having a false start at Sandbanks on 23 January 1942 (where they had had to wait, with drawn blinds, for the return of Churchill by air from meeting Roosevelt in the West Indies), going on to Portugal via Shannon, then Gambia, Lagos,(where he had to remain in a 'cage' as his Yellow Fever vaccination was queried) Kano, Maiduguri, Khartoum, finally arriving at Addis Ababa to enable the formal signing of the Anglo-Ethiopian Agreement by the Emperor and Mitchell to take place on 31 January. It is no wonder that the photograph of the signing shows him looking rather tired as he leans over the table to show the Emperor where to sign. Mitchell records the signing with much mutual goodwill and the stand-up supper given by the Emperor for 100 mixed Ethiopian and British staff: 'Very cordial indeed; I found the Emperor, Empress and the Princes and Rases all beaming smiles.' The Emperor asked him to help over getting Prince Makonnen into Oxford. This was followed rather improbably, since there were few women present, except the Emperor's young daughter, by a dance at which Mitchell gamely led off with Princess Tsahai.

Mitchell left afterwards and was later to take up a similar role in the South Pacific, which had become a war zone following the opening of the war with Japan. In his biography he regretted that the Emperor and the Ethiopians had taken the British effort both in the fighting and in the reconstruction for granted and had given little thanks, which was typically Ethiopian, but admitted that he might have played his cards better with the Emperor.

Two days later Chapman-Andrews continued on to Cairo to report and pack up and return to Addis Ababa in time for the arrival on 12 February of Robert Howe, the new Minister, with whom he was to work for a time to assist in getting the Legation set up. Lush was leaving. The Emperor had told him that he did not wish any of General Cunningham's officers to remain. Lush wrote in his Memoirs that he considered that this was part of 'a Foreign Office design backed by Sandford and Chapman-Andrews' who he thought, wrongly, was being formally appointed to the restored Legation. A few days later Lush lunched at the Legation with Howe and Chapman-Andrews, until a few days before being used by Lush as OETA's mess and, according to rumour, now empty of the large wine supplies left over from the days of 1936.

Lush describes the occasion: 'I handed over a few files which I thought he should have – including my full report. Mr Howe never asked a single question about the country, the situation or the Emperor . . . I took my leave of the Emperor. I received a polite message of farewell, not a word of thanks, nor an expression of goodwill. To the Emperor I was personally non grata for 30 years. I was not included in the party of British officers invited 25 years later for a week's festivities to celebrate the return of the "little man" to his throne in 1941.' Understandably, he felt that he had only been doing his duty and actually doing a very difficult job in trying to reconcile conflicting British and Ethiopian interests and priorities with energy, devotion and, in fact, great success. However, the story had a happy ending: in the late 1960s a message was received by Lush, probably via Sandford, that the Emperor would be happy to receive him again in Addis Ababa and the hatchet was buried.

The Agreement represented a triumph for Chapman-Andrews' strongly argued view and the Emperor never forgot the part he had played and awarded him the Order of the Star of Ethiopia – fifth class!

His concern about OETA, which was sometimes, as he tells us, rather forcefully expressed, was shared by an anonymous bit of doggerel which he retained in his papers:

As pales the blush on maiden's cheek, OETA fades away,
New lands to conquer, fame to seek, in cities far away.
They traversed miles of desert sands to reach fair Ethiopia,
Though powers untold were in their hands, they all had bad
    myopia.
We'll show the habash [Ethiopians] how its done, we've
    done it oft before;
Its all just simple, good, clean fun as in the days of yore;

You open miles and miles of files and 'minute' every
    second.
"To you" from me? Oh gosh! Oh gee! This really is great
    fun.

"LA to speak", "CA to see" no matter when its done.
Just fill the file with merry smile with comments meant to
    flatter
All those who may be worth your while, the subject doesn't
    matter.
You ask about the captive race we fought so hard to free?
I know they only own the place, but first of all comes Me.
When war is over, fighting done, you rest at home at leisure
Relating proudly one by one the triumphs of your tenure,
Of ordered peace all due to you; it really is quixotic.
You know it really wasn't true, but chaos thrice chaotic.'

The Emperor in Control

For the Emperor the Treaty was a turning point and he was now
able slowly to regain control over his Empire and its adminstration. During 1942 OETA handed over the adminstration, except
the 'Reserved Areas' of Tigre and Ogaden and the Railway, while
retaining in various forms control for the next eight years over
Eritrea and Somalia. The Emperor steadily regained control
over the Rases and the Feudal Aristocracy and over the Patriots,
who had to be rewarded with appropriate posts. Outside the cities
law and order remained precarious and in some areas local
rebellions and *shifta* made control and communications difficult.
There were many conspiracies and a number of more significant
uprisings and one in Tigre had to be suppressed with the help of
RAF bombers from Aden. Ras Hailu remained in effective house
arrest, to be joined later by Ras Seyum and others who had played
a part in Gideon Force and Mission 101. Some, such as Belai
Zelleika and Lij Mammo, plotted and were executed, but the
Emperor's tried and tested method of ever-changing patronage, by
which Governors and senior posts were frequently switched,
together with the strong commitment of the Church, ensured that
he was always in command and one step ahead. While the years of
exile and adversity had quenched some of his desire for reform and

'progress', he ensured that a new class of civil servants grew up outside the feudal class devoted only to him and the country experienced increasing order and prosperity over the succeeding years.

Relations with Britain improved following agreements in 1944 and again in 1954, but the experiences of 1936-1942 had left their mark and the Emperor, however much he was grateful and loyal to many British individuals, was more than ever determined never again to be dependent on Britain or on any other power. He became experienced in playing off Britain, Egypt, Sudan, the United States, Russia, the United Nations and the 'Non Aligned Powers'. In the 1940s his priority was the union of the British-administered Eritrea with Ethiopia and he devoted considerable efforts both on the ground and internationally to achieving this and frustrating UN ideas of merging Muslim parts of Eritrea with the Sudan. He was equally resistant to pressures for Britain, Egypt and the Sudan to come to an agreement on Lake Tana and the Blue Nile dam, still on the drawing board since the begining of the century and still a pawn in the endless Anglo-Egyptian negotiations. Ethiopia was developing its own ideas – never carried out – of creating a new capital and industrial base on Lake Tana and its own hydroelectric dam.

In 1952 the United Nations mandates were terminated. In Eritrea the British administration left and Eritrea was federated with Ethiopia under the Emperor, a Union which did not long outlast him. The presence of a strong US communications base near Asmara helped to ensure the increasing enmity of Egypt and the Arab world. Against strong Ethiopian objections and increasing Ethiopian claims, Italy was given a ten-year mandate over its old colony, Italian Somaliland, which was terminated in 1960 when Italian and British Somaliland, to the Emperor's dismay, merged in the independent and Muslim Somalia, later to be a threat to Ethiopia in the Ogaden and an African friend for the Russians in the Cold war.

Although Chapman-Andrews never served again in Ethiopia, he kept closely in touch with the country from his posts in London, Egypt and the Sudan and visited it again many times. Relations between him and the Emperor remained warm, based on mutual respect, the Emperor's great sense of loyalty and, on Chapman-Andrews' side, a degree of objective hero worship.

137

Chapter Nine

Egypt and The Sudan

For the next 12 years Chapman-Andrews' career was mainly in Egypt and Lebanon and it wasn't until he went to the Sudan as Ambassador in 1956 that more frequent contact with Ethiopia took place. Christmas cards and other messages were regularly exchanged with the Emperor and Ethiopian friends, but, apart from a brief visit in 1948 as an Inspector, he did not visit Ethiopia again during this period.

His posting in 1942 was to the Egyptian desk at the Foreign Office, where he received a flood of usually indiscreet letters from his old chief at Cairo, Sir Miles Lampson, now Lord Killearn. It was an anxious time in Cairo, with Rommel's army poised near Alexandria and the need to keep the political situation in Cairo under control. Many Egyptians, including King Farouk, were by no means certain that the Allies would win. In January 1942 Lampson faced down the King at the 'Siege of the Abdin Palace' with an ultimatum, supported by British troops and tanks, to accept British wishes that he appoint the Wafdist leader, Nahas Pasha, as Prime Minister or abdicate. The King gave in, but the humiliation had a profound effect both on him, the country and on future relations with Britain. Lampson wrote to Chapman-Andrews that, if he hadn't been called off by HMG, he would have completed the job by getting rid of Farouk. He had had reluctant support from the Allied GOC Egypt, General Stone, whom he mistrusted as being 'so terribly thick and "matey" with so many locals (including Copts)'. To Eden he wrote, 'I was personally never so sorry as when at the very last second the Monarch yielded'.

138

With Rommel's offensive in June and his capture of the besieged Allied forces in Tripoli, there were many in Cairo who feared that Egypt would fall; Chapman-Andrews was sent out to reinforce the Embassy late in June during what was called 'The Flap', a rather inglorious time when the Cairo skies were reported to be obscured by burning files. Foreign diplomats, Allied civilians and 'essential', and not so essential, officials competed for space on the trains leaving for Palestine. The 'Monarch', as Lampson called King Farouk, made it clear that, as an Egyptian, he had no intention of leaving *his* country. Sir Walter Smart, the Oriental Secretary, wrote later that he would 'always remember with gratitude when you came to my help during Alamein days and ably handled for me the stream of applicants seeking to fly from Egypt before the Germans got in, particularly the unfortunate Jews'.

However, by July the situation had stabilized and confidence, and those who had fled, returned; the Flap was over and he was able to return to London. As with all flights to and from Egypt at that time, his was quite eventful and between Gibraltar and England they lost their bearings and ran into some Messerschmitts over Ushant, fortunately without sustaining any damage.

In 1943 he was transferred, as one of only three staff, to the newly formed personnel department under Sir Ivo Mallet, whom he succeeded as Head six months later. After years of discussion, it had finally been decided to accept the recommendations of a report written by Mallet and Sir David Scott to merge all the British Diplomatic, Consular and Levant services into a single Diplomatic Service – not an easy task in three famously conservative and long established services – and, with the War going rather more the Allies' way, Parliamentary time was found to pass the Foreign Services Act.

As always, the role of Head of Personnel was never popular and his old chief, Lord Killearn, as Lampson had become in 1943, writing in 1946 in his usual forthright style from his new post as Special Commissioner in South-East Asia was strongly critical about the transfer of many of his staff: 'In Cairo we were a milch cow that has been milked until the udders squeaked'. Chapman-Andrews found no difficulty in rebutting his comments: 'You are the Caesar and I am the dust under the chariot wheel. I learned much from you but could never hope to emulate you. All I can do is to be disarmingly frank and that will be in saying that your letter

139

is the most masterly back-hander that I have ever had the advantage of studying.' He now had the confidence that he was moving fast up the career ladder and could afford to be firm and dismissive with his seniors!

His role at that time created many friendships, particularly among the Foreign Office's many new recruits returning from the War. Bevin, who had become Foreign Secretary when the Labour Government had taken power in 1945, summoned Chapman-Andrews to ask why he seemed to be selecting so many 'Public School Boys' for the post-war Foreign Office. Chapman-Andrews, whose West Country background was not disimilar to that of Bevin, pointed out that his rule was a simple one: 'We take only the best, whatever their background'. The matter was not raised again and Bevin remained a good supporter. The Egyptian press later referred to him often as 'Bevin's Boy'. On Chapman-Andrews' retirement in 1961, Lord Home, then Foreign Secretary, wrote that 'it was largely due to your efforts that it was possible to re-staff so many posts at short notice in the difficult and trying days at the end of the war.' In 1948 he was made a CMG in recognition of his services.

Among those who were not recruited was Evelyn Waugh who noted in his diary in March 1945: 'I have had interviews at the Foreign Office with Chapman-Andrews, an old friend from Abyssinia, who is now in charge of personnel; he is very hopeful of my getting an appointment if I wished it'. The imagination boggles; Chapman-Andrews was, no doubt, being diplomatic.

In November 1945 he received a personal letter from the Emperor: 'We had no news of you for a long time and we were glad to receive your letter, the contents of which we note with interest. Your letters from time to time would indeed be welcome.'

Late in 1946 he was made an Inspector, an important career move which involved him visiting and reporting on the performance of British Embassies abroad. This included Addis Ababa, where he was again received by the Emperor and was appointed a Grade 3 officer of the Star of Ethiopia – an upgrade of the 1930 Coronation award ' in recognition of his services during the Liberation'.

Cairo Again

Later in 1947 he was appointed Minister at his old Embassy in Cairo, the number 2 post in what was still, and remained until the Suez Crisis in 1956, a strategically highly important Grade 1 British Embassy, and for the next three years he devoted all his energies to trying to achieve a lasting Treaty agreement with Egypt.

The independence of India and Pakistan in 1947 had paradoxically – since the 'Route to India' had originally been the main *raison d'etre* of the need to control Egypt, the Suez Canal and the Red Sea – made the British government even more determined not to surrender their dominant position in the Near and Middle East either to Russia or the United States or to any local states. It is difficult, sixty years later, to understand how British policy with regard to Egypt became for successive British Governments and Army leaders the touchstone of Britain's survival as an imperial and military power. With India 'gone', the Middle East, with its growing importance in oil, was the only area where the two world wars had given Britain and the British Empire increased status and power; the need to preserve this became something of a 'last ditch stand'. As a result, both the Labour and the Conservative governments and Cabinet meetings from 1945 to 1956 devoted a disproportionate amount of time to the Middle East generally and to Egypt, and hence the Sudan, in particular. Britain maintained a Middle East Office in Cairo, although from 1945 no longer headed headed by a British Government Minister; the Commander-in-Chief Middle East was still based in Cairo. The Suez Canal base had become in the 1940s the largest overseas base in the world estimated to have cost over £200 million. For Britain some form of control over Egypt and the Suez Canal was the keystone of this policy, in which the Sudan and the control of the Nile Waters, including the Blue Nile in Ethiopia, were important components. In addition, Egypt, with its sterling balances from war payments, had become, after the USA, one of Britain's largest creditors.

Unlike the Commonwealth and Colonies, where Britain had a clearly defined and long-established constitutional role, her relations with Egypt, and even more with the Sudan, could be described, in more senses than one, as being built on sand. Egypt had since 1922 been recognized as an independant country and had become a member first of the League of Nations and then

141

of the United Nations. In theory Britain's relations were based on the 1936 Anglo-Egyptian Agreement which allowed her to retain 10,000 troops in the Canal Zone, in which she had the major shareholder interest through the Suez Canal Company. In practice, Britain had used the exigencies of the Second World War to re-occupy Egypt in the interests of her 'Imperial' Middle East role and to try and manipulate her Governments accordingly. For most of the 1940s Britain continued to keep some 80,000 troops in Cairo and the Canal Zone, as well as their enormous base, both of which were outside the 1936 Treaty. While the Foreign Office was happy to point out the mutual defence interests of the two countries in relation to the growing Russian threat to the Middle East and, more relevant to the landowning Egyptian political classes, of the communist threat to their existence and power, it was clear that after 1945 no Egyptian Governments would survive unless they demanded the evacuation of the British forces and a fundamentally different Treaty with Britain

With regard to the Sudan, the constitutional position was even less clear. The 'conquest' of the Sudan by Kitchener in 1898 had been carried out in the name of, and largely at the expense of, the Egyptian Khedive. Cromer had concluded the one-sided Con-dominium Agreement of 1899, by which, in effect, Britain would provide the leading adminstrators for the Sudan on Egypt's behalf through a British Governor-General who was appointed by both powers. After 1924 and the forced evacuation of Egyptian forces and civil servants from the Sudan, this fiction had largely broken down and the Government, Administration and Security of the Sudan were entirely in British hands. Although the two flags were flown side by side, the Governor-General reported to the British Government, technically through the British High Commissioner to Egypt in Cairo, but in practice direct to the Foreign Office in London.

To this already highly controversial situation must be added the problem of the Nile Waters, the key to Egypt's economy. While before the First World War Britain had had effective control of the Nile waters, with the exception of the Blue Nile in Ethiopia, and had been happy to manage these in the interests of Egypt, pressure from the growing population in Egypt and the political need for the Sudan to become financially independent from Egypt through its own irrigation schemes resulted in an increasing divergence of

142

interests. While the 1929 Nile Agreement between Britain and Egypt provided some breathing space, by 1945 Egypt's ever-increasing water requirement allowed Britain to use its interests in Uganda and the Gezira (whose cotton-growing was key to the viability of the country) and other schemes to put additional political pressure on Egypt. To reinforce this, it became important for Britain to bring to a conclusion her endlessly abortive negotiations with Ethiopia for an Anglo-Ethiopian Agreement to give Britain control over Lake Tana and the Blue Nile waters, but Haile Selassie still would not play.

The Labour Government of 1945 were anxious to conclude a fresh agreement with Egypt on all these issues and were prepared to make some concessions towards Egypt's concerns. In this Britain was also conscious of a changed world attitude towards, as well as US suspicions of, Britain's 'Imperial role', although rising US worries about Russia's ambitions in the Middle East meant that defence arguments still carried weight. However, it was not until the military regime took over from King Farouk in 1952 that any agreement was possible, and then largely on Egypt's terms.

The main problem until then lay in the highly volatile Egyptian political situation, where rival forces made any agreement impossible, except on terms of total British evacuation and return of the Sudan to Egypt. The irresponsible King Farouk, now in his thirties, had lost most of his original popularity, but remained constitutionally powerful. The politicians were drawn from the land-owning classes, often of Turkish, Albanian or Coptic origin. There were various parties, of which the main one was the Wafd, who were 'anti-Palace' and strongly nationalist, led by Nahas Pasha with whom Killearn had found he could do business, in preference to the others usually more sympathetic to the King. Eden described them as 'a party of rich men, many of whom had grown fat at the expense of the state'; Wavell had never trusted Nahas Pasha and the Wafd, but accepted Killearn's conclusion that it was better to work with them than against them. During the War the Wafd had concluded that even the British were a lesser evil for Egypt, and the political classes, than the Germans and Italians and had been generally supportive of the Allies. However, there were two other groups who were emerging after the War and were to be of increasing importance: the Muslim Brotherhood and the educated native Egyptians, particularly in the Army and professions. And underneath were the fellahin in the rural areas and the restive masses in the towns, both increasingly volatile.

In the Sudan the Sudanese had been pushing for a greater say in their affairs and the Sudan authorities had realized by 1943 that some form of constitutional evolution was required. However, any form of assembly or legislature would still require the agreement of the other 'co-dominus', Egypt, and successive Egyptian governments were insistent that any agreement to this with Britain must cover both the evacuation of British troops and recognition of Egypt's sovereignty over the Sudan. In March 1947, after lengthy negotiations, the Labour Government, who were increasingly preoccupied with how to solve the problem of Palestine, hastily agreed with the then Egyptian Prime Minister the Bevin/Sidky agreement by which Britain agreed to complete evacuation of Egypt within three years with the position over the Sudan being left, in the British eyes 'as it was' – deliberately imprecise wording which allowed two interpretations: the Egyptians inferred that this confirmed that the King of Egypt was also King of the Sudan and trumpeted it as a victory. An uproar arose in the Sudan where many Sudanese, as well as the Sudan Political Service, raised strong vocal objections and the British Government insisted that they had never agreed to any such thing. As a result neither side ratified the Treaty and the British troops remained in Egypt. The Egyptians then took the dispute over the Sudan to the United Nations – to little avail, since the UN considered that the Sudanese themselves must in due course be allowed their say. It was against this background of stalemate that Chapman-Andrews arrived in Cairo in November 1947.

He was expected, as the new British Minister with his wide range of previous contacts both in Egypt and the Sudan, to play an important part in breaking through the diplomatic impasse. Over the next four years this took up most of his time, but, as has been seen, it was not to be: the policies of the two countries were for the time being irreconcilable. He threw himself straight into the evolving diplomatic and political life and thrived on it. As second-in-command to the elderly Ambassador, Sir Ronald Campbell, he played a prominent role as Britain's spokesman in Egypt. Many caricatures of him appeared in the volatile Egyptian Press: 'Reassuring News. Mr Chapman-Andrews to Nahas Pasha [the Prime Minister] "No evacuation. No unity of Egypt and the Sudan.

No Sterling Agreement . . . but I have pleasant news: Mr Bevin says that *you* are Egypt's leader – and not the King."' He was on first-name terms with many of the leading Egyptians and, in particular, with the influential Egyptian Ambassador in London, Abdel Fattah Amr Pasha, who was responsible for the negotiations with the British Government. Whatever the political differences, personal relations between the British and the governing classes remained good and social life involved continuous contacts between the two at receptions, the Gezira Club, the races and, at weekends, in country houses, houseboats or at the sea in Alexandria. Once Lord Killearn had been succeeded in 1946 by Sir Ronald Campbell official visitors were again received politely at the Palace.

Meanwhile negotiations to break the impasse over the Sudan continued. In March 1948 Sir Robert Howe and Chapman-Andrews were recalled to London for consultations with Bevin, following which a further attempt was made to agree the proposals for the Sudanese Assembly. Howe, a career diplomat, had been posted from Addis Ababa to succeed Sir Hubert Huddleston as Governor-General of the Sudan the year before. Any hope on the part of the Foreign Office that he would be more conciliatory towards the Egyptians was quickly disabused and Howe proved to be as strong a defender of Sudanese interests, as seen by the Sudan Political Service, as his predecessor. Before long Chapman-Andrews found himself complaining that his old colleague seemed unable to appreciate the need for some compromise form of words to meet Egyptian objections in the broader interest of an Anglo-Egyptian Agreement. Although an agreement was reached with the Egyptian Minister for Foreign Affairs, Kashaba, in May, the latter was unable to get his Government to accept it and the British Government then authorized Howe to go ahead with his constitutional plans involving limited self-government notwithstanding.

The next few months were dominated by the end of the British Mandate in Palestine, the emergence of the State of Israel and the Arab invasion. After initial successes, the Egyptian army had to withdraw and, following the assassination of the Prime Minister Nokrashy Pasha by the Muslim Brotherhood, a ceasefire was concluded in January 1949, leaving widespread unrest in Egypt, not least among the Army officers. Whilst Britain had been neutral, if instinctively during this period pro-Arab, the arrival of the state of Israel, with Russian and US support, involved further de-stabilization in the Middle East and confirmed the British Government and Army in the need to remain in a strong position on the Canal and not to compromise further with the Egyptian Government. Chapman-Andrews was personally sympathetic to the problem of the Palestinian refugees and his wife worked hard in Cairo in fundraising for their relief. He was accused later of giving 'an Unholy Guarantee to the Palace that the British Army in the Canal Zone would supply the Egyptian army with arms', which was certainly untrue: the Egyptians, seeking any excuse for the inadequacy of their army, accused the British of having denied them promised arms supplies. Chapman-Andrews thought that the revelation of the evident weakness of the Egyptian army offered a further opportunity to press for a new Treaty with Britain, and the King and some senior politicians appeared to share this view. In March 1949 he visited Khartoum to explore again with the leading British and Sudanese the possibility of some form of joint Anglo-Egyptian committee which could open the route for Sudanese self-government, but feelings in both places were too high to allow this to be pursued. Following elections in 1949, the King appointed another Wafd government under Nahas Pasha. It was widely thought in Egypt that this had been supported by the British and by Chapman-Andrews in particular, but, although initially relations improved, the Wafd Government proved no more decisive and certainly no more pro-British than its predecessors. Chapman-Andrews foresaw that unless strong domestic measures were taken to face the problems of a growing population and a distorted economy, some form of revolution was inevitable and the King and the 'Old Guard' would be swept away.

There were many important visitors to Cairo in 1950: Bevin, as Foreign Minister, and other Ministers, Montgomery, Slim, the Duke of Edinburgh, on an 'educational' tour with Bevin, all of whom had the entrée to King and Government, but the stalemate continued. Little emerged from the Bevin visit, although British troops were withdrawn from Cairo to the Canal Zone, but Nahas's government were too preoccupied with internal problems and unrest and the aftermath of the Palestine War to tackle contro-versial international agreements.

The Maclean Affair

Apart from this, Chapman-Andrews had the problem of an unhappy Embassy. The Ambassador, Sir Ronald Campbell, who he respected, was a bachelor, which put much of the responsibility for entertaining on Chapman-Andrews and his wife. The Head of Chancery was Donald Maclean, whose drinking and erratic behaviour, which has often been described, made him a serious responsibility. The two families lived in neighbouring houses, although their contacts were strictly formal. In 1969 Chapman-Andrews took up with the Foreign Office some references to himself, suggesting that he had been sympathetic to Maclean and Philby, in a book *The Third Man, the Story of Kim Philby.* He wrote:

'My alleged sympathy with Maclean must have come from Toynbee whom I did not trust and who seemed to me at the time to be exercising a harmful influence over Maclean. [Philip Toynbee had recently come to Cairo as correspondent for the *Observer*] He was in fact staying with the Macleans during that last night in Cairo when Maclean beat up the American Secretary's flat. In fact having spent the latter part of that morning [10 May1950] with the Ambassador discussing Maclean's strange behaviour and the entire afternoon with Maclean himself, having first told Toynbee to clear off and leave me alone with him, I went to the airport with him to make quite sure that Maclean got on the plane. (As for Philby, so far as I know, I never set eyes on him . . . although I did come across his father.)

'I certainly did not suspect that Donald Maclean, a brother officer, was a Communist, a traitor and a spy: but I was quite certain that his "breakdown" in Cairo was not due to overwork or anything of that sort and I wrote a personal and private letter to the Foreign Office at that time stating that opinion. We used not in those days to pry into the private lives of people in the service. I knew that Maclean was weak when it came to drink and thought that was an end of it. I was wrong but I was not sympathetic. On the contrary, as soon as I had a good opportunity, I wanted to get him out of Cairo and I advised the Ambassador very strongly in this sense in the meeting I had with him on the morning of 10 May 1950.'

Chapman-Andrews had several times expressed to the

Ambassador his concerns about Maclean's behaviour, but had met with a brick wall. The Ambassador had throughout been supportive of Maclean, whom he had know earlier in his career, and sent him home with a good report for reasons which remain incomprehensible. However, it was popularly supposed that Campbell was homosexual and that this might have laid him open to a degree of blackmail and made him more sympathetic to Maclean, who certainly had homosexual tendencies himself.

Campbell was replaced shortly afterwards by a married career diplomat, Sir Ralph Stevenson, who was new to the Middle East and did not always share Chapman-Andrews' views. When the latter was appointed as Minister to Lebanon in May 1951 Stevenson wrote warmly to the Foreign Office, 'His wide circle of friends and acquaintances among Egyptians made his advice of the greatest value to me and he has played an important role in the maintenance of tolerable relations in despite the many political differences between ourselves and the Egyptians.' This was generous, although the Egyptian press believed that Chapman-Andrews' departure reflected some differences of opinion between the two men. The fact that he was a fluent Arabic scholar certainly helped in his relations with politicians and the Press, with whom he had a high profile. Whilst articles about him were often critical – and frequently inventive – there was a clear thread of respect and even affection: when he left in 1951 Akhbar El Yom noted 'his resemblance between "Mr Andrews" and the British fruit salt of this name; always effervescent, active and soothes the nerves'. Another caricature said, 'Our Pasha [Nahas] will turn the British out one by one; this week he started with Mr Chapman-Andrews'.

Whilst it was coincidental that relations deteriorated after 1951, this was due mainly to the increasing internal unrest in Egypt, although the Press and a number of influential Egyptians drew attention to the loss in the British Embassy of all staff with any Egyptian experience. In October 1951 Nahas, in a last throw, declared the Unity of Egypt with Sudan and the abrogation of the 1936 Anglo-Egyptian Treaty and the withdrawal of Egyptian civilian workers from the Canal base, which finally convinced the British Defence Chiefs that the base was unusuable without an agreement with Egypt. The next few months saw a number of violent incidents, some indirectly encouraged by members of Government, concluding on 'Black Saturday' in January 1952 with the extensive attacks on British, and other, property in Cairo to which the new British Government under Churchill took strong exception. In July the King was replaced, following the Army *coup d'état* by a Republican Government under General Neguib, with Nasser as it main leader. Initially this was able to break the stalemate and led to the Anglo-Egyptian Agreement of 1953, under which the Sudan was allowed to decide its own future and Britain would withdraw its troops from the Canal Zone while retaining a civilian-staffed base. However, by that time trust between the two countries had largely broken down and Nasser's increasing relations with the Soviet Bloc, the breakdown of the High Dam negotiations with the USA and the World Bank and the concerns of Sir Anthony Eden and his government, with the loss of the dominant British role in the Middle East and 1930s precedents, made the Greek tragedy of the Suez affair inevitable.

Lebanon

All of this Chapman-Andrews saw from his new post as British Minister in Lebanon, to which he had been appointed in May 1951, and didn't hesitate to comment on to London. In 1953 he wrote to Sir Anthony Eden, still Foreign Secretary, arguing that there was little point in pursuing the idea of a treaty of mutual defence which would allow the return of the British forces in time of war, that they should leave Egypt and seek an alternative base in Cyprus or elsewhere and that early agreement should be reached with General Neguib before he was undermined by the Muslim Brotherhood or the Communists or other disruptive forces. He also added a word of warning about the need for Israel to come to some form of cohabitation with its Arab neighbours and to the difficulty of working with the Americans, whose 'overriding fear of communism obscures the realities of the situation and their desire to be loved comes to look very like appeasement', all very relevant to the forthcoming Suez crisis.

Lebanon in the early 1950s was going through a period of comparative political calm and attracted a stream of British visitors, many of them en route by air to the east via this new Middle East staging post. These included the Queen Mother and Princess Margaret, straight from the Coronation of Queen Elizabeth II, the Mountbattens, Anthony Eden, as Foreign Secretary, and his wife, as well as Aldous Huxley and Freya Stark. Many of these expected to be put up at the attractive Residence. In addition there was a summer house at Brumana and opportunities for exploration of archaeological sites and the marvellous countryside. With a young family, it was a very happy time and, although politically less demanding than Cairo, Chapman-Andrews had the excitement of this being his first command of his own; many Middle Eastern leaders could be expected to pass through Beirut and be greeted by the British Ambassador. In 1952 the Legation was upgraded to Embassy status and in 1953 he was made a Knight Commander of St Michael and St George. Among those who congratulated him was the Crown Prince Asfa Wossen, who was otherwise seldom in agreement with his father, who sent a message on behalf of the Emperor saying that 'Your name will always be associated with the triumph of those days [1941]'. During the Emperor's state visit to Britain in 1955 Chapman-Andrews sent him a message with a Biblical quotation: 'The Lion of Judah fought the fight and has prevailed', which he knew would appeal to him. A prompt reply came: 'His Imperial Majesty has immediately commanded me to let you know how much your greetings meant to him . . . and provided a warm recollection of the sympathetic comprehension which graced your so-well-remembered days in Ethiopia. Your name will always be associated with the triumph of those days. He trusts that that the turn of the days may one day bring you back to Addis Ababa.'

Return to The Sudan

In 1955, with the imminent independence of the Sudan, after 47 years of so-called Anglo-Egyptian Condominium, but effectively British rule, his was an obvious name for the proconsular role of first British Ambassador. So, shortly after Independence Day on 1 January 1956, he took up his post in Khartoum where he was to stay for five years until he retired in 1961. As one from a poor background whom a Kitchener scholarship had enabled to go to University and as a romantic with a great sense of history, he considered his posting to Khartoum as 'a great reward'.

He found a very different Sudan from his last visit in 1949. The coming to power in Egypt of the half-Sudanese Neguib in 1952 and the disappearance of a King determined to be recognized as 'King of the Sudan' removed the main obstacles to an agreement on a new Sudanese constititution based on the right of self-determination. A Sudanization Committee was to supervise the replacement of the old British Sudan Political Service and by 1954 most of the latter had left. The Governor-General, still Sir Robert Howe, continued to exercise extensive powers, but with an elected Prime Minister and Government. The Egyptian aim was to achieve a union of the two countries through a mixture of wooing and bribery; the British hoped that the anti-Egyptian Umma party of Sayed Sir Abdel Rahman El Mahdi would win the elections and work closely with Britain. In the December 1953 elections the winners were the Pro-Egyptian NUP party under Ibrahim El Azhari who formed a government in coalition with the party of the Khatmia, followers of Sayed Sir Ali El Mirghani, Sir Abdel Rahman's great rival ever since the Khatmia and the Mirghanis had been persecuted by what they had regarded as the upstart Mahdists and forced into exile in Egypt in the 1880s. When Neguib came to Khartoum for the opening of the new Parliament with the hope of an early union of the two countries, the Umma rioted with the loss of life of a British Police Commisssioner and twenty police. However, the popular Neguib himself was replaced shortly afterwards by Gamal Abdel Nasser, whose priorities lay more with Egyptian domestic problems and with the rest of the Arab Middle East. Unrest in the Southern Sudan, believed to have been provoked partly by Egyptian meddling, and disagreements over the Nile Waters and the effect of Nasser's Aswan High Dam on Sudanese water needs resulted in a cooling of relations and late in 1955, with the tacit support of Britain, El Azhari's Government declared the Sudan independent with effect from 1 January 1956 and the Governor-General and fifty-six years of what in effect had been British rule ended.

Chapman-Andrews quickly took up the reins and over the next five years ensured that successive Sudanese governments followed generally pro-British policies. While this meant continuing to favour the Umma and the military, good relations were also maintained with the rival Khatmia and with the more independent urban liberals. Within a few months of Chapman-Andrews' arrival El Azhari was ousted by a coalition of the two traditional enemies, Sayed Ali and Sayed Abdel Rahman, both religious conservatives and increasingly concerned about Egyptian influence, the appearance in the Sudan of the Egyptian Muslim Brotherhood and the rise of left wing and communist influences. Their new coalition was headed by an ex-officer, Abdulla Bey Khalil, who had served with the British in 1916 at the Dardanelles. This stood him in good stead during the Suez crisis that November when diplomatic relations with Britain and law and order were maintained in spite of general sympathy with Egypt, supported by peaceful protests in Khartoum. An attempt to sever diplomatic relations was defeated in Parliament. The Government continued to look to Britain, as well as to their conservative neighbours in Ethiopia and Saudi Arabia, to support them against Egypt, but their main attention was on internal politics and the economy, rather than international affairs.

The interaction of the two Sayeds and of Britain and Egypt continued to dominate Sudanese politics for the first years of independance. Chapman-Andrews had called on both men during his visit in 1949 during his attempts to find a way to an Anglo-Egyptian Agreement and had probably met them during his time in Khartoum in 1940. He reported to the Foreign Office: 'The Mahdi impresses as being undoubtedly the better man of the two. He may have ambitions but I think very few fears. He is probably a bully. The other may have no ambitions but is full of fears. Sayed Ali, I think, nurses feelings of frustration, disappointment, envy, hatred and malice and an ambition to see the Mahdi's power again destroyed. Sayed Abdel Rahman, on the other hand, is a full man and I think could be persuaded to compromise on pratical issues if given assurances.' Sayed Ali had been appointed KCVO in 1919, but this was followed by Sayed Abdel Rahman's KBE in 1926. With his close relations with Egypt and many Khatmia followers in Upper Egypt, Sayed Ali exercised his considerable indirect influence with his generally urban and educated Sudanese followers in Egypt's favour. Sayed Abdel Rahman's deep suspicions of Egypt and his considerable powers of leadership over his 'Ansar', the largely rural descendants of his father's warriors, naturally endeared him the British Administration, and to the Foreign Office. To the romantics, and there were many in the Sudan Political Service, there was something historically poignant in the reconciliation with Britain of the son of the man who had killed Gordon and had indirectly had such an influence on Britain in the 1880s and 1890s. While Chapman-Andrews was punctilious in maintaining good relations with Sayed Ali and in helping to bring him closer to Sayed Abdel Rahman, there is no doubt that it was the latter whom he admired, rather as he did the Emperor, quite apart from official British Policy. This policy had its costs: Sayed Abdel Rahman was always in need of money. The White Nile estates which the British Administration had granted him after the First World War provided the base for an expanding agricultural cotton business which, particularly after 1950, was hungry for capital and made him even more anxious to ensure that Sudan obtained its share of Nile waters in negotiation with Egypt. The British banks in the Sudan, and particularly Barclays, were encouraged to assist through the Foreign Office and the Bank of England, on occasions with Treasury guarantees. At the same time the expenses of running the Umma party and of the Ansar continued to increase. With elections looming in 1958, Sayed Abdel Rahman turned to the Emperor, with whom he had maintained good relations since the latter's exile in Khartoum in 1940, and to Saudi Arabia for support. Whatever the source, £1,750,000 was received, almost certainly not from the British Government; Sayed Abdel Rahman told Chapman-Andrews that the election had cost him over £500,000.

The lack of experience of Khalil's government had produced an economic crisis, mainly as a result of the failure to sell the Sudan Gezira cotton crop and he was forced to call an election early in 1958. This resulted in the Umma emerging as the leading party, largely thanks to President Nasser's extraordinary ineptitude in laying claim to Sudanese territory north of the 22nd parallel in the middle of the election. El Azhari's pro-Egyptian NUP party lost seats and the coalition under Khalil continued with equal ineffectiveness. However, relations soon deteriorated as Sayed Abdel Rahman was determined to become President and this was more than Sayed Ali was prepared to accept. As a result, the Khatmia started to manoeuvre with Egypt and the NUP to undermine the Coalition government, of which they remained members. To forestall this, General Ibrahim Abboud, the Head of the Army, seized power through a bloodless *coup d'état* and formed a military Government. Both Sayeds issued statements of support: it appeared likely that Khalil had at the least connived at the plot and that the two Sayeds with varying degree of reluctance acquiesced.

Abboud and most of the military leaders had served with the

Sudan Defence Force in the Eritrean campaign of 1941 and relations with Britain as a result remained good. Chapman-Andrews found Abboud easy to get on with: he was an admirable front man for the Sudan both internationally and nationally, but had little understanding of the problems of the economy and administration. However, thanks to a successful cotton harvest and the sale of the carryover cotton stock, his government was able to benefit from a rapid upturn in the economy. Abboud experienced some unrest in the Army which gave rise to two attempted coups by officers and it was not until 1960 that affairs settled down, although the Umma then became increasingly restive.

The Death of the Mahdi

Sayed Abdel Rahman died in March 1959. Chapman-Andrews reported to Selwyn Lloyd, Foreign Secretary, who wrote a personal reply acknowledging Chapman-Andrews' 'moving account' of the death and its implications:

> There is a strong sentiment, shared by Sudanese and foreigners here alike, that the death of Sayed Abdel Rahman El Mahdi (S.A.R) has closed not a chapter but a whole volume of Sudanese history. He himself lived it. Both he and his father had the stamp of men of destiny. A Dongolawi of humble origin, SAR's father, Mohamed Ahmed, received in the cramped and dark hole in the rock of Aba Island whither he repaired for prayer and thought, a revelation direct from Allah. He was El Mahdi "the Messiah". "There is no God but Allah. Mohamed is the Messenger of Allah and El Mahdi the successor of the Messenger". Banners bearing this device led his dervishes, ill-armed except by fanatical faith in him and in Allah, against the boots and puttees, the tarbouches and accoutrements, the rifles and close formations of the Khedival troops occupying the country. The army of Hicks Pasha was wiped out to a man, Slatin a prisoner, Emin missing in Equatoria and Stanley to his rescue, Gordon slain, the relieving force under Wolseley in hazardous retreat, the entire Sudan, one million square miles of it (except for a narrow strip at Suakin on the Red Sea Coast) bore witness that the

Mahdi was indeed the revelation of the unconquerable will of Allah. Far more than the founder of a heretical sect, he was the inspired creator of a patriotism of irresistable force, a fierce mysticism, a religion of strict discipline, constant prayer and prideful austerity.

His son, Abdel Rahman, was born in 1886, a few months after his father's death, which followed within a year of Gordon's. The boy spent the first twelve years of his life in the camps of the Khalifa Abdullahi, the strong administrator who spared no effort to keep his treasury full, but was ruthless, headstrong and, in times of crisis, irresolute. When the Khalifa's power was broken by Lord Kitchener at Omdurman in 1898, the young Mahdi was sent in care of a tutor to Aba island with a government grant of £5 a month for his keep. Mahdism was in eclipse and the boy's education was purely native in character. Abdel Rahman thus grew to manhood in the closest touch with the remnant of his father's followers, the tribesmen who are the backbone of the country. They acknowledged him as the true successor to his father, whom in feature he strongly ressembled and he, for his part, knew from his youth that he was their natural leader, that he had it in him to fill the role and that one day his star would rise.

His opportunity came in 1915 when, in response to the Turkish Caliph's call to a Holy War, the Khedival faction amongst the officers resigned from the Egyptian army and adopted an attitude of veiled hostility to Britain in both Egypt and the Sudan. To rally the country for the war effort and to raise reliable troops, Sir Reginald Wingate [the then Governor-General] turned to Abdel Rahman El Mahdi, then aged 29. The subsequent Allied victory was also the Sayed's victory and he was amply rewarded with grants of land, licences for irrigation water and with help both to cultivate his estates and market their produce. He attended the victory celebrations in London in 1919 (as did the 'senior Sayed' Sayed Ali El Mirghani who was rewarded with the KCVO) and it is said here that he took the opportunity during an audience with King George V to tell His Majesty that his intention was to lead the Sudan in the steps of his father towards independance. Be that as it may, as the Mahdi prospered, so he extended his political influence.

155

His estates at his death must be worth many millions, though they are overburdened with debts. This is partly due to rapid expansion, undertaken to give employment to his needy followers, to the fall in cotton prices and, regrettably, to unwise, not to say extravagant, spending. The late Mahdi himself lived austerely but he loved to surround himself with regal spenledour and he was generous to a fault. No foreigner who paid him court left without a gift and the demands made upon him by his numerous family and their progeny, by followers and dependants, were unrelenting. For the Mahdi was three things in one: the Imam or religious head of the Ansar; the patron of the Umma Party which is the political expression of Mahdism, and the head of the agricultural estates company called the Dairat El Mahdi. People associated with him in any of these capacities applied to the common till for sustenance. His political expenses alone, covering two election campaigns and the maintenance of the Umma Members of Parliament and their political supporters, must have run into little short of £1million during the last six years of his life. He himself told me that the two elections had brought him nearly to ruin but that the sacrifice was neccessary if the country was to be saved from subversion by Egypt. An autocrat by nature, he was never really convinced that the parliamentary system of democracy was fitted for this country and its tribal structure.

Throughout the greater part of his life he was in conflict with Sayed Ali El Mirghani (S.A.M.) the leader of the orthodox Khatmia sect. There was a mutual antagonism between them, born perhaps of the association of the Khatmia with Egypt, their expulsion from the Sudan by the first Mahdi and their return under S.A.M., then a young man of 18 years of age, at the end of 1898 after the battle of Omdurman: but the difference went deeper than that. The two men were in sharp contrast with each other. Where S.A.R. was generous, S.A.M. was mean; where S.A.R. was politically minded and determined to take the lead, S.A.M. publicly disclaimed interest in such worldly affairs and professed only his religion; where S.A.R. was bold, S.A.M. was cautious and where [the one] forthright, the other cunning. The Mahdi was a man of good physical staure, a full man, while S.A.M. is small and usually in indifferent health. Though the senior by perhaps six years, S.A.M. has outlived his old rival.

The differences between them did not persist until the end. In 1956 the breach was healed. Six months after the attainment of Sudanese independance the two Sayeds drew together. They seemed both at last to recognize that together they represented the strongest traditional and conservative elements in the country and that by remaining apart they would tend only to weaken one another and increase the rapidly growing strength of non-sectarianism. Azhari, the President of the Unionist party and the first Prime Minister, had won the Parliamentary General Elections in 1953 largely because of Khatmia support; but once established as the ruler of the country he had found it convenient to go back on his declared policy of union with Egypt and had come out as the champion of complete independance and what he called National Union. By doing so he not only betrayed the Khatmia who had supported him only in order to save the Sudan from independence under Mahdist control, but also stole S.A.R.'s thunder as the begetter of independence and the father of his country. From Azhari's fall in June 1956 until the General Elections in February 1958, the political parties of the two Sayeds, the Umma and the PDP in coalition, ruled the country, albeit lamely.

The truth was already apparent. The two parties, like the two sects from which they sprang, would not mix. S.A.R. had had misgivings from the first but had allowed himself to be overruled by those who persuaded him that it was the surest means to attain the Presidency of the Republic for himself. This he had set his heart on and S.A.M. (so S.A.R. was given to understand) had agreed to it to seal the bond between them. The inconclusive result of the 1958 elections, of which the prime purpose was to elect a Constituent Assembly, put a severe strain on the coalition. The only Constitution the Umma could approve was one creating a single President, but the Umma could not obtain the neccessary majority for this in the Constituent Assembly with the support of the PDP alone. The Umma's search for ways and means to satisfy the Mahdi's presidential ambitions bedevilled the political situation to such an extent that S.A.M., to reinsure himself and his party against a possible combination of the Umma and the NUP, publicly declared his support for a three-man presidency, thereby infuriating SAR, and set to work to strengthen his political ties with Egypt. At the beginning of last November there were indications that the PDP were about to come to an understanding with the NUP under Egyptian patronage. This precipitated the Sudanese Army *coup d'état* of 17 November.

These events clouded the last days of S.A.R.'s life. The *coup d'état* must have come as no surprise to him, though it is generally accepted that he did not instigate it. He came out in public support of it, as did S.A.M. (the latter with reservations visible to the reader between the lines). The second coup, of 2 March, seemed to S.A.R. at first to be intended to limit his own influence in the Supreme Council by removing at least three of his adherents from it. He was persuaded that this was not so, though he accepted the new situation with the greatest reserve. He feared the reshuffle might herald a shift towards the left, weaken the Sudan's independence and eventually enable the Egyptians to realize the aspirations he always believed they harboured to dominate this country. He accordingly put the new régime unmistakenly on notice that any move in this direction would immediately encounter his open hostility.

He died as he had lived, the uncompromising champion of Sudanese national honour. His death came two hours after sunset on Tuesday, 24 March and an English doctor, summoned hastily by myself, in response to Sayed Siddiq's [the Mahdi's son and heir] urgent appeal was with him at the end. He was conscious, uncomplaining and courteous to the last few moments of his life. It was in the middle of the Holy Month of Ramadan. The moon was at the full and as his body was being brought down from the upper rooms of his house at Khartoum to be taken at night to lie in state during the night in his palace at Omdurman the moon was seen to be in partial eclipse. The wailing of women and the loud and unrestrained lamentations of the mourners mounted to a crescendo as the eclipse grew, dying away gradually as full moonlight was restored.

'When beggars die there are no comets seen; The heavens themselves blaze forth the death of Princes'.

Having rapidly checked with President Abboud on the correct protocol, Chapman-Andrews immediately went back through the gloom of the eclipse in the Embassy Rolls Royce to the Mahdi's house to present his condolences to Sayed Siddiq and his brother Sayed El Hadi: 'Chairs were quickly brought round a large square carpet and Sayed Siddiq took an armchair in the middle and placed me on his left. As the mourners arrived they stood just short of the carpet, with the palms of their hands raised until Sayed Siddiq rose to receive them. They then advanced with great dignity but briefly offered their condolences. By now the wailing was loud and everywhere people were rolling about, beating the ground and howling. Women were streaming in carrying infants in their arms to touch the corpse (they believe it brings luck to young children). After about half an hour Siddiq turned to me and gave me leave to go. As I took leave he shook me with great warmth and strength by the hand, holding my elbow tightly in his left hand. I thought he would not let me go. He was obviously very deeply affected.'

All that night and in the following days thousands of the Ansar, many dressed in the Mahdist gibbas in which their grandparents had fought 'the Turks', poured into Omdurman from all over the country, peacefully, if noisily, to mourn their Imam. It was the same when Sayed Siddiq himself died only two years later.

The Military Government

Chapman-Andrews considered that the military government and the end of parliamentary democracy was acceptable and largely in Britain's interests: after all, Britain had ruled the Sudan for fifty years as an autocracy under a Governor-General without a parliament. One of the Abboud Government's earliest decisions was the populist one of ordering the removal of the statues of Kitchener (on a horse) and Gordon (on a camel) which stood in central Khartoum. Chapman-Andrews ensured that this was done with due dignity and the 'imperialist emblems' shipped back to the UK. But otherwise Abboud's rule, which continued until 1964, provided stability and an upsurge in investment in schools, health and the economy generally. Communist and Egyptian influences were kept well in check. Relations with Sayed Siddiq, who had inherited his father's role but played it in a lower key, deteriorated; while the military were conservative and shared many of the Umma policies, they tended to be led by men from the east bank of the Nile who were more likely to be Khatmia followers of Sayed Ali. Siddiq saw the possibility of Mahdi leadership of the country receding in the absence of a parliamentary system. He died in 1961 before relations could deteriorate further, leaving his son Sayed Sadiq as his political heir and his brother Sayed El Hadi as Imam. While Sadiq and the Umma continued to play an important part in future political life, Mahdism would never again be the major force in the Sudan.

Chapman-Andrews urged Abboud, 'as one who has lived with the Nile waters problem for 30 years, whether in Egypt, Ethiopia and the Sudan, and who wishes to see real progress made with Nile water projects in the Sudan by general agreement to seize the opportunity of the services of the IBRD (World Bank)', to reach agreement with Egypt. In November 1959 a new Nile Waters Agreement was signed which allowed the Aswan High Dam to proceed, with Egypt paying full compensation for the resetting of the Sudanese Nubians whose land would be flooded and which gave the Sudan a fourfold increase in the quota of water which it could use for irrigation and to allow the start of the Roseires dam on the Blue Nile and the Jonglei canal on the White Nile. In view of the sixty years of intermittent negotiations with Ethiopia (and Uganda), the Sudanese were concerned that this might damage their close relations with the Emperor, but he accepted it. Early in 1961 improved relations with Egypt and the Sudan's self-confidence allowed a state visit from President Nasser, which passed off well. Nasser's eyes were looking more towards his role as an Arab leader than towards troublesome and poor Sudan.

One subject of increasing concern was southern Sudan. Here the ending of parliamentary government had the effect of sharply reducing the involvement of the southern Sudanese in national affairs. The understandable policy of the British Administration of treating the three southern provinces until the late 1940s as different from the north had left the new independent unitary Sudan with a major problem, which much concerned Chapman-Andrews. A mutiny in 1955 before the handover had resulted in a number of largely northern deaths. In January 1957 he visited the

south and saw the implications of the still largely northern administration and the 'nationalization' of the hitherto largely Christian,
often British, missionary educational system. While giving credit
to the genuine attempts of the Goverment to improve the southern
economy and situation, he was concerned that almost inevitably
these involved the takeover of the south by the north and of
Christianity by Islam. His efforts with the Sudanese government
were recognized on his departure from the Sudan by the award by
the Pope of the Knighthood of St Gregory. For many years after,
he maintained close relations with the Church leaders in the south
and did not hesitate to bring the growing problems and abuses to
public attention.

One additional benefit of his post in Khartoum was the opportunity to resume contacts with Ethiopia, Sudan's important
neighbour to the south and east. Earlier, UN-inspired attempts to
merge the Muslim parts of Eritrea with the Sudan had been
dropped and Eritrea was by 1952 moving towards union with
Ethiopia. Relations between the newly independent Sudan
and Ethiopia were generally good and particularly between the
Mahdi and the Emperor who had met first in Khartoum in the war
years.

In June 1956 Chapman-Andrews was invited to Addis Ababa to
take part in the unveiling by the Emperor of a War Memorial in
the Anglican Church commemorating the Allied men who had died
there during the liberation. He lunched with the Emperor – 'short
jacket and striped trousers'; the Emperor always insisted on strict
and detailed protocol.

On the occasion of the Sudan's fourth Independence Anniversary celebrations in 1960, the Emperor paid a state visit to
Khartoum and was well received everywhere. Any sensitivities over
the Nile waters were forgotten and the Emperor inaugurated the
work on the new Sennar hydroelectric power station on the Blue
Nile, wholly dependent on the Ethiopian rains. The Emperor
greeted Chapman-Andrews as an old friend. '"Still holding my
hand," he asked me, "How long is it since we first met?" On my
reply, "Thirty Years", the Emperor turned to President Abboud
and said, "Thirty years Sir Chapman has been my friend".'
Abboud was impressed and told him later, 'The Emperor was
always talking about you'. Chapman-Andrews told the Emperor
that he had just come back from a tour on the Ethiopian frontier

and the Emperor asked whether this was near Roseires 'where we had first started off' in 1941. When leaving, he was insistent that Chapman-Andrews and his wife should be his guests in Addis Ababa before he left the Sudan

Later in the year he was able to play a small part in advising the Emperor during the attempted *coup d'état* which had occurred when the latter was on an overseas visit to Brazil. He wrote:

When the Emperor passed through Khartoum on his way to Brazil I naturally saw him and had a talk. When the rebellion broke out, Asrate Kassa and two or three others contacted Sir Denis Wright at the British Embassy who reported by wireless to the Foreign Office, with a copy to me. It was quite natural that, in the general confusion, the Ambassador could not possibly ascertain what was going on. Many Ethiopians, including, for example, Azaj Kabada, told me that they themselves did not know for two or three days. The Ethiopian Chargé d'Affaires in Khartoum, however, was the brother of Ato David, the Minister for Foreign Affairs, who was one of the ministers who the Emperor had left behind in Addis Ababa with the Crown Prince, and he established regular contact by telephone with Abeye Ababa, the Emperor's son-in-law (he had been married to the late Princess Tsahai), Governor of Eritrea. Abeye, who was a first-class man in every way, calm, courageous, sensible and moderate, very soon established wireless contact with Ethiopian forces still loyal to the Emperor outside Addis Ababa. He thus discovered that the Air Force was loyal and the landing ground usable. I kept in touch with the Chargé d'Affaires and tried to keep Sir Denis Wright and the Foreign Office informed.

When the Emperor returned, having cut his Brazilian visit short, he was received at Khartoum airport by General Abboud and members of the Sudan government and a guard of honour. I was given the opportunity of ten minutes' conversation with him and was thus able to tell him what I knew of the internal situation. Having discussed things previously with General Abboud and agreed with him, I advised the Emperor to fly to Asmara rather than to Addis Ababa. The situation was not by any means desperate and it was thought not only safer but more satisfactory in every way if the Emperor could assess the situation with Abeye before moving into the capital.

The Emperor accepted this advice, though he said he had no doubt that he could equally well go straight to Addis. The only thing was that at that time he did not know exactly the cause of the trouble. He was rather puzzled by the whole thing, though not for one moment was he in the slightest doubt about what he should do or his ability to do it, namely to return to Addis Ababa and straighten things out. What struck me at that time was his utter and complete calm confidence. He was puzzled but by no means alarmed, though he was understandably a little anxious about the Empress, the Crown Prince, and his family. It was the same during the war. In fact I have never known him in any circumstances other than calm, quiet, serene even. Anxious I have seen him, but never frightened or in any doubt about what he should do and what he was going to do. This was never clearer than at that moment.

In the event the Emperor returned and quickly re-established control, but not until the instigators of the Coup, the Neway brothers, had killed a number of the leading Ethiopians in the Massacre of the Green Velvet Room.

In March 1961 Chapman-Andrews retired from the Sudan and from the Foreign Office only to embark on a second career which was going to bring him again close to Ethiopia and to the Emperor. He had greatly enjoyed his Sudan experience and particularly his close relations with the Mahdi. Khartoum was still an important air staging post and there had been many interesting visitors: British ministers and generals, old friends like Thesiger and Boustead, his friend George Steer's widow and son, en route for Ethiopia, Alan Moorehead writing his *White Nile* and *Blue Nile*, who tried to persuade his host to take him up the Blue Nile to Lake Tana, but accepted his advice that this was not possible; a helicopter was the only way. Travelling in the Sudan was still an adventure for an Ambassador, whether by road to Suakin on the Red Sea or round the Southern Sudan in a broken-down taxi. The memories of Gideon Force were not forgotten.

Chapman-Andrews' experience of the independent Ethiopia and even Egypt and the Sudan gave him a strongly anti-colonial bias, in advance of many of his colleagues in Whitehall and the British colonies. After all, he had seen an African Emperor running his country in 1930, whatever the imperfections of his rule, and in1941 stuck his neck out with OETA and the British military establishment that it was the Emperor's right to run his own country without British intervention. He saw the Russians and the Egyptians playing the 'liberation' card and winning widespread support in the Third World, especially in Africa, for doing so. In 1959 he again put forward to Lord Dalhousie, then Minister for State, the urgent need for all the relevant British ministers and civil servants to get together to produce a coordinated and forward-looking policy for Africa rather than relying on the traditional piecemeal and defensive approach and being picked off one by one, country by country. But his was a lone voice, ahead of his time.

Chapter Ten

Thesiger and The End of The Emperor

Chapman-Andrews first met Thesiger in Addis Ababa when the latter, aged 20 and at Oxford, had been invited by the Emperor to his coronation. Their friendship continued until the end of their lives. For both of them the Emperor's sad end was a desolating experience, as expressed in both their writings.

Thesiger, of course, already knew Ethiopia well since he had been born there in 1910, his father having been Minister at the time. Chapman-Andrews was 7 years older and could hardly have come from a more different background, but the two got on well together. They both appear in the formal photograph of the British Delegation to the Emperor's Coronation in 1930 led by the Duke of Gloucester. Shortly afterwards Thesiger left on his first exploratory expedition to the wilds of Aussa, the first of many adventures.

Their paths separated and it was probably not until Khartoum in 1940 that they started to have regular contact again, but Thesiger would have been aware of Chapman-Andrews' distinguished service at Harar in 1936 in the Italian War, which he had followed closely and with indignation from his post as a District Officer in the Western Sudan. In November 1940, before leaving on Mission 101, Thesiger was received by the Emperor and Chapman-Andrews duly recorded this in a film which he took during the Ethiopian Campaign (now in the Imperial War Museum). Thesiger wrote that the Emperor had 'in Chapman-Andrews, his Political officer, and above all in Sandford, two men devoted to his cause'.

The diary has only one reference to Thesiger, largely because he was fully engaged on the front line while Chapman-Andrews remained with the Emperor. However, there are several references to their meeting and spending time together after they all reached Addis Ababa. Again their paths separated with Thesiger going to Syria, then to the Western Desert, back for a frustrating year with the Crown Prince in Ethiopia and then in Saudi Arabia with the Locust Research Organization. It is likely that they did not meet during this time, but within ten days of Chapman-Andrews taking up his new post as Minister in Cairo in 1947 Thesiger turned up seeking help over the mundane question of clothes and the two men spent a long evening together. It was clear that Chapman-Andrews had kept up to date with his activities and knew about Thesiger's unusual and largely secret expeditions; the latter's first book about them was not published until 1959. Chapman-Andrews dictated a diary covering the first fortnight of his return to Egypt and recounted their conversation at length. (The diary quickly stopped as the pace of business accelerated.)

29/10/47. Wilfred Thesiger turned up at the Embassy to ask me if I would look after his one and only European suit if he posted it to me from Aden. I brought him home to dinner. Wilfred has become undoubtedly our leading British explorer. His last journey was across the empty quarter of Arabia on a line parallel to the journeys of Bertram Thomas and Philby but starting from a point several hundred miles to the east and following an almost waterless track previously used (and rarely) by raiding Bedouin when either from dire necessity or because they had a special reason to believe there was unusually good grazing. He was away and out of touch with Europeans for nine months clad in Arab rig and accompanied only by the wildest Bedouin walking barefoot like them most of the way. His feet must be like leather. The last lap of his journey involved a stretch of 12 days with only 20lb of flour, about a pound of rancid butter and 4 goatskins of water between himself and his four companions. The other Arabs could not face the seemingly endless sand dunes and deserted him at a nearby village before the final treck began. These dunes, he says, are often 700 feet from top to bottom. He admitted that he had cut it rather fine at times. This time he is off to do a yet more hazardous thing, the south to north journey starting somewhere near Mukalla. Officially he is visiting the Hadramaut for he would certainly never get permission from anybody, let alone the joint permission of HMG and Ibn Saud, to do a journey that has never yet been done by any man, even Bedouin, as far as is known. Shepherd, the Political Officer at Mukalla (Ingram's successor) is alone privy to the plan and Wilfred will inform him of any last minute change before setting off. He expects to be on the march about three weeks from now and come to the surface again about June or July next. The longest stretch he has in mind is a waterless region of sand dunes which with hard going he thinks he will cross in twenty days. I hope he is right.

There was rather a strange look about him and he spoke to me with an eloquence and volubility I have never found in him in all the years that I have known him. He has fined down and has a slightly fanatical look in the eye, though there is no doubt that he is completely sound and as balanced in western society as any normal person. He knows, however, that he is now two men; half of him which lives only when he dons Arab dress and scouts around to contact suitable Bedouin, is very nearly a pure Bedouin type. Of this he tires after about a year and begins to be his other self. Towards the end of this period he said that the ineradicable Bedouin habit of discussing every mortal thing for half an hour before settling anything, even a camping place for the night, interminable courtesies of the frugal meal and the rare cup of coffee, the everlasting punc-tilious formality of religious exercises and practice, begins to wear and grind on his nerves. He could never become Moslem though he does not profess to be a very noticeable Christian. He says that when, at the beginning of his acquaintance with the Bedouin, one calls him a Nosrani [Christian], he ups and hits him, abusing him roundly, as a result of which they regard him as one of their own people of the book like them-selves, even though of a different book, and respect him for his stout championing of his own volume. He said that were it not for the fact that he can almost at will bring down a sort of iron curtain between his mind and his companions he would not be able to stick it for so long.

He told me that before leaving London the BBC had asked

him to record a talk in a series called *The Lure of the Desert*. At first he refused, but when his mother heard of it she persuaded him to ring them and say that he would do it. In actual fact he much enjoyed analysing for himself the undoubted attraction the desert has and holds for him. Freya Stark and Stewart Perowne were among others contributing to the series and they are all lying in wait for Bertram Thomas. He said that when he got back from his last nine months wanderings he checked up with St John Philby at Jeddah and was pleased to find him a mellow reasonable being. He rather expected Philby to be ready to criticize, rather carping; but not at all. The reason, Wilfred thinks, is that Philby now fully realizes that he is long past hazardous journeyings so Wilfred cannot in any sense be regarded as a competitor. Rather, if he wins Wilfred's friendship, will Wilfred be regarded as his disciple. I have no doubt in my mind that Wilfred is our greatest desert explorer and traveller since Doughty. Unfortunately, as someone said, he is a walking gold mine and does not know it. He seems hitherto to lack the ability to turn his unique experience and encyclopaedic knowledge of Bedouin tribes, customs, religious sects and general philosophy of life to financial account. He always despises material things and always has. During the war when we were together in Sudan, he forwent his SDF pay because he said that he did not wish to profit personally from the war and could live quite well for nothing with his men. During the past two years he has been employed under the Colonial Office to hunt down the breeding places of the locust, but this job recently came to an end so he is making the present trip entirely on his own expense. He told me that he had saved £20,000 in the past few years and was investing so many hundred on this new journey. He thinks that amount should be sufficient to last him until well after the middle of next year.

He said that the punctilious courtesies of the Bedouin at meals were most irritating sometimes. For example, no one would take it upon himself to be the first to dip his hand into the bowl or to take the proffered cup of coffee even though water and coffee were in extremely short supply. A companion might, whether out of sheer cussedness or for the fun of it, refuse the proffered cup until the one sitting next to him should take it. To do so then would be for that one an insult so he with all formality declines the gesture, 'after you, Claud'. This goes on Box and Cox for some minutes until finally the servant, to settle the question, propels the precious liquid over his shoulder, spilling it in the sand and pours out another cup piping hot. If the one to whom it is proffered should feel equally inclined to play tricks the same wasteful performance is played out until finally in some way or another the cup is taken by someone as though absent-mindedly or alternatively no coffee for tonight. Again if one or two arrive at a camping place in advance of the other they will not sit down without them. The same applies when arriving at water. None will drink until all arrive, though this will mean waiting sometimes for hours, thirsty though they may be. If one should say he feels sick and will not eat tonight, others will say in that case nor will we and if they are to eat one has to satisfy his honour by at least once dipping his hand into the dish then he may withdraw as soon as he likes. They have queer habits too and will not milk a camel or goat until they have washed their hands, even though in the wilderness this may mean washing them under standing camel.

They think ill of a man who changes his religion and it is no advantage in the desert to have done this; even of Philby they say if someone should remark that he is a Moslem like themselves: 'Yes, so he says.' They have, however, told Wilfred, when approaching a particularly fanatical village which they must enter to get food or perish, that he must pass himself of as a Syrian, a member of a race which these remote tribesmen have heard of but never encountered. At the time of prayer or just before he has withdrawn behind a sand dune in order to escape observation, and when questioned his companions have said that he prefers to pray alone and this has been accepted. Had he not done this or got away with it, he says they would have undoubtedly been chased out of the villages like dogs and refused even a drink of water and this for them on at least one occasion would have meant perishing in the sands.

The Bedouin are most interested in the flora and fauna of the desert. Wilfred has collected dozens of different specimens

169

of flora and plant life. Some of these, though looking alike, have been declared by the Bedouin to be different and, on microscopic inspection afterwards in London, the Bedouin have been proved to be right. They can always tell him when he is collecting whether he has already put away a specimen of this or that plant. They have names too for all the varieties and these Wilfred knows as he goes along, as he does the compass bearings and the description of the soil. His topographical notes are afterwards made up in the form of a map and he has collected a lot of very valuable information for the Royal Geographical Society in this way. His friends too are most expert trackers and it is common for them, on seeing a track of a camel or camels that might to his eye be well blown over by sand and obviously to have been made some weeks ago, to say to one another, 'Ah, these camels, or this particular camel, belonged to such and such a section of such or such a tribe and they passed this way from a raid three weeks ago bearing with them so many camels of such or such a tribe,' or 'Hallo, the last time I saw this camel . . .', or 'Hallo this looks like so and so's camel. I haven't seen that one for four or five years'. 'Oh', said another, 'Didn't you hear that he had sold it to so and so.' 'Mm – then it must have been through here last in such or such a raid.' Wilfred says it is a constant source of revelation to him to find such accurate knowledge revealed to their minds on such scanty visual evidence. Many of the tribes in that part of the world are very savage and owing to good raids in recent years they can assemble in raiding parties 200 strong. They invariably cut the throats of men they encounter, carrying off their arms, goods, chattels, and herds with them.

As Wilfred left us bound for the Carlton Hotel which he will leave at five o'clock tomorrow morning by air for Aden he said, 'Well right then, expect this suit back in about three weeks in a parcel and for heaven's sake when I send for it get it to me by the quickest possible route for I shall otherwise be compelled to remain in Arab dress!'

History doesn't relate whether the suit appeared and was subsequently called for, but, knowing both men, it almost certainly was; the story in the family is that it was two years later. Chapman-

Andrews' comment on the 'two Thesigers' was perceptive. The ability of this man from such a very 'establishment' background to switch from Chelsea and worrying about suits to long periods in totally austere surroundings is one of Thesiger's great attractions. One of his fellow soldiers in Gideon Force, Major Harris, wrote, tongue slightly in cheek, of how he met Thesiger first in Gojjam, bathing naked in a pool from which he emerged describing how he liked to live off the land with his fellow soldiers, ignoring all discomfort. He then proceeded to demolish Harris's carefully saved-up store of Cooper's Oxford marmalade in the course of one breakfast. This went the rounds in Gideon Force; it is not known whether Thesiger was amused or not.

Return to Ethiopia

It was fourteen years before Thesiger was able to return to Ethiopia, years spent largely in Arabia, Iraq, Pakistan and Afghanistan. During this time Chapman-Andrews remained in the Middle East and it is likely that, even if they didn't often meet, they would have kept in touch through mutual friends and the rumour market. So it is not surprising that they were writing to each other in 1959 when Thesiger was back travelling in Ethiopia and Chapman-Andrews en poste in Khartoum. Once again the subject seems to be clothes: writing from the Embassy in Addis Ababa, Thesiger explains that he would have loved to stay with him in Khartoum on his way back to London: 'The trouble is that I have no dinner jacket, etc. which I'm sure would be necessary. I shall be too shabby after three months trekking. Air travel makes it impossible to carry enough clothes except at exorbitant cost . . . Did you ever get to Lalibela? It is a wonderful place and as yet quite unspoilt, only two tin roofs. I am hoping to get off to the south towards the end of the month starting from Soddu and going down to Omo, Rudolph, Mega, the Boran country and Aussa and getting back here at the beginning of June', journeys described in *The Life of my Choice*.

The next exchange, in August when Thesiger wrote from where he was staying in Ireland, is rather surprising: 'I am extremely flattered that you should wish to include me as one of the subjects in your book *Three Men*. I should find myself in distinguished company [the others in the planned, but never consummated, book were Wingate and Boustead]. I am perfectly willing that you should do so and would give you what help I could and put you in touch with various people who could give you some of the information you would want. We have, as you say, known each other for a long time. Certainly if I am to appear in a book I would as soon you undertook what I think will be a thankless task as anyone else I know. I am sure that you would do it very well. I hope to go back to Addis Ababa towards the end of December and will come by way of Khartoum in the hope of seeing you for a day or two. I hope you are having a good leave. I am sure you need it. My book comes out on October 19th [this was *Arabian Sands*]. Yours, Wilfred'

In November, writing from his flat in Tite Street, he says, 'I'm glad you enjoyed the book. Eventually I might try another book on the marshes but it would have to simmer for a bit. I am leaving here on or about December 16th on my way to Addis Ababa and hope to pass through Khartoum. Could I stay for a day or two with you then? I plan to travel in the North Gojjam, Simien, Tigre and Wollo for about 5 months.' In the event this did not work out and it was not until his return journey from Ethiopia that the visit took place.

In June 1960 he writes from Beirut: 'I arrived here after a very tedious journey. For no apparent reason we were two hours late leaving Cairo. I have never liked Egypt and the worst of all places in any country is the airport. However, it is nice to be here and the weather is surprisingly cool – I find it too cool to bathe. I go to Tripoli on Friday.

'I do hope you realise how much I enjoyed my stay in Khartoum and how grateful I am for all you did for me. I felt very guilty when you stayed up till 1 o'clock on the last night, but I greatly enjoyed our talk . . . Thank you again so much. I really cannot tell you how much I enjoyed seeing you.'

The 25th Anniversary of the Liberation

In March 1966 they both received from Taffara Worq, now Minister of the Imperial Court and who had been Chapman-Andrews' Amharic teacher 35 years before, an invitation from the Emperor to attend the 25th Anniversary of their entry into Addis Ababa on 5 May 1941: 'Special ceremonies will be held to commemorate and honour the men who participated in the Campaign to drive out the fascist invader.' It was to be as the Emperor's guest, including the cost of air travel. His staff had spent many months tracing the current whereabouts of the officers of 1941 all over the world. In spite of the fact that they had been given only two months' notice, twenty-five comrades in arms were able to accept, many of whom, of course, figured in Chapman-Andrews' diary. Thesiger wrote, 'Dan Sandford was already in Abyssinia [as it always was to Thesiger, rather than Ethiopia]; the rest of us arrived by air. I was delighted to see them all again. Hugh Boustead was there, and Chapman-Andrews, Clifford Drew, Donald Nott, the former Sergeant-Major Grey, now a Lieutenant-Colonel, Laurens van der Post, Neil McLean, W.E.D.Allen, Akavia and others whom I had not previously met.'

With great imagination the Emperor had also asked Lieutenant Wingate, Wingate's posthumous son, and George Steer, the son of George Steer, for whom the Emperor had stood as godfather the week before he left London in 1940. Lush, as we have seen, was not invited. But this was also to be a celebration of Ethiopia's armed forces as well, and senior representatives of the US, Soviet and British Armies were also invited. It was also to make a political point: the Emperor wanted to emphasize that the West should not assume that he was a committed member to their side in the Cold War and that the Russians, who were supporting Somalia, should not assume that Ethiopia, too, could not be a useful player in Africa and the Third World.

The day must have demanded a lot of stamina on the part of all the guests as well as of the Emperor. Starting at 8.30 with a Thanksgiving service, a Military parade ('in the presence both of the Lion of Judah and of a King of the Beasts safely sitting on an armoured truck just behind'), a Sports and Gymnastic display, and Air Display, it ended with a Banquet for 2000 at the Palace. Van der Post described it in rather more colourful language: 'Preceded by a frightening display of fireworks, when dinner came it was as moving as it was impressive, because it was like a sacrament of the history of all that kings and their captains, who are so fast disappearing from the scene, represented in the life of Man. There was a footman for every two guests: they stood behind their allotted chairs in tailcoats of bright green velvet, faced with gold brocade lined with gold braid at the hems and glittering with gold buttons.

They wore waistcoats, satin knee breeches and silk stockings all in white with black patent leather pumps with silver buckles. The menu was not long but superbly chosen: for every European course, there was an Ethiopian course to match it. At the end, the Emperor remained seated at the head of the main table whilst all his guests rose and departed.'

The Emperor's speech paid tribute to 'the noble fighting men of Ethiopia and of many other nations . . . like General Wingate . . . Present on this occasion are a few of the valiant British officers who twenty-five years ago travelled the long and arduous path to victory. We recall with deep pride the magnificent accomplishment of many brave men like Brigadier Sandford who joined in that glorious and triumphal march.' No reference was made to the fact that it was to the Allied armies of Platt and Cunningham to whom the greatest credit for the defeat of the Italians was due.

The Emperor, as always, rubbed in the failure of the League and of the big powers like Britain and France to support Ethiopia in 1935. 'Our appeals were unheeded, our warnings ignored. We placed our faith in the League. The story of that betrayal is one of the acknowledged tragedies of our time. The most futile sanctions were half-heartedly called for, and less than half-heartedly enforced. But at last those who had turned their backs on us were themselves driven to the very brink of destruction. The victory over fascism in Ethiopia became not only a triumph for Ethiopia and for Africa but the first inspiring landmark for the allied nations on the long road back to the re-establishment of liberty and justice for themselves.'

The Emperor personally spoke to each of his British guests – Van der Post typically reported that he alone was specially selected for this honour! – and presented them each with a commemorative cigarette case. In return the guests decided that they should make a presentation to the Emperor which Chapman-Andrews later duly arranged; among those who contributed to it was a Mrs Lorna Smith, Wingate's widow, now remarried and living in Scotland. It was, perhaps, typical that the Emperor suggested that the wording 'from the British officers who fought in the campaign for the Liberation' should be amended to read 'with their Ethiopian comrades, fought against the fascist invader.' The silver tray was presented by Sandford (now 85) later in the year.

Thesiger continued on to Saudi Arabia, with his usual problems about luggage and clothes; from Jeddah he wrote to Chapman-Andrews, thanking him for arranging for the Presentation to the Emperor and for getting his suitcase to London and looking forward to seeing him there in the autumn. From one or two later letters it would appear that, apart from occasional meetings in London, their paths again diverged. Thesiger remained based for much of the next twenty years mainly in Maralal on the Kenya/Ethiopian border, while Chapman-Andrews, based in London and with various directorships, was often away on missions in the Middle East and elsewhere.

The End of the Emperor

Chapman-Andrews' busy life after retirement from the Foreign Service gave him many opportunities to revisit Ethiopia, whether as a Director of Mitchell Cotts and Massey-Ferguson or as Chairman of the Committee on Middle East Trade. On most occasions he was received by the Emperor and this and his long connection with the country was recognized in the Press and radio. In 1971 he was there for the 30th Liberation anniversary and again was received by the Emperor and stayed with the Crown Prince and other Ethiopian friends and with the Sandfords at Mulu. Writing then, he reflected on the extraordinary transformation which he had seen in the country in education, agriculture, the administration and the armed forces.

The Ethiopian political situation, however, was deteriorating and the Emperor was growing old. A Foreign Office report some years before (1959) comments on the fact that 'the Emperor no longer enjoyed the unquestioning devotion of all his subjects. Surrounded by a clique of reactionary, self-seeking and often corrupt ministers, he and particularly his family were by no means free of taint. He has made great strides in the promotion of education, so much so that he is in danger of creating a force which sooner or later will be in danger of undermining his regime. He is sincerely anxious to develop the economic resources of Ethiopia for the benefit of Ethiopia as well as of himself and has introduced a constitution which provides for an elected Chamber of Deputies with considerably increased powers and an appointed Senate. His character is in fact a strange mixture of good and of bad qualities. Devoutly religious, he can behave with ruthlessness on occasions, yet he has shown remarkable humanity in his treatment of those who deserted to the enemy during the Italian invasion and who have plotted against him since; at times disinterestedly generous, he is often acquisitive to the point of rapacity; instinctively liberal and progressive, he has surrounded himself with some of the most conservative and oppressive elements in his realm – and these, in time, may prove his undoing. [He is] intensely suspicious by nature and determined that his country shall never fall under the domination of any one Power but shall derive the maximum assistance from any country which is prepared to help. While admiring British education and grateful both to Great Britain for wartime help and to the United States for aid, he is becoming increasingly neutralist and Pan African.'

Writing after his 1971 visit, Chapman-Andrews comments that at 78 the Emperor was rather frail but pretty tough, still leading a regular, hard-working, disciplined life. 'He is a complete fatalist and he himself has no doubt about the future stability and prosperity of his country. In his day he was "the greatest reformer of them all" but the project of land reform has been held up since he realized that it would bring down on his head and that of the Government the non-cooperation of the great landowners.' He was becoming increasingly lonely: the Empress had died in 1968 and of his six children only two were still alive: the Crown Prince was described by the Ambassador as 'neither a strong character nor particularly clever, but he is serious-minded and has a reputation for relative honesty'. Inevitably seen by the Emperor as a potential focus for disaffection, he kept him on a short rein under discreet supervision and for years did not allow him to leave the country. Thus the Emperor remained as lonely and autocratic as ever.

Early in 1974 came the news that, following a *coup d'état*, the Government had been replaced by a 'reformist' regime. The severe famine which had been affecting Ethiopia as well as other countries of the Sahel had brought many issues to the fore and its belated revelation in the world press had deprived the Emperor of much international support. In September, after several changes of Government, a group called the Dergue, mainly consisting of Army officers, announced that the Emperor had been placed, together with most of the Imperial family, in prison. In a letter to *The Times* to rally support for the Emperor, Chapman-Andrews emphasized: 'By his wisdom and statesmanship and the strength of his two frail shoulders, Haile Selaissie raised his country from the 15th to the 20th century.' On 23 November many of the Emperor's men and many of the 'old guard', including some of the Imperial family were rounded up and killed. Callaghan, as British Foreign Secretary, protested, with European Union support, and this may have delayed the Emperor suffering the same fate. In August 1975 it was announced that he had died 'following an operation' and years later it was confirmed that he had indeed been murdered, probably by Mengistu, the Dergue's leader.

For both Thesiger and Chapman-Andrews it was a terrible loss. Thesiger was in Addis Ababa in April, just in time to see Mrs Sandford before she died and before the Dergue took over the Sandfords' farm at Mulu. Just before, the Dergue formally abolished the monarchy and declared the country a communist state. Thesiger asked the then Ambassador if it had been Chinese or Russian agents who had introduced communism to Ethiopia. He had answered: 'There was no need. The revolution was largely brought about by British and American communist school teachers and university lecturers', which might well have had a grain of truth, although the underlying reasons were different.

Chapman-Andrews visited an unhappy Addis Ababa in October and wrote, 'I went to Addis on business in the hope of being able to find out a little more of what had happened to the Emperor, but it was most disappointing and very disagreeable from my point of view. Some twenty members of the Imperial family – all women, some no more than teenage girls – are locked up in a room in prison and allowed out in the yard for something under an hour a day just for change of air. There is an open lavatory, if you can call it that, in one corner of the room. These conditions are inhumane, to put it no worse, but nothing has so far succeeded in changing the attitude of the so-called soldiers in power towards the families of the Emperor's former entourage who survive. It is very distressing, especially if you are amongst those of us who were so closely identified with earlier events.'

For the next two years, before his health broke down, Chapman-Andrews devoted himself to trying with a dwindling band of old Ethiopian friends to help the Ethiopian exiles with money and jobs and in drawing public and Government attention to what was happening to the prisoners in Addis Ababa and to the country as it rapidly deteriorated. During his October 1975 visit he had read in the *Ethiopian Herald* of the death in London of his old adversary General Platt, aged 90, and that the Ethiopian Government had, surprisingly, sent a message of sympathy to Lady Platt, indicating that even the Dergue saw some mileage in recalling the 'Liberation'. On his return he arranged with her to write a plea to the Dergue that the female members of the Imperial family be released from prison. He tried to persuade the British Government to take a more positive role but readily understood that there was little they could usefully do. He helped arrange a memorial service at St Margaret's, Westminster, for those who had been killed in November and accompanied the Crown Princess to the service, attended loyally by Anthony Eden, who was to die not long afterwards, and many others. The Crown Prince and Princess had been living in London for the previous two years, following a stroke which had largely incapacitated the Prince. In October there was a Memorial Service for the Emperor at St George's Chapel, Windsor, where the Emperor had once been installed as a Knight of the Garter.

In 1977 Chapman-Andrews suffered a stroke which left him largely incapacitated and he died in February 1980. At the family funeral the Crown Princess appeared, a kind gesture to an old friend whose life had been so bound up with her family and country. Her son, the heir to the Emperor's throne, Prince Asfa Wossen Asserate, wrote to Lady Chapman-Andrews: 'Through his departing, Ethiopia and the Imperial family have lost an old and trusted friend. My countrymen and I will never forget his uncompromising stand against Fascism in the thirties and his unswerving friendship to us all after the Revolution. His council and his sense of optimism will be terribly missed.'

There is one further small postscript: in 2000 the Ethiopian Government, who had taken over following the ousting of the disastrous Dergue, allowed a Funeral Service to be held for the Emperor in Addis Ababa. It was to be a private service since they did not wish to encourage an Imperial revival, but it was attended by thousands of the Emperor's old followers and followed the full ritual and ceremony of the Ethiopian church. The Emperor's last surviving daughter, now freed and who herself was soon to follow her father, was there. Although none of the 'class of 1941' had survived, Lord Deedes, who had been there as a journalist in 1936, attended and recorded it in his book *To War with Waugh*.

178

Perhaps the last word should be Thesiger's, which Chapman-Andrews would have echoed, at the end of *The Life of My Choice*: 'Many of the present inhabitants of Ethiopia must look back on Haile Selassie's long reign as on a golden age, and remember their former monarch with the appreciation he deserved. It is my hope that in time historians will assess at its true worth all he did for his country. I was privileged to have known that great man.'

Appendix 1

Brief Biographies
of Sir Edwin Chapman-Andrews
and of Other Major British Names

Many of these names are, or were, well known; they have been included only where it was felt necessary to throw additional light on the papers. Since both Wingate(1903–44) and Thesiger (1910–2002) are well covered elsewhere, they have been omitted. The numerous military names who were involved in Gideon Force are listed with brief details in Appendix 3.

SIR EDWIN ARTHUR CHAPMAN-ANDREWS was born in Exeter on 9 September 1903, the son of Arthur John Chapman-Andrews, stationer's assistant, and Ada Allen. To his family and his Exeter friends, and later to those who did not know him well, he was always 'Edwin' or 'Ed', but to his wife and his Foreign Office colleagues he was 'Andrew'.

The family were not at all well off but were determined that their sons – a second was born in 1907 – should have the best possible local education. Both won scholarships to the fee-paying Hele's School in Exeter. Their father was an enthusiastic Territorial and, as a result, Chapman-Andrews was eligible to enter for, and in 1922 won, a Kitchener Scholarship which enabled him to go to University College, London, which would otherwise have been financially out of the question. He gained his BA II in English Literature in 1925.After a brief flirtation with a possible lectureship at Rangoon University, he was accepted to apply for the Consular service and stayed for further year at UCL, spent partly at the Sorbonne and gained an Honours Degree in French. He passed 8th in the Consular examinations in 1926 and chose the Levant Service, which involved spending a first year studying oriental languages at St John's, Cambridge

His service details show his subsequent appointments: 1928, Acting Vice Consul, Port Said; 1929, Acting Vice Consul, Addis Ababa; 1930–32, Foreign Office; 1932, Vice Consul, Kirkuk; 1935–6, Consul, Harar; 1936, OBE; 1936–7, Foreign Office; 1937–40, 2nd Assistant Oriental Secretary, Cairo; 1940–42, seconded as Political Liaison Officer to Emperor Haile Selaissie (Major Royal Sussex Regt) and Middle East Intelligence Centre; 1942, Order of Star of Ethiopia; after secondment to Legation, Addis Ababa, returned to Foreign Office, London; 1942–4, in Egyptian Department; 1944–6, Head of Personnel Dept, Foreign Office; 1946, Foreign Office Inspector; 1947–51, Minister, Cairo; 1948, CMG; 1951–6, Minister, later Ambassador, Lebanon; 1953, KCMG; 1956–61, Ambassador, Sudan; 1958, Knight of St Gregory the Great – for service in the Sudan; 1961, retired from Foreign Office.

1962 Director, Massey-Ferguson(Export) Limited and Mitchell Cotts; College Committee, University College, London (Fellow 1952); Council, London Chamber of Commerce, Royal Albert Hall, Anglo-Arab Association, Committee of Middle East Trade (Chairman 1963–8), Lord Kitchener National Memorial Fund; Knight of St John.

He married in 1931 Sadie Barbara Nixon, a textile designer, whom he had met when he had come to University College where she was based the Slade School. Her father, who had died in 1925, had been a successful engineer and his widow had a house in Hampstead Garden Suburb which provided a UK base for the Chapman-Andrews for the rest of their lives, although they had a small house in Devon near Ottery St Mary during the war and later in West Bay near Bridport in the 1950s and in the 1960s a holiday home in Minorca. But after retirement from the Foreign Office, London was their main home. There were four children of the marriage: David born 1933, Charlotte born 1938, Harriet born 1939 and John born 1943.

Sir Edwin died on 10 February 1980, after having had a stroke

181

in 1977. Lady Chapman-Andrews died on 6 November 2002 aged 97.

This story, told as far as possible in his words, helps to explain the contribution he made and the remarkable man he was: a great diplomat and a loyal friend.

W. E. D. ALLEN (1901–1973) Gideon Force. Author of the very entertaining *Guerrilla War in Abyssinia,* 1943 and many other works, mainly about the Caucasus. An Etonian and an Ulsterman, he had had a varied career as a Mosleyite MP, businessman and journalist in the Caucasus, Ukraine and Morocco, during which he worked for MI5. He joined up in 1939 and volunteered for camel duties in Gideon Force, but he may also have had an Intelligence role. He and Laurens van der Post enjoyed sparring together. He retired to Ireland after the war, where he died.

SIR SIDNEY BARTON (1876–1946) arrived in Addis Ababa as Minister in 1929, having spent the whole of his career in China in the Consular service. Chapman-Andrews describes him as a highly competent and demanding Minister, very different from the fictional Minister whom Waugh caricatured in *Black Mischief*. He was impressed by what Haile Selassie was trying to achieve and was strongly supportive of his resistance to the Italians, both before and after their invasion, whilst the Foreign Office was much more equivocal. After successfully protecting the British and foreign community during the sack of Addis Ababa prior to the entry of the Italian army, he was withdrawn and retired to England where he remained in close touch with the Emperor and his family, now in exile, and helped co-ordinate the Ethiopian pressure group. He played an important part in advising the Emperor in his approaches to the British government in 1940. He had two daughters of whom the elder caused him considerable embarrassment in Addis Ababa; she eloped with the Italian military Attaché and then left him for another Italian and had to leave the country. His younger daughter, Esme, who once flung a glass of champagne at Evelyn Waugh, whom she considered had insulted her and her family, subsequently married George Steer. The Emperor invited her and her son to Ethiopia in 1959. They described the warmth of their reception in letters to Chapman-Andrews with whom they had been staying in Khartoum en route.

182

Count **ARTHUR BENTINCK** (1887–1952) Mission 101 in 1940. An Army Officer, he served in WWI and from 1917–20 in the Legation in Addis Ababa where he returned in the British Ambulance Unit during the Italian invasion. He was recruited to work alongside Sandford in 1940 in the Beghemder sector, where he had a difficult time and was replaced in April 1941. Thesiger, who had first met him when Bentinck, having been badly wounded, was working for his father in Addis Ababa, described him as having 'a gruff manner, a game leg and a pronounced cast in one eye'. Another elderly, self-reliant and improbable volunteer, he showed how it was possible to survive in really adverse conditions in enemy-held territory.

Colonel **HUGH BOUSTEAD** (later Sir Hugh 1895–1980) was a remarkable character. Chapman-Andrews had planned to write a book on three men from the 1940s whom he had known well: Wingate, Thesiger and Boustead. KBE, CMG, DSO, MC and bar (WWI) he was at various times in his life a deserter from the Navy, a soldier under an assumed name, served with the White Russians in the Caucasus and later in Turkey and the Sudan, was captain of the British Olympic Pentathlon team and member of 4th Everest expedition. He joined the Sudan Political Service in 1931 as a District Commissioner, Darfur. Raised the Sudan Defence Force Frontier battalion in 1940 which formed the fighting core of Gideon Force. Later served as Resident Adviser in Mukalla, and later in Oman and Abu Dhabi. Thesiger described him as small wiry man with a lined, leathery face, intensely energetic and, although by no means an intellectual, widely read and with an endearing playful sense of humour. 'All his life he had sought adventure and revelled in hardship and danger.' He was very sociable and when word went round that 'Hugh is back' friends flocked round. He and Chapman-Andrews got on well and remained in touch. Boustead and Wingate did not. Boustead thought the later lacked military experience and was disorganized; Wingate intolerably accused him of cowardice. The two men had a number of flare-ups, the last being in Cairo after Wingate's attempted suicide. Thesiger admired Boustead greatly, but felt that he could not have done what Wingate did, lacking his originality of thought, bold imagination and ruthless single-mindedness. A bachelor, he retired to Tangier and died there. His autobiography *The Wind of Morning* was published in 1971.

Colonel **ROBERT CHEESMAN** (1878–1962), after serving in WWI in India and Iraq, was appointed by the Sudan Government as Consul in North-West Ethiopia from 1925–34, based at Dangila, an important sounding board from the point of view of frontier troubles with Ethiopia and, more importantly, of British and American interest in Nile Waters. It was in that role that Chapman-Andrews first met him and they remained good friends thereafter. Whilst at Dangila Cheesman travelled extensively in the borderlands of Ethiopia and the Sudan on which he wrote in *Lake Tana and the Blue Nile*. CBE 1935. He was thus a natural recruit in 1939 to run the Ethiopian intelligence section in Khartoum. He served as Oriental Counsellor at the Legation in Addis Ababa from 1942–4, when he retired to farm in Kent His wife was godmother to Chapman-Andrews' youngest son, John. In 2001 his papers were donated to the Royal Geographical Society, of which he had been an active member and medal holder. His brief account of his work in 1939–41 has been most useful in filling in some of the intelligence details of this story.

Brigadier Sir **ILTYD CLAYTON** (1886–1955) appears as Chief of the Middle East Intelligence Centre. A regular officer, he had been involved in the Middle East since WWI when he had worked with Lawrence. Whilst working behind the scenes he knew everyone and played a part in the appointments of Wingate, Sandford, Steer, Bentinck and Chapman-Andrews in 1940.

ALEXANDER (SANDY) CURLE DSO OBE (18 –198?) A Scot, he served in the Colonial Service in British Somaliland, in which capacity he was Vice Consul in Jijiga in 1930. In 1940 he raised an Ethiopian force (the 2nd Irregulars) in Kenya and had some success in the Galla/Sidamo area. After the liberation he worked in Addis Ababa briefly for OETA and then in the revived Legation, where he stayed for 10 years, and was close to the Crown Prince. He retired to the Borders, attended the 1966 reunion and was active in supporting the Imperial family once again in exile in 1974.

Sir **DOUGLAS DODDS-PARKER** (1909–) served in the Sudan political service until 1938 when he left to travel in Europe. He joined up in 1939 and was commissioned in the Grenadier Guards, from where he was recruited by the embryo Special Operations

Executive under General Gubbins. He worked on the Ethiopian plans and was probably largely behind the scheme to bring the Emperor out to the Middle East, where he joined him in September1940. He played an important part in Gideon Force, not least in its financing and acting as Wingate's intermediary with GHQ, which role, to his great disappointment, kept him in Khartoum and away from the front line. Later a politician and a junior Foreign Office Minister. His book *Setting Europe Ablaze (Some Account of Ungentlemanly Warfare)* published in 1983 makes it clear that Mission 101 and the 'setting light' to the Ethiopian resistance was in some ways a model for the later and much more famous SOE activities in Europe.

ANTHONY EDEN, later Earl of Avon, (1897–1977) became Foreign Secretary in 1935 when he took over following the resignation of Sir Samuel Hoare over the Abyssinian crisis. He resigned in 1938, but returned to Government in 1939 as Dominions Secretary, then became War Minister in Churchill's Government in May 1940 and Foreign Secretary from late 1940 – 1945. When Churchill returned to power in 1951 he was again Foreign Secretary, during which time he and his second wife, Clarissa, stayed with Chapman-Andrews in Beirut. He was Prime Minister from 1955 to late 1956. Conscious of Britain's failure to support the Emperor in 1935/6, he was later a good supporter and in his last years attended the Memorial service for the victims of the Dergue in St Margaret's, Westminster, in 1975.

Sir **MILES LAMPSON** cr **LORD KILLEARN** 1943 (1880–1964). Professional diplomat who served mostly in Asia until posted as High Commissioner for Egypt and Sudan in 1934; as Ambassador in Cairo played an important part in Chapman-Andrews' career. The last of the British Pro-Consuls in Egypt, he was a forceful and rather larger than life character. He greatly enjoyed his powerful position in Cairo during the war. Endless hand-written letters winged their way to Churchill and Eden from him and also from his (second) wife, who played a large part in the social and political life of Cairo. She was the daughter of Marchese Aldo Castellani, well known for his work for Britain and Italy in tropical medicine, but, potentially more embarrassingly, as Physician to the Italian Royal family and to the Italian Ethiopian Army. It was a tribute to

the Lampsons that this was never held against them, except by King Farouk, who enjoyed teasing Lampson on the subject. From 1946 till 1948 when he retired Killearn was Special commissioner for South-East Asia. It is interesting to see the change of social habits: letters start 'Dear Chapman-Andrews' or even 'Dear Chapman', but his congratulations on the latter's KCMG begin with 'Dear Andrew'.

LORD LLOYD (1879–1941) was High Commissioner in Egypt from 1925 until 1929 when he resigned due to a difference with HMG over British Egyptian Policy. He was Chapman-Andrews' first chief in Egypt. A formidable figure, he was always known as "God" to his staff in Cairo; his successor, Sir Percy Loraine, a very different character, was known as 'The Two Minutes Silence'. A supporter of Churchill, Lloyd became Secretary of State for the Colonies in 1940 and died in office in 1941.

Colonel **MAURICE LUSH** (1896–1992) was awarded an MC and bar in WWI and joined the Sudan Political Service, serving initially as Secretary in the Legation in Addis Ababa and then in many posts in the Sudan and Cairo, rising to Governor, Northern Province, in 1938. His experience made him in many ways an excellent candidate for Political Officer in Ethiopia; as we have seen, his role in OETA inevitably caused friction with the Emperor and with his brother-in-law Sandford during that period. Later he filled a similar role in Madagascar,Tripolitania and Italy. His administrative experience was well used after WWII in the International Refugee Organization and later as Political adviser to Shell in Libya. Chapman-Andrews and he were never close, but learnt to respect each other.

Sir **RICHARD LUYT** (1916–1993) served in Gideon Force as a sergeant, later officer. He was a South African Rhodes scholar who joined the British Colonial Service and retired as Governor General of Guyana. Many of the NCOs in Gideon Force were subsequently commissioned; often the only reason why they weren't already officers was because it was a quicker form of volunteering for military service to join up in the ranks.

NEIL MCLEAN DSO (1918–86). A Lieutenant in the Royal Scots Greys, he joined Gideon Force in 1941 and won the DSO, later

rising to Lieutenant-Colonel. He subsequently entered politics and was MP for Inverness from 1954–64. He attended the 1966 reunion.

SIR PHILIP MITCHELL (1890–1964) Colonial civil servant who served in WWI in the Tanganyika Campaign. Governor of Uganda 1935–40, which helped to confirm the Emperor's suspicions of British intentions when he was appointed Chief Political officer, OETA in 1941. In his *African Afterthoughts* he admitted that his failure to consult with the Emperor early on made for many of his future difficulties as CPO. Afterwards Governor of Fiji 1942–44 and Kenya 1944–52.

General Sir **WILLIAM PLATT** (1885–1975) GBE KCB DSO. Regular Army 1905, served WWI; appointed Commander Troops in Sudan 1938; GOC East Africa 1941–45 when he retired. Victor of the Battle of Keren and a good leader, although a difficult colleague, as the story shows. Lieutenant-Colonel Barton, when writing the official record of the Campaign told Cheesman that Platt was 'his usual unpleasant self'. Steer said that his switches from humour to fierceness were alarming for a new junior officer who could never make out when the car would go into reverse, but they got on surprisingly well. In later years he and Chapman-Andrews established a more amicable working relationship.

Brigadier **DANIEL SANDFORD** (1882–1971) plays a major part in the story. After serving in the artillery from 1900–1910, he joined the Sudan Political Service, first as District Commissioner and then in 1913 as Sudan Liaison Officer in Addis Ababa. He rejoined the army and ended the war as Lieutenant-Colonel and DSO. He married in 1918 Christine Lush and returned to Ethiopia in 1920 as General Manager of the Abyssinian Trading Corporation and in practice it remained his home until his death. The ATC closed in 1921 and from then until the Italian invasion he was variously a trader (in hides and skins), part-time journalist and farmer. Clearly, with his background, he was a leading member of the British community but also became close to the Emperor, who made available to him land at Mulu near Addis Ababa, where he died. He followed the Emperor to England in 1936 and returned in 1940/1 as his Chief Political Adviser. He was

187

made CBE in 1942. He continued serving the Emperor as Director General of the Ministry of the Interior and then of Addis municipality until 1949. Thereafter he was involved with his wife in many social and educational initiatives, based at Mulu farm where Chapman-Andrews visited him many times. Although, and because, he played no part in Ethiopian politics, he remained close to the Imperial family and the Emperor who insisted that his funeral in 1971 was delayed to allow him to attend. His wife wrote two books about Ethiopia and the Emperor. Sadly she died in 1975 after the *coup d'état* which resulted in the death or imprisonment of many of their friends, and shortly afterwards of the Emperor himself. They had six children, a number of whom remained in Ethiopia. The family donated the Sandford Archive to the Ethiopian Studies Institute in Addis Ababa in 2002.

SIR DAVID MONTAGU DOUGLAS SCOTT (1887–1996) KCMG, OBE Foreign Office 1911, Assistant 1938, then Deputy-under-Secretary 1944–7; was Chapman-Andrews' great inspirer and later close friend and supporter in the Foreign Office. He was the author, with Sir Ivo Mallet, of the unification of the six 'Foreign' services and brought Chapman-Andrews in from the Levant service in 1944 to run the new Personnel Office to implement the unification. This was a key role which made Chapman-Andrews known throughout the new Foreign service. They remained close friends for the rest of their lives. His only son, Merlin, was killed in action in 1941. Chapman-Andrews wrote to Clayton in Middle East Intelligence in 1940 to ask that Merlin should be allowed to join him in Gideon Force. He did not.

GEORGE STEER (1909–1944) played an important part in Ethiopia in the period 1935–41, as a journalist and author and as Propaganda Officer in 1940/41. Born in South Africa, he was educated at Winchester and Oxford, where he got a First. Bright and forceful, he achieved distinction in several worlds. As *The Times* Special correspondent aged 30 in Ethiopia during the Italian invasion, he quickly achieved a special relationship with the Emperor and, as a result, his coverage of news was much the best, to the irritation of Evelyn Waugh, who was probably also irked by Steer's superior education, if lesser social contacts, and some of the other Ethiopian press doyens. He married his first wife, a fellow

journalist, at the Legation during the sack of Addis Ababa in May 1936, just before his expulsion by the Italians. Already passionately committed to the Emperor and Ethiopia, he published *Caesar in Abyssinia* later that year. He then covered the Spanish Civil War and Guernica and published two more books. In 1938 he was back in Somaliland and actively promoting support for the guerrilla war, including the clandestine visit of the French Monnier into Ethiopia. His first wife having died, he married Esme Barton, Sir Sidney Barton's second daughter. The Emperor was godfather to their son in early June 1940 and immediately afterwards he joined Special Operations Executive and accompanied the Emperor on his flight to Khartoum. His work as Propaganda Officer for the campaign was recognized as being highly innovate, effective and influential. His hand can be seen in the Emperor's statesmanlike Liberation speech on 5 May setting out his vision of a new Ethiopia. After writing the official, unattributed, HMSO account of *The Abyssinian Campaign* and *Sealed and Delivered*, he did further Propaganda work during the Madagascar and Burma campaigns. He died in a car accident in India on Christmas Day 1944.

Writing to his widow in 1944, Chapman-Andrews said: 'George was a great adventurer, a magnificent brain, full of guts and energy and ideas and utterly resilient. Nothing ever got George down long and everything, every occasion,brought that little one-sided twisted smile of humour and real deep human understanding to his face. I know I shall never forget him as long as I live'. He remained close to her and her son, George. She remarried and died Mrs Kenyon-Jones in 1988.

Sir **LAURENS VAN DER POST** (1906–99) served in Gideon Force as a volunteer. He wrote many books in two of which he makes brief references, partly exagerated, as his biography *Storyteller* by J.D.F. Jones makes clear, to his time in Ethiopia: he later wrote to Chapman-Andrews that he did not like 'reliving the past though paradoxically nothing means more to me than doing all I can to preserve the human relationships evolved in such past'. He joined up in 1940 in London and, as an African, was probably thought suitable for a transport role in Ethiopia. In spite of then having no experience of camels, he managed to bring all his animals through alive to Debra Markos. Allen gave him credit: 'He managed five

blasphemous British sergeants and a tough crowd of Sudanese camel men with equanimity'. He attended the 1966 reunion.

EVELYN WAUGH (1903–1966) contributed greatly to making Ethiopia – or rather Abyssinia, as he always called it – a household name in the 1930s through his books: *Remote People* (1931), *Black Mischief* (1932), *Waugh in Abyssinia* (1936), *Scoop*(1938) and *When The Going was Good (*1946), as well as a number of contributions to the newspapers, mainly in 1930. These were excellent for Waugh's literary career, but gave a misleading impression of Haile Selassie's Ethiopia, with which he had little sympathy. Indeed his early sympathies were with the Italians, although he recanted in the 1940s. To be fair, Waugh always made clear that his works of fiction did not reflect historical people or circumstances, but, as always, this did not prevent people thinking otherwise. Lord Deedes' book *At War With Waugh* puts a proper perspective on this and describes Waugh as a rather more practical and attractive companion than his own writings suggest. Certainly Waugh's warm anonymous commendation of Chapman-Andrews in 1936 shows him in a more human light. They maintained good relations into their 70s.

ARNOLD WEINHOLT (ca1880–1940) Mission 101. An extraordinary character; an Etonian, a lion hunter in South-West Africa who served in the Boer War and the German East African campaign in WWI, DSO and MC, a rancher in Australia, and a Senator, a volunteer in the Red Cross during the Italian invasion. He wrote *The African's Last Stronghold* in 1938. He waited in Aden until the Italians entered the war and then volunteered for Mission 101 in 1940; he was over 60, but was killed in an ambush by a Gumz *banda* in August. Thesiger was probably the last European to see him: 'I was hauntingly reminded of "Rocky" in *Jock of the Bushveld*, gun in shoulder, stick in hand, starting with his donkeys on his last journey into the interior.'

Appendix 2

Ethiopian Biographies

The diaries and other papers refer to a number of Ethiopian notables. Where these are of lesser importance, an explanatory note accompanies the reference to them, but some played a major part in the history of Ethiopia and these are covered by the brief notes below, based mostly on a 'Report on Leading Personalities in Ethiopia' submitted to the Foreign Office by the Ambassador in Addis Ababa in 1959.

Wide variations are found in the transliteration of Amharic names and titles: Ras very roughly equates to Duke, Dejazmatch to General, Fitaurari to Commander and Lij to Prince or 'the Hon', i.e son of a noble; titles played a very important part in Ethiopian life and ranking and had all sorts of additional significance.

1) *The Imperial family.* **HAILE SELASSIE** was born Tafari Makonnen in Harar in 1892, the son of Ras Makonnen, a leading Shoan noble and cousin and trusted supporter of the Emperor Menelik. He was educated at the infant French Catholic Mission in Harar under Père Jarosseau, later to become Monsigneur and first Catholic bishop in Harar, and later at Menelik's Academy of Nobles. His father died in 1906 and he succeeded him as governor of Harar. In 1916, following the deposition of Lij Yasu, Menelik's grandson, he was appointed Regent under the Empress Zauditu, becoming Negus(King) in 1928 and Emperor, taking the name Haile Selassie I, on her death in 1930. He visited Europe, including the UK, in 1924. He and his family spent 1936–40 in exile in Bath, returning as ruler in 1941. He was deposed in 1974, murdered in 1975 and was finally buried in Addis Ababa in 2000.

He has been the subject of many books including his own very formal *Autobiogaphy* translated by Ullendorf (OUP 1976). His character and the loyalty he inspired comes over very clearly in Chapman-Andrews papers. The early emergence of 'Rastafarianism' in the Caribbean and USA amongst the black population made him widely known in the USA.

He was devoted to his wife and family; he had married the Empress **MENEM**, the granddaughter of the King of Wollo, in 1916 and they had six children, four of whom predeceased him. Her death in 1962 was a loss not only of a wife but a wise adviser. **ASFA WOSSEN**, the Crown Prince, (1916–97), returned from exile in UK in 1941 and lived very much in the shadow of his father. He had a severe stroke in 1973 and spent the rest of his life in exile in London with his wife **CROWN PRINCESS MADFARISH WORQ**. They had four children all of whom went into exile, including Prince Asfa Wossen Asserate, the senior representative. Prince **MAKONNEN**, 1923–1957, the Duke of Harar, was a favourite son of the Emperor and his death in a motor accident in 1957 was a major loss. This was less true of Prince **SAHLE SELAISSIE** (1931–62), described by the Embassy as 'irresponsible, ill-mannered and unattractive' and as 'treated by the Emperor with some justification as a naughty small boy'. Of the Emperor's daughters, one died in childbirth in 1933, Princess Tsahai in 1942 and only Princess Tenagne Worq (1913–2001) survived to be imprisoned under the Dergue and die after eventual release in 2001. Her son, Prince Alexander Desta, was murdered by the Dergue in 1974.

2) *The Rases.* **RAS HAILU** (1868–1953), son of the King of Gojjam and Governor 1907–32 until replaced by the Emperor, who kept him under house arrest. He accompanied the Emperor to Europe in 1924. He took advantage of the Italian invasion to escape in the traumatic days of May 1936 and collaborated with the Italians, under whom he returned to Gojjam in December 1940. His surrender to the Emperor at Debra Markos and suborning of Lij Belai Zelleka in April 1941 is well covered in the Diary. He remained under house arrest for most of the rest of his long life. **RAS KASSA** (1881–1956), cousin and loyal supporter to the Emperor, under whom he was ruler of Salale and custodian of the monastery of Debra Lebanos. In exile in Jerusalem until 1940

when he joined the Emperor in Khartoum. He represented Ethiopia at the Coronation of the Queen in 1953. Of his four sons, three were murdered by the Italians and the survivor **RAS ASRATE KASSA** (1919–1974), who was in exile with his father, returned in 1941 with the Emperor and succeeded his father as Ras. He was murdered by the Dergue in 1974.

RAS GUGSA, the Tigrean Ruler of Beghemder and husband of the Empress Zauditu, whose severed head makes a brief appearance in 1930, was the father of Dejazmatch **HAILE SELASSIE GUGSA**, who married the Emperor's daughter in 1932, but was the first to join the Italians in 1935. For this the Emperor never forgave him. Captured by the Allies in 1941, he was first imprisoned in the Seychelles and then, after trial and condemnation to death in Addis Ababa, for the rest of his life in Ethiopia. **RAS SEYUM** (1887–1960) Tigrean noble and grandson of Emperor Johannes, was Governor of Tigre 1910–1960. He played a rather equivocal role with the Italians, but rallied to the Emperor in 1941 and was killed in the 1960 coup d'etat. **RAS IMRU** (1894– 1980) was a cousin of and brought up with the Emperor, with whom he did not enjoy close relations. He was imprisoned by the Italians and returned in 1943. He was the only member of the 'Old Guard' who was tolerated by the Dergue, who gave him a State Funeral when he died in 1980.

3) *Church leaders.* Traditionally the Head of the Ethiopian Church and the Bishops had always been appointed by the Head of the Coptic Church in Alexandria. Haile Selassie had been determined to break this and to enhance the role of the **ECHEGE** or Itcheguey, an Ethiopian usually the chief of Debra Libanos monastery, to ensure that the Church remained strong supporters of his rule. It was important to him that the Church leaders should return from exile to join him in Khartoum in 1940. **ECHEGE GABRE GIORGIS**, who had been in exile since 1936 in the Ethiopian Monastery in Jersualem returned and accompanied the Emperor on his return in 1941, as we have seen, together with **ABBA HANNA** (1895–1960). The argument with Alexandria continued, but in 1959 Haile Selassie secured the Coptic Patriarch's agreement to the independant appointment of an Ethiopian to head the Ethiopian Church and Archbishop Gabre Giorgis became Patriarch Abuna Basilios. Abba Hanna's role was rather obscure,

but he remained very close to the Emperor who relied on him both as his priest and as an adviser. His importance was recognized in his death in the 1960 *coup d'état*.

4) *Courtiers*. Haile Selassie made full use of educated men, usually of non-noble birth, as his closest supporters and administrators. An early example was **DEJAZMATCH NASIBU**, the son of a courtier of the Emperor Menelik, who was one of Ras Tafari's 'Young Ethiopians' in the 1920s and whom he promoted to Governor of Harar. Elegantly dressed with kid gloves and a fluent speaker, both Waugh and Steer found him congenial. Unfortunately he had TB and died in exile in Switzerland soon after his escape from Harar in 1936. **LORENZO TAEZES** (1900–1946) was one of his protégés. A Tigrean from Eritrea, he found that he had no future in the Italian colony and was sent by the Emperor to Paris and returned as one of his most loyal supporters, accompanying him in exile in Bath. He served as Ethiopian Representative to the League of Nations and in 1939 made a secret visit to Gojjam to report on the Patriots. As the diary shows, he was a key player in the Emperor's return and became Foreign Minister in 1941. He was married to Ras Imru's daughter, but died young. Two others who entered Gojjam with the Emperor and became great rivals were **WOLDE GIORGIS** GCVO(1902–?) and **TAFARA WORQ** KCVO (1904–?), both of comparatively humble origin who rose through the Emperor's patronage. Both were fluent in foreign languages and accompanied the Emperor into exile and returned with him in 1940. Wolde Giorgis served, not very successfully, as the Emperor's representative to the Northern (Bentinck's) part of Mission 101. He became Minister of the Pen in 1941, but was dismissed in 1955 since he had become too powerful. Taffara Worq had been a translator in the British Legation, but was imprisoned by the Italians in 1936. Eden, at Barton's urging, secured his release and he joined the Emperor in 1940, where he served as Private Secreatry. He replaced Wolde Giorgis as Minister of the Pen in 1955 and was a 'power behind the throne' for many years. The Embassy did not find him easy to deal with: 'Shifty in appearance and somewhat pompous in manner, but can usually be relied on provided a certain amount of flattery is used.'

5) *Other notables*. The Emperor was joined in Khartoum by a number of other notables, most of whom had been in exile in Jerusalem. Dejazmatch (later Ras) **MAKONNEN ENDALTKATCHEW** (1892–1963), a Shoan noble, married to the Emperor's neice, Princess Yashasheworq, 'a tall handsome man, is courteous and friendly'. He played an active military role during the Italian invasion. After his return he became briefly Prime Minister in 1943. Dejazmatch (later Ras) **ADAFRISAU** (ca 1880–1950), a Menz nobleman of the old guard, had fought at Adowa and been commander of the Imperial Guard in the 1930s and again on his return. Served also as Provincial Governor. Fitaurari (later Ras) **BIRRU WOLDE GABRIEL**, had been Minister of War in the 1930s and was the Emperor's representative to Mission 101 in Beghemder. He served later as a provincial governor. Reputed to be an illegitimate son of the Emperor Menelik, he was regarded by Haile Selaissie with caution. Dejazmatch **MAKONNEN DESTA** (1910–1966) had been educated at Beirut and Harvard, served later unsuccessfully as a Minister. Described by the Embassy as 'well read and socially affable, but a weak character, conceited and lazy. Drinks to excess and on such occasions is intolerable.' Dejazmatch **AMDA MIKAEL** was a cousin of the Empress and head of the Shoan clan of the Mojaz. He served in various capacities after the war. Brigadier-General **ASFAU WOLDE GIORGIS** (1902–?) had been in exile in Kenya. He served in many different Governorships after the war: 'inclined to be anti-British . . . one of the cruder Ethiopian personalities'. Ajaz **KABADA TESEMME** (19? –1986) had been Court Chamberlain before the war and was the Emperor's representative with Sandford in Mission 101, where he had done well. He served in many different posts after the war and played an important part in the collapse of the 1960 *coup d'état*. In 1969 he published (in Amharic) an account of the 1940/1 campaign which revealed his unhappiness about the Allied role and particularly of Sandford. It has been said that the leader of the Dergue, Mengistu, was his illegitimate son. Certainly he survived the 1974 massacre of the Notables.

Other characters who appear had a rather different background. **MESFIN SILESHI** (later Ras and KCVO – 1902–1974) had been a member of the Imperial Bodyguard and remained in Ethiopia as a Patriot leader in Gojjam. He later served as Provincial Governor and other key roles: 'shrewd, active, prompt at decisons and hot

tempered . . . perhaps the most corrupt of Provincial Governors'. As Court Chamberlain he accompanied the Emperor on his 1954 State Visit to London. Executed by the Dergue. **DEJAZMATCH MANGASHA JEMBERIE**, son-in-law of Ras Hailu, was an active Patriot leader in Gojjam. **NEGASH BEZAHBU** (1908–?) a nephew of Ras Hailu, remained in Gojjam as a loyal but not very effective patriot fighter. He was appointed Governor of Debra Markos in April 1941 and later President of the Senate; he was involved in a plot and was denounced by Gerassu Duki and subsequently imprisoned. Dejazmatch **GERASSU DUKI** (1892–?) was of obscure Galla birth. He remained in Ethiopia as a Patriot and became an important figure in 1941 in Jimma of which he later became Provincial Governor. 'A man of virtually no education but of considerable charm, he is a brilliant leader of men but a poor though energetic administrator'. Lij (later Brigadier and KBE **ABEYE ABABA** (1918–1974), a Shoan noble, joined the Emperor in exile in Bath and returned with the Crown Prince in 1940 to Khartoum. Later he married Princess Tsahai, who died shortly afterwards, and subsequently the daughter of Dejazmatch Nasibu. He attended the Coronation of the Queen in 1953. As Governor of Eritrea he played an important part in the suppression of the Coup in 1960. In 1974 he was executed by the Dergue. Blatta **TAKELE WOLDE HAWARIAT** (1900–69), described by Mockler as 'Childhood companion and lifelong bane of the Emperor', was a strong nationalist and later a republican. He never accepted the Emperor's decision to leave the country in 1936, remained as a resistance leader and in 1940 urged the Emperor to enter Ethiopia and recover the country without British help. He was kept in Kenya until after the liberation and spent the next 25 years alternately rebelling and being rehabilitated and given office by the Emperor. In 1969, after his last release from prison, he attempted to blow the Emperor up and died resisting arrest. In some sympathy with him was Dejazmatch **ABEBE DANTEW** (ca1900–?), Shoan war leader and brother of Ras Desta Damtew who had been married to the Emperor's elder daughter and had been killed by the Italians in 1937. He was in exile in Jerusalem, returned to Khartoum in 1940, but went with Takele to Kenya where they tried to raise the flag in the Galla-Sidamo.

Appendix 3

Ethiopian Campaign Officers
1940–1941

(* campaign awards; +attended 1966 reunion;
see brief biographies: App 1)

1) GHQ and others

Gen Sir Archibald Wavell (later Earl Wavell) GOC Middle East

Gen Alan Cunningham (later Sir) GOC East Africa

Maj Gen Weatherall (later Sir H.) o/c 11th African Div

Brigadier C.C.Fowkes (later Maj-Gen) o/c 22nd East Africa Brigade

#Brigadier Iltyd Clayton (later Sir) i/c Middle East Intellence Centre, Cairo

#Lt Gen W Platt (later Sir W.) C-in-C (Kaid) Sudan

#R. Cheesman Col i/c Sudan Intelligence office in Khartoum

Maj R. Tuckey DAAQMG Ethiopian Irregulars Khartoum

Lt-Col Terence Airey (later Lt-Gen Sir) SOE i/c GR unit, Khartoum

#Capt Dodds-Parker Capt GSOII Khartoum staff officer (SOE)with Kaid

Lt J. Bagge i/c Transport Khartoum (later Sir John)

Capt Whinney W Yorks instructor Ethiopian OCS Khartoum

Lt Col Athill, i/c Ethiopian Officer Training (Soba-Khartoum)

GIDEON FORCE

2) Staff

OC Wingate	Maj wef Feb 41 Col and CO
#D.A.Sandford+	Brigadier Chief Political Officer from Feb 1941
#E.A. Chapman-Andrews+	Maj. Dep CPO from Feb 1941 sec Foreign Office
A. Akavia+	unofficial Chief of Staff to Wingate Palestine civilian.
#George Steer	i/c Propaganda (SOE)
Perry Fellowes	Propaganda Unit Khartoum and Gideon Force
Lt Palmer	official photographer
Staff Sergeant Pollitt	Chapman-Andrews' staff

3) Sudan Defence Force – Frontier Battalion

i/c	#J.E.H. Boustead+Lt.Col DSO* MC		Sudan Pol. Service
2I/c	J.R.Maxwell	Maj DSO OBE	ex Reg R. Scots Fusilers
i/c Aco	T.G. Johnson	Bim DSO*	Sudan civilian
2i/c	- Riley	Lt	
i/c Bco	W.A.B. Harris	Bim MC*	ex R. Scots Fusiliers
2i/c	S. Creeden	Lt	
i/c Cco	A.J. Jarvis	Maj	Sudan civilian
2i/c	J. Holcombe	Lt	UK civilian
i/c Dco	P.B.E. Acland	Maj OBE DSO MC* Sudan Pol. Service	
i/c D	- Barlow	replaced wounded Acland Apr 41	
2I/c	- Carroll-Leahy	Lt	
i/cMtr	J.G. Turrall	Maj DSO MC*	civilian -Ethiopia
Adj	C. Macdonald	Capt (killed Mar 41) Sudan Pol. Service	

4) Mission 101

i/c -Feb 41#Col D.A. Sandford DSO CBE*+		to Feb 41

i/c +Feb 41 Maj A.C.Simonds MBE		reg. R. Berkshire
i/c Patriots Lt Col B. Tarleton		from May 41
2i/c-Apr41 Maj R.A.Critchley DSO MC*		reg. 13/18 Hussars
2i/c +Apr 41Bim W.P.Thesiger DSO*+		Sudan Pol. Service
DAAQMG Maj D.H.Nott DSO+ OBE MC		reg. Worcs

4) Mission 101 (cont)

i/c Eng	Lt T. Foley MC*	mining in Eritrea
MO	Capt C.B.Drew+ MBE	Sudan Med. Service
MO	Lt Hunt	Sudan Med. Service -- retd
MO	Dr Haggar	self-styled SM0 ex Syria
i/c signals	Sgt G.Grey later Lt Col MBE*+	reg. R Signals later CBE
i/c North	#Col Count A. Bentinck	to Feb 41
i/c North	Lt L.F.Sheppard(killed 44)	from Feb41 -civ Cairo
	#2LtA.Wienholt(killed Sep 40)	Australian senator
TptO	Lt J.LeBlanc	Canadian civ
Vets	Lts J.Jack and I.Gillespie	Sudan service

5) Operations Centres

i/c Opcentre1	Lt A.Brown+	Australian civ bank
2i/c	Bim P. Hayes	Sudan civilian
Sgts	Body,Burke,Howell	Civs Australian
i/c Opcentre2	Lt Mackay	Canadian, wounded Apr 41
	#Lt N.McLean+ from Apr 41	reg. R. Scots greys
i/c Opcentre3	Lt G. Naylor	reg. Beds and Herts
i/c Opcentre4	Lt Bathgate	Kings Own. civ SA
i/c Opcentre5	#Cap L.van der Post+	civ S African – Apr 41
	Lt M.Pilkington (killed 42)	reg Life Guards +Apr41
	#Lt W.E.D.Allen+	civ. ex MP

i/c Opcentre6	Lt Welsh	civ. schoolmaster
i/c Opcentre8	Lt Stanton+ later Lt Col	Yorks Hussars
	Lt Cope+ later Maj	from Apr 41

5) Ethiopian Battalion

CO 2nd Bn- Apr 41	Maj E.M.Boyle	Civ in Kenya
2i/c and 1/c Bco	Lt A.S.Beard	civ N Rhodesia-ex reg..
CO 2nd Bn+Apr 41	Lt Col G.Benson OBE	reg.R.Ulster Reg
Adj -Apr41	A.Smith	civ missionary N Zealand
i/cA co	Lt S. Downey	civ Kenya
i/cC co	Lt K.Rowe (killed May 41)	civ Kenya
i/cD co	Lt M.Tutton (killed Nov 41)	DO Tanganyika
Sgt	#R.Luyt(later Sir R.)	civ S African Rhodes Sch
Sgt	A.Botha	
QM	Sgt Stewart	Black Watch
Sgt	G.Clarke	S. African
Guard Pln	Lt Phillips	
	Lt Shaw	
I/C Emps Bodyguard	Col Morough-Bernard Apr 41 ex Indian Army	
I/C Tps in Kenya	#Lt-Col A.T. Curle+ DSO OBE ex Col Civil Servant	

6) OETA from Apr 41

CPO	Maj Gen Sir Philip Mitchell	Gov. Uganda
CPO Ethiopia	Brig Lush	P.C.Sudan
CPO Res. Areas	Col T.R. Blackley	P.C. Sudan

Appendix 4

Bibliography

Allen, W.E.D., *Guerilla War in Abyssinia*, Penguin 1943
Avon, Earl of, *The Eden Memoirs Vol III*, Cassell 1962
Barker, A.J., *The Civilising Mission*, Cassell 1968
Bierman, John, and Smith, Colin, *Fire in the Night*, Macmillan 1999
Birkby, C, *It is a Long Way to Addis*, L.W.Muller 1942
Boustead, Sir Hugh, *The Wind in the Morning*, Chatto & Windus 1971
Brit. Docs at End of Emp., *Egypt and Defence in the Middle East Vol I*, HMSO 1998
Brit.Docs at End of Emp., *Sudan I*, HMSO 1998
Bullard, Sir Reader, *The Camels Must Go*, Faber 1965
Cecil, Robert, *A Divided Life*, Bodley Head 1958
Churchill, Winston S., *The Second World War, Vol 2*, Cassell 1948
Connell, John, *Wavell*, Collins 1964
Cooper, Artemis, *Cairo in the War*, Penguin 1995
Davie, Michael, *Evelyn Waugh Diaries*, Weidenfeld & Nicolson 1976
De Monfried, Henri, *Le Masque d'Or*, Grasset 1936
Dimbleby, Richard, *The Frontiers are Green*, London 1942
Dodds-Parker, Douglas, *Setting Europe Ablaze*, Springwood 1983
Evans, Trefor, *Killearn Diaries*, Sidgwick & Jackson 1972
Farago, Ladislas, *Abyssinia Stop Press*, Robert Hale 1936
Gandar-Dower K., *Abyssinian Patchwork*, L.W. Muller 1949
Glover, Michael, *An Improvised War*, Leo Cooper 1987
Greenfield, Richard, *Ethiopia*, Pall Mall 1965
Haile Selassie, *My Life and Ethiopia's Progress (ed. Ullendorf)*, OUP 1976
Harmsworth, Geoffrey, *Abyssinian Adventure*, Hutchinson 1935
Henderson K.D.D., *The Making of Modern Sudan*, Faber 1953
—— *Sudan Republic*, Benn 1965
Hoare, Geoffrey, *The Missing Macleans*, Cassell 1955

Jones J.D.F., *Storyteller*, Murray 2001
Keown-Boyd, Henry, *The Lion and the Sphinx*, Memoirs Club 2003
Lewis, I.M., *A Modern History of Somalia*, James Curry 2002
Little, Tom, *Modern Egypt*, Benn 1967
Lush, Maurice S., *A Life of Service*, privately printed
Macfie, J.W.S., *An Ethiopian Diary*, Univ Press 1936
Mansfield, P., *The British in Egypt*, Weidenfeld & Nicolson 1971
Mitchell, David, *The Fighting Pankhursts*, Cape 1967
Mitchell, Sir Philip, *African Afterthoughts*, Hutchinson 1954
Mockler, Anthony, *Haile Selassie's war*, OUP 1984
Money, George., *Nine Lives of a Bush Banker*, Merlin Books 1990
Moorehead, Alan, *African Trilogy*, Hamish Hamilton 1965
Mosley, Leonard, *Gideon Goes to war*, Arthur Barker 1955
—— *Haile Selassie*, Weidenfeld & Nicholson 1964
Nelson, Kathleen et al, *John Melly of Ethiopia*, Faber 1936
Page, Bruce et al, *Philby, the Spy who Betrayed a Generation*, Dent 1968
Playfair, Maj Gen I.S.O ed., *Offical History of WWII Vol 1*, HMSO 1954
Ranfurly, Countess of, *To War with Whittaker*, Heinemann 1994
Rankin,Nicholas, *Telegram from Guernica*, Faber 2003
Raugh, Harold E., *Wavell in the Middle East*, Brasseys 1993
Rennell of Rodd, Lord, *B.M.A. in O.T. in Africa*, HMSO 1948
Robertson, Sir James, *Transition in Africa*, Hurst 1974
Rooney, David, *Wingate and the Chindits*, Cassell 2000
Rosenthal, Eric, *The Fall of Italian East Africa*, Hutchinson 1942
Sandford, Christine, *Ethiopia under Haile Selassie*, Dent 1946
Shirreff, David, *Barefoot and Bandoliers*, Radcliffe Press 1995
Slim, Sir William, *Unofficial History*, Cassell 1959
Spencer, John H., *Ethiopia At Bay*, Ref Publications 1984
Stannard, Martin, *Evelyn Waugh, The Early Years*, Dent 1986
Steer, George L.-ed, *The Abyssian Campaign*, MOI / HMSO 1942
—— *Caesar in Abyssinia*, H&S 1936
—— *Sealed and Delivered*, H&S 1942
Sykes, Christopher, *Orde Wingate*, Collins 1955
Symes, Sir Stewart, *Tour of Duty*, Collins 1946
Thesiger, Wilfred, *The Life of My Choice*, Collins 1987
Thompson, Sir Geoffrey, *Front Line Diplomat*, Hutchinson 1959
Van der Post, Laurens, *First Catch Your Eland*, Hogarth Press 1977
    Yet Being Someone Other, 1982
Waugh, Evelyn, *Waugh in Abyssinia*, Longmans 1936
—— *When the Going was Good*, Duckworth 1946
—— *Remote People*, Duckworth 1931

Weller, George, *The Belgian Campaign in East Africa*, N York 1941
Wienholt, Arnold, *The African's Last Stronghold*, J. Leng 1938

National and Other Archives

Sir Edwin Chapman-Andrews, Films, Imp.War Museum
—— Papers, held privately
Robert Cheesman, Papers, R. Geog. Soc
Akavia, Avram, War diaries, WO217/37
Barton, Col J.E.B., Mission 101, CAB 41/81
Churchill,W. S., PM's Papers, PREM 3/278/3
Sir A. Eden, Sundry Papers, FO954
Harris, Maj W.A.B., Guerrilla War in Gojjam, WO201/365
Wingate, Lt Col Orde, Despatches from Gojjam, CAB 106/648

I am grateful to Mr Julian Lush for permission to quote from his father's book *A Life of Service* (privately printed) and to Mr Nicholas Rankin and Mr George Steer for permission to quote from the former's book *Telegram from Guernica*.

Index

El Mirghani, Sayed Sir Ali, 151, 153, 155, 156–8
Elles, Captain, 103
Elphick, Dr, 20
Emperor Haile Selassie, xi, xii, 3, 13, 15, 18
  and Brocklehurst affair, 60
  and Syrian doctor, Haggar, 80
  and Wingate, 55, 57, 130
  announcement of death, 177
  appoints Chapman-Andrews Grade 3 officer of the Star of Ethiopia, 140
  arrives in Jerusalem, 23
  biography, 191–2
  codename 'Mr Smith', 38, 39–40
  coronation, 4–5
  coronation gifts, 5–6
  crosses Ethiopian border, 62
  death of wife, 176
  deposed and imprisoned, 176
  Ethiopian government allows funeral service in Addis Ababa, 178
  gives Chapman-Andrews Order of the Star of Ethiopia – fifth class, 135
  helps with revolt, 49
  improves infrastructure of Ethiopia, 11
  in exile in Bath, 32
  invites Chapman-Andrews to 25th Liberation Anniversary celebrations, 172
  leads forces into battle at Mai Chew, 19
  memorial service in St George's Chapel, Windsor, 178
  murdered, 177
  progress of march into Ethiopia, 63–4
  promotes sons to rank of general, 104
  returns to Addis Ababa, 106–9
  sends Imperial family to Palestine, 22
  sends message to King George VI, 65
  signs Anglo-Ethiopian Agreement, 134
  speaks to League of Nations, 23
  supporters and family members murdered, 177
  takes salute at Um Idla, 65
  threatens to form government in exile, 41
  triumphal entry into Addis Ababa, 102
  unveils war memorial in Addis Ababa, 161
  urged to leave Ethiopia, 20–1
  visits Italian prisoners, 92
Emperor Menelik, 1, 2, 14, 60, 191
Empress Menem, 176, 192
Empress Zauditu, 2, 191
Endalkatchew, Ras Makonnen, 16, 20, 195
Engiabara, 75, 85, 89
Enterprise, HMS, 22
Erskine, Major, 60
Ethiopian Church, 2, 23
Ethiopian Herald, 178
Ethiopian monarchy abolished, 177
Ethiopian Officers Training College, 61
Ethiopian Studies Institute, 188
Exeter Express and Echo, 26

Farouk, King of Egypt, 138, 139, 143, 186
Fellowes, Perry, 65, 66, 90, 93, 94
Fergusson, Sir Bernard, later Lord Ballantrae, 126
Fikre Mariam, *see* Sandford, Colonel
Foley, Captain Tim, 86, 98, 104, 107
Foreign Office records, xi
Fort Emmanuel, 83, 91, 94, 97, 100, 101
Fowkes, Brigadier, 116–18
French Catholic Mission, Harar, 2, 24
French Hospitals, 14,19, 24

Gabriel, Fitaurari, later Ras, Birru Wolde, 195
Gazzera, General, 105, 115, 116, 118
Geneva Convention, 73
Genock, Edward, 64
George V, King of Great Britain, 5, 118, 155
Gideon Force, xi, 33, 51, 54, 55, 56, 58, 59, 62, 71, 74–5, 76, 77, 85, 87, 105, 107, 109, 110, 121, 122, 133, 136, 171, 185, 186, 189
Giorgis, Echege Gabre, 193 (see also Itcheguey)
Giovannone, Dr Ernesto, 103

208